THE POLITICS OF NAMES

R. URBATSCH

THE POLITICS
OF NAMES

Attitudes, Identity, and the Naming of
Children in American History

Columbia University Press / *New York*

Columbia University Press

Publishers Since 1893

New York   Chichester, West Sussex

cup.columbia.edu

Copyright © 2026 Columbia University Press

All rights reserved

Cataloging-in-Publication Data is available from the Library of Congress.

ISBN 9780231221689 (hardback)
ISBN 9780231221696 (trade paperback)
ISBN 9780231563857 (epub)
ISBN 9780231565080 (PDF)

LCCN 2025035493

Printed in the United States of America

Cover design: Chang Jae Lee
Cover image: © Shutterstock

GPSR Authorized Representative: Easy Access System Europe,
Mustamäe tee 50, 10621 Tallinn, Estonia, gpsr.requests@easproject.com

For my parents

CONTENTS

ACKNOWLEDGMENTS

In our very first conversation, Stephen Wesley mentioned an upcoming paternity leave. My immediate thought, of course, was "If you really want to support the book manuscript, you should name the child *Eleventh Amendment*,[1] then let me interview all concerned after the ensuing break-up." He didn't do that, but otherwise was everything one could hope for in an editor: incisive, responsive, and gracious. My thanks to him, and the whole team at Columbia University Press, including Alex Gupta and Kathryn Jorge, for their support. The anonymous reviewers also were paragons of thoughtful professionalism (even if Reviewer 2 seemed a bit puzzled by the whole project). Helen Glenn Court copyedited with heroic patience, and Amanda Wilson expertly compiled the index.

Before this project got to Columbia, several other colleagues provided helpful feedback. In its extremely early days, when it still concerned political trends in names in Norway rather than the United States, Jonathan Rodden discussed the ideas with encouragement and Jeffry Frieden did so with bemused tolerance. Nell Gabiam, Jonathan Hassid, and Christina Gish Hill read and commented on parts of the manuscript in progress. Boom Boom Peterson, Matt Potoski, and Emilia Justyna Powell gave advice on bigger-picture framing. I am grateful to them all.

THE POLITICS OF NAMES

INTRODUCTION

Alternative measures of public opinion . . . Names as identities . . . Strengths and weaknesses of name-based indicators . . . The generalizability-clarity trade-off . . . Anthropologists, sociologists, and names

Suppose someone told you that Theodore Roosevelt emerged from the Spanish-American War as the most popular person in the United States.[1] If the assertion arose in casual conversation—if your interlocutor were, unprovoked, spouting claims in some very strange bar about Teddy Roosevelt—you might just shrug your shoulders and move on. After all, fate rarely hangs in the balance on Theodore Roosevelt's popularity, at least not in most theologies. But sometimes claims like this matter for our understanding of past or current events and thus guide reactions to circumstances. If we did want to take such claims more seriously, how could we assess them?

Had the question concerned not Roosevelt but later history, we would probably look for surveys asking the public what they thought about

Roosevelt and other figures of the day. Alas, the Spanish-American War preceded the development of modern public-opinion polling techniques by several decades, so the survey-based approach is unavailable.

The problems that arise from restricting oneself to survey evidence extend well beyond understanding Theodore Roosevelt's allure.[2] Having more comparison cases available facilitates the formulation and testing of hypotheses about society. Having a larger number and broader variety of historical episodes to draw on would allow more general and more precise conclusions about many questions underpinning big, important outcomes in politics and policy: the rise and decline of social movements, the ways war transforms public values, what shapes popular views of government, and so on. When we can only consider contexts for which polling data is available, much of history closes to us—we sacrifice an enormous wealth of experience. Even current events may slip from our grasp; when no pollster happens to ask a question at the time we retrospectively want it to have been asked, we lack survey data about the episode ever after. That problem is especially acute when the unexpected happens. We can only compare survey responses from before and after the terrorist attack (or earthquake or stock market crash) if people knew in advance what topic would eventually be of interest.

Moreover, survey data—indispensable though it is for divining what people believe—has unavoidable flaws, as any methodology does. Entire books focus on plumbing the difficulties of understanding public preferences from surveys.[3] Polls are obtrusive measures: Survey respondents are acutely aware that the survey taker is paying attention to their answers and to any political implications of those answers.[4] This self-consciousness pulls respondents away from their natural reaction toward saying what they think the survey taker wants to hear or what might come off as relatively cultured or well informed. Respondents may even self-censor to avoid a true answer they fear the survey taker will find contemptible or offensive. Such dissimulation is especially easy because suboptimal survey responses have few if any serious consequences: One can blithely tell a survey taker that the United States should bomb Canada or radically cut taxes without worrying about making any practical difference. In consequence, even if pollsters could magically formulate a neutral question wording that all respondents understood in the same way, and even if they could avoid having any element of survey design contaminate opinions, the relationship between survey responses and respondents' actual views is murky.

Hence alternative sources of information about public opinion can help confirm the findings of traditional survey research as well as extend its reach to times and places without surveys. Many such alternatives are possible. We can look at evidence from protests, or petitions, or referendums, for example. But the self-spoiling nature of titles for academic research—sorry!—correctly indicates that this book proposes to look instead at baby names.

In particular, names reflect and reveal identity. Names are after all how people most immediately identify themselves.[5] And identity is deeply entangled with politics, even beyond narrow struggles over "identity politics." Someone who identifies with a particular place, party, or group will naturally, even automatically, take that identification into account when contemplating political action and when considering what name to give a child. This is not to say that identities wholly determine behavior in either politics or naming, but they are considerations and constraints in both realms. Because they are, names can organically capture whatever dimensions of political identity resonate at a given time and place. Indeed, one lurking theme of the following chapters is that, across the centuries of American history, issues have waxed and waned as the central fixations of politics and identity, and hence as names. The stark cleavage between North and South, the public's desire to associate itself with the incumbent president, the increasing partisan animosity: Names can shed light on each of these and on when they mattered for the public. Indeed, increasing uses of the names *Theodore* and *Roosevelt* might show identity as a Roosevelt fan, allowing comparison with other potential namesakes.

THE AIM OF THE NAME

The idea that names can shed new light on public opinion is by no means original.[6] People have repeatedly returned to that insight because names circumvent some of the problems with survey responses even if they have other drawbacks. As a consequence, they complement those more conventional measures and other indicators of public sentiment.

For one thing, a baby name is less obtrusive a measure than a survey response is. When selecting the name for a child, people rarely consider the possibility that some oddball academic might a century later examine the name for what it says about politics.[7] Of course, names are publicly visible, so name choices do incorporate social constraints. However, the audience of relatives and neighbors whose views constrain name choices are, unlike survey takers, an ongoing part of the social context, people whose views also play into many everyday life decisions. Their influence in naming therefore better reflects real-world decision-making than statements inflected by an academic researcher or pollster do: Any bending of name choices to perceived standards of acceptability helps reveal local political currents.

Social visibility, moreover, adds real stakes to the naming choice. People have prejudices about names: Contemporary Americans' expectations about a person named *Dorothy* differ from those about a *Lakisha*, or a *Cletus*, or a *Poindexter*.[8] Those prejudices matter. A misbegotten name can potentially lead to worse life outcomes for the child, from childhood teasing to fewer professional or social opportunities,[9] risks captured by one old-time book of baby-naming advice's forthright title, *How to Name Baby without Handicapping It for Life*.[10] Name-givers who care about the child's prospects accordingly have strong reason to carefully consider their naming choice. Studies from many disciplines and societies confirm that most people do, indeed, take the naming of children very seriously.[11] The potential personal costs of an ill-advised name choice are more pointed than the more diffuse consequences of other nonsurvey expressions of public opinion such as referendums—which furthermore tend to be both more rare and more limited in their issue coverage than baby names can be.

Names also incorporate groups that other appraisals of public opinion likely underrepresent. Society long denied women much voice in public politics; their lesser access to schooling also limited their literacy rates and hence ability to write books, editorials, or letters that historians could draw upon.[12] But names directly connect to family and children, fields more often accepted as within women's purview. This sometimes allowed women to assert their voice as name-givers, though to be sure the role of mothers and other women in that process varied across time and location. The impoverished, the persecuted, and the newly immigrated all likewise had greater scope for naming children than they did for expressing political views in many other ways widely recoverable in the historical record.

Names do have several limitations as measures of public opinion to weigh against these potential benefits. For one thing, they only directly reveal the attitudes of name-givers, who in the United States are overwhelmingly though not exclusively the child's parents.[13] Parents are not a representative sample of the population at large. They tend to fall in particular age bands, with women above their mid-forties in age scarcely represented, even as considerable over-time variation in the age of parenthood further complicates assessments of changes across generations. Parents do not include various groups of people who, for reasons from a celibate priestly vocation to health struggles, never have children. Not even all parents are involved in name-giving; death or separation may remove the father by the time of childbirth, and even within stable couples one parent may choose a name with limited input from the other. If, for example, conservative couples systematically delegate the task of name selection to the father, names might underrepresent conservative women's views. Although many of these sorts of unrepresentativeness likely change only slowly and thus may not bias some over-time comparisons, they leave unavoidable uncertainty about what groups uninvolved in naming would have chosen as names.

Nor is uneven coverage the only weaknesses of names as barometers of public opinion. Using names to see how people responded to social changes requires knowing when naming happened. The modern bureaucratic state tends to compel people to choose names at or by the time of birth, but this was not consistently the historical norm. Perhaps because infant mortality was high, or perhaps because of more concern for observing the child's personality before selecting a suitable name, it was not unusual for much of U.S. history to hold off on naming for weeks or months after the child's birth, or to put in official records a name contrived months or years later even if some other name had been used for the child in early infancy. Conversely, some social strata today often select names well in advance of birth, also separating the time of name selection from the actual birth (though name-givers' not allowing subsequent events to dissuade from the original choice is itself informative). Even when a data source provides an exact date of birth, then, it can be unclear when any political signals embedded in a name were sent: A name might not reflect the contemporaneous political moment, but instead a later, retrospective inspiration.

In light of these imprecisions of timing, this book's analysis mostly focuses not on specific birth dates but on birth years; only on occasion does the discussion touch on more time-sensitive but uncertain questions of interpretation. The focus on years is, admittedly, also a matter of necessity because year is as specific as the information gets in the main data sources used. But a survey could normally provide much more precise information about the timing of attitudes than this, so the fuzziness on dating is another relative drawback of names for studying some questions.

Even bigger ambiguities surround the meaning of a particular name choice. A baby named *George* in 1776 could mark a loyalist celebrating George III, a patriot celebrating George Washington, or a political apathist celebrating someone else entirely—a family member, say, or perhaps the Anglican cleric William George, whose sermons were popular at the time, or even nobody in particular. Americans' names tend not to be explicitly narrative, unlike those in some other cultures,[14] so birth-certificate information will generally not conclusively identify the namesake. Muddiness of meaning also plagues survey responses—the earlier point about survey takers not always expressing their genuine opinion binds here—but the specific meaning of names often is hazier still.

This problem of ambiguity tends in the case of names to trade off against frequency. Read enough books about Abraham Lincoln, and you will run across mentions of the Coggeshalls, White House hangers-on who named their daughter *Emancipation Proclamation* in 1862.[15] We can probably agree where that name, unlike our *George* of 1776, came from. Names like that are immediately identifiable as deriving from particular sources in part because virtually no one else used them as names. (Not to say that such unmistakably political names were always unique; the 1800s saw *States Rights* come up as a name across the South,[16] and *Wilmot Proviso* several times in the North.) Names generate their own cultural momentum. Once someone gets a previously unknown name, other people may be named for that person, a process that can then echo through the generations. Consider *Winfield*. It was not, historically, a common name, but the record of Winfield Scott—general, popular icon of the War of 1812, and 1840 presidential candidate—gained the name some popularity, especially among military families.[17] Hence Winfield Scott Hancock (Civil War general and 1880 presidential candidate) or Winfield Scott Featherston (a Mississippi representative and Confederate general) or Winfield Scott Kerr (an Ohio representative) or Winfield Scott Hammond (a Minnesota governor), to name just politically prominent examples. It eventually becomes unclear whether any particular *Winfield* is named after the original general, was instead named for one of the subsequent namesakes, or had parents who just liked the sound of the names *Winfield* and *Scott* without associating it with any particular person as it floated around with multiple familiar associations. Or *Winfield* could be a family name, as it was for Winfield Scott himself, his maternal grandmother's maiden name having been Elizabeth Winfield.

Screamingly political one-off names such as *Emancipation Proclamation* therefore compellingly indicate what was of importance to the child's namegiver in a way that examples like *George* or even *Winfield* cannot precisely because a name's uniqueness equally signifies that the political event being commemorated did not similarly inspire very many other choices of name, or at least not in the same direct way. The name *Emancipation* could be dismissed as a striking but meaningless fluke. Conversely, substantial proportions of the population starting to use a formerly obscure name (or abandon the use of a formerly common one) indicates that something has had widespread cultural purchase, but that "something" could be a political message, inspiration from some nonpolitical figure, or a meaningless embrace of random trends. Even some of the individuals who chose the name in question may not know why it spoke to them, and the inspiration for the name is necessarily even less clear when considering trends across the population as a whole, commingling several name-givers' possibly divergent motivations.

When names do derive from politics, moreover, they capture unusually intense political feelings. Most people have only a few opportunities to name children and so tend to reserve those opportunities for expressing their most central preferences and identities, often less explicitly political ones. Only positions and politicians with passionate support, even among a tiny minority, will tend to find that support translating into names. Those with broader but less ardent support may not. Although intense supporters are sometimes exactly what one aims to assess, this disconnect between the depth of support indicated by names and the breadth of popular feeling cautions against too rigidly interpreting increased prevalence of a name as wider support for the name's political associations. It more specifically indicates wider intense support for the namesake cause, which will often but not always track the cause's overall popularity.

THE NAME IS AFOOT

Although a broad look at American political history through baby names is unusual, scholars—anthropologists, historians, sociologists, and economists—have assembled a vast literature about names in other contexts.[18] Indeed, the study of names, or to use its technical name onomastics, has its own dedicated journals and scholarly societies around the world: the American Name Society, the International Council of Onomastic Sciences, *Names, Onomastica Canadiana, Вопросы Ономастики, ONOMA*, and so on. This academic apparatus complements a lively informal community avocationally unearthing insights from naming patterns.[19]

All sorts of names can provide clues about society. Names for places, pets, business enterprises, and much more have been scoured for what they reveal about society and culture.[20] Even restricting oneself to personal names still leaves many ways forward. Academic analysts have found many uses for family names (surnames). A small sampling of examples might include examinations of social mobility across centuries;[21] of women's roles in societies East and West,[22] as well as in international law;[23] and of specific historical episodes, as with Turkey's Surname Law of 1934, which as part of a national modernization campaign mandated the use of family names in a society that traditionally lacked them.[24] Nicknames or names taken on as adults (sometimes involving formal rites of passage or change in identity, sometimes less officially) can similarly reveal elements of culture.[25] Here, though, the focus is on forenames given at or around the time of birth: mostly first names, with a smattering of middle names when possible.

Even given names offer a huge range of previous studies and themes to build upon. Religion is a major social force and also a much-remarked source of names: *Muhammad* is often cited as the world's single most prevalent given name,[26] and use of gods' names has been ubiquitous from medieval Norse paganism up through the modern Hindu world.[27] Religious expression's connection to names is so tight that *Christian name* was long the commonest term in English for a given name, and *to christen* is to bestow a name. Although this invocation of religion through name choices occurs in many contexts, it can be particularly pointed in societies divided across multiple faiths.[28] Having an opposing religious group nearby to define oneself against imparts special significance to religion-tinged names.

Similarly, societies divided across other dimensions also can see those divisions spill into naming practices. Names follow predictable trends based on socioeconomic status: education, income, and social class. Higher-status groups in the United States, for instance, more often prefer traditional names, whereas lower-status groups are more drawn to current vogues or complete idiosyncrasy.[29] In modern society—less so in feudal, warrior cultures—high status can also associate with a preference for names that signal gender less intensively.[30]

Ethnicity, too, appears in names. Multiethnic societies frequently see names polarize by ethnicity as ethnic differences come to matter for social relations.[31] In line with the centrality of Black–White racial distinctions to much of United States history, ethnic differences in naming have been particularly notable in the form of distinctively Black names. These have a long past. Several names basically unused among the free were commonly given to babies born into enslavement (or to adults bought therein, with little regard to what they had formerly been called). Common examples included classical and biblical names (such as *Juno*, *Samson*, or *Pompey*), adaptations of traditional African names (such as *Juba* or *Quash*), and in some cases outright racial slurs.[32] Even after emancipation, when Blacks had more control over their own names as recorded in official documents, they maintained distinctive naming traditions,[33] especially with the rise of the Black consciousness movement from the 1960s on.[34]

Non-Black ethnic minorities have notable naming patterns, too. Indigenous peoples' naming practices, though diverse, can differ substantially from those of European-origin cultures.[35] Conversely, recent-generation immigrants have chosen names distinctively from the early republic to the present.[36] Because an ethnic group's using the same names as others in society do suggests assimilation,[37] it is especially noteworthy that many migrants give sons names typical of their country of ancestry but daughters names associated with the country of residence.[38]

As that sex distinction suggests, gender is another social division featuring in naming practices. Many societies' traditional naming practices conspicuously distinguish between girls' and boys' names,[39] some countries going so far as to legally require names to be identifiable by sex.[40] Even when language and culture do not formally differentiate names by sex, names given to girls often sound different from those given to boys.[41] In English, one frequently used example is that names ending in the letter *A* tend, with the signal exception of *Joshua*, to be primarily given to girls. Names are in consequence widely used to infer gender, and to study gendered differences.[42] Just as girls are less likely among recent migrants to receive a heritage name, their names tend to go in and out of fashion more quickly, are less likely to be passed directly from parents (or other close kin) to children, and are more likely to be spelled idiosyncratically: People tend to be more conservative with sons' names, conceiving them as carrying forward the family legacy.[43]

These sorts of findings, illustrating possible roles of important social identities in naming, build a foundation for exploring political influences on names. However, skepticism that politics matters much for naming is widespread. One landmark work in using names to examine the development of American culture over the centuries sniffs that "newsworthy events produce only minor or temporary fads for naming of infants after national or cultural heroes."[44] Other major book-length social-scientific examinations of names typically mention politics only glancingly, if at all.[45] Even when an essay specifically examines the politics of naming, it is as likely to focus on the use of names (when it is politically acceptable for me to call you by your given name, or to change my own name?),[46] or who has the power to choose names and what consequences come from that power,[47] as on the specific name chosen. It is true that political names can have short currency—you meet tragically few *Wilmot Provisos* these days[48]—and with the vast range of influences on baby names, politics is only rarely the primary determinant involved.[49] But as anyone who has been a teenager can attest, even a temporary social trend can be intensely meaningful while it is trending: The episodes when something political breaks through to become a popular naming choice, however briefly, uncover something about people's interests and concerns at the particular historical moment. And personal names have been found to have sustained connections to nationalism, monarchy, and other political questions throughout modern European history.[50] There is no obvious reason why people in North America would be any less susceptible to analogous influences, especially given the relatively long U.S. tradition of popular participation in government. In fact, it might be the mark of responsiveness to politics that the names in question constantly change. When a name that was originally derived from political events escapes that orbit and just becomes a permanent, nonpolitical part of the naming landscape—like *Grant*, to draw on an example explored in chapters 2 and 3[51]—it is not a "temporary fad" only because it was so overwhelming that it transcended its political roots and people fail to recall that it originally referred to a specific person.

Furthermore, although individual names often fade as fashions change, broader relationships may endure. One study found that those who lean to the political right systematically favor more "masculine" names, and that those on the left prefer cultural allusions.[52] Such patterns could be consistent even if the particular masculine names, or the particular referents of the allusion, evolve over time. Ongoing trends, that is, may involve several related names increasing or decreasing slightly in use and thereby collectively having a large effect. These trends, moreover, may reflect a broader conception of politics than names noting powerful figures, significant though those can be. They might instead speak to factors such as political equality between sexes being reflected in more similar (or even androgynous) naming choices for girls and boys, or the increasing status of a minority ethnicity being matched by increased use of names from that ethnic culture even among nonmembers, or the turn toward or away from biblical names as the public role of religion changes.

This book hopes to synthesize all these strands of the literature, to show some of the range of possibilities for using names as an indicator of public opinion; thus it is fundamentally exploratory, illustrating some of the hypotheses that names might speak to rather than conclusively testing a specific case.[53] Focusing on breadth by galloping across multiple centuries and issue areas necessarily sacrifices depth. One could write entire books exploring names in any one historical episode covered here. Part of the goal of this book is to inspire you to think about how you might do so, or how you might draw on other nontraditional measures of public opinion to help expand our understanding of history, society, and policy. With luck, baby names can offer an accessible gateway to those weighty questions of substance and methodology.

1

BEGINNINGS (CA. 1760–1800)

Monarchs and aristocrats ... American naming practices ... Recordkeeping ... The ambiguities of Warren ... Patriots, heroes, and partisans of the early republic

C alvin and Lydia Manning of Coventry, Connecticut, welcomed a child into the world in early October 1776, and so had to settle on a name. They had a wealth of traditional options. The most common choices in eighteenth-century New England for a firstborn son, which the baby was, might have included one of the names of the baby's grandfathers (*Hezekiah* or *Samuel*, in the Mannings' case), or some other male relative's given name, or possibly Lydia's maiden name (*Robertson*).

But the year was 1776, and politics was in the air. Only a few months after the colonies had declared independence, concerns of war and rebellion—the clash between pro-revolutionary patriots and anti-revolutionary loyalists—particularly asserted themselves in Coventry: It was the hometown of Nathan Hale, a sacrifice to the revolutionary cause, who had been hanged by the British army barely two weeks before Lydia

Manning gave birth. The exact circumstances of Hale's death were still unclear in Coventry at the time, and his purported last words regretting having "but one life to lose for [his] country" would not pass into general circulation for decades.[1] Grim rumors, however, had already reached Coventry that Hale had been arrested and almost immediately executed as a spy for the patriot cause against the king; Hale's family and friends lurched between grief and outrage.

The Mannings named their new son *Royal*, the most literally royalist option imaginable.

One might assume that the mid-1770s were an inauspicious time for royals in the soon-to-be United States. As revolutionary currents coursed, relations between Britain and its colonial subjects spiraled from acrimony to outright warfare, the king went from being widely revered to widely reviled, and feelings toward the institution of monarchy went down with him. Naming a baby *Royal* could then seem somewhat provocative, or would so seem if people linked the name *Royal* to the royal cause. They need not have: *Royal* and its twin *Royall*, as the name (and word) was often written in the eighteenth century's rakishly promiscuous approach to spelling, had long traditions as boys' names in the colonies as well as in the United Kingdom. People could easily have ignored any political overtones entirely. They may not even have considered them, simply thinking of *Royal* as a pleasant-sounding name, or one that reminded them of some local worthy. It was in fact often a family name, passed down from father to son or grandfather to grandson. Those with the surname Blood, understandably, could not resist: Many boys named Royal Blood appear in colonial records in the 1700s, in several colonies. Less fortunately, various Paines also adopted *Royal* as a recurring name, the name-choosers shortsightedly having failed to anticipate the negative idiom "royal pain" of two centuries later. People in this type of heritage situation may have serenely continued to use *Royal*, heedless of public debates on the merits of monarchy and republicanism. If anyone did happen to raise an eyebrow, the awkwardness could easily be explained away by alluding to the relatives or other namesakes that might have motivated the name.

But as waves of strident anti-monarchical sentiment swept through the thirteen colonies, one might imagine that people would shy away from naming a child *Royal* notwithstanding any innocuous justifications they had for wanting to do so. Even people who did not care about the name's regal associations might have feared that their neighbors did care: Few things encourage circumspection about one's parenting choices like the possibility of tarring and feathering. In any case, the political tumult supplied new alternative name sources that might have crowded out royal choices. Many upheavals, from Oliver Cromwell's English Revolution in the 1640s to the Russian Revolution, have inspired a wave of supportive names.[2]

On the other hand, bolder members of the anti-independence, pro-monarchy loyalist faction might actively have felt moved to signal their allegiance to their embattled king. Had they surmised that their fellow loyalists were a silent majority who could win the day if only their partisans would know the broad popularity of their own cause, the draw of a name like *Royal*, with its potential ability to show the pro-British flag, might even have increased. Or these two forces might have canceled out, with the hardest-core loyalists' increased gestures of support for monarchy balanced by independence supporters and moderates who abandoned the name.

One obvious way to see whether the name *Royal* gave people pause during the Revolutionary War is to see whether and when it was in fact used. To this end, the top panel of figure 1.1 looks at how many births in New England, the region for which at least partial data is most available during the colonial era, involved the name *Royal* (or *Royall*) in each year from 1760 to 1800. The number of recorded births per year is not constant over this period; the colonial population was growing, records gradually became more complete over time, and a wartime baby bust occurred as some potential fathers were off fighting and other families may have held off on having children amid the uncertainties of conflict. To better assess the relative attractiveness of the name, the figure thus shows not the raw count but instead the count as a proportion of the estimated total number of recorded baby names for the year; the book's methodological appendix discusses many more details about this and other measurement issues. For

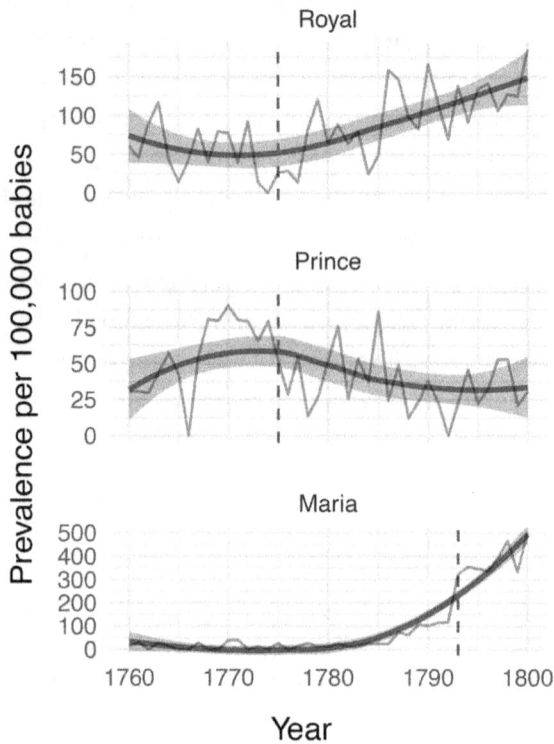

FIGURE 1.1 Number of babies with royal-suggestive names in available New England birth records, by year, 1760–1800, with trend line and shaded 95 percent confidence interval. Dashed line marks onset of the war between Britain and the United States (*top and middle panels*) or execution of Marie Antoinette (*bottom panel*).

comparison, the single most popular name in the United States in 2020, *Liam*, had a prevalence just under six hundred per hundred thousand babies. That followed several decades of name choices becoming much less concentrated.[3] In 1920, the most popular baby name, *Mary*, was used for more than 3,100 per hundred thousand; in 1970, the champion *Michael* was given to slightly more than 2,300 per hundred thousand.

As the country slid into rebellion, use of *Royal* proves to have been less popular than its trend would otherwise have suggested; a run of years around 1776 have lower usage than would have been statistically probable had the underlying propensity to use the name remained constant. Any bashfulness about potential association with royalty, however, seems to have dissipated relatively quickly. By 1778, well before the end of the war (though coinciding with the conclusion of most active fighting in the North, from which these name records come), the prevalence of *Royal* had recovered to its levels of a decade earlier. Perhaps indicatively, the one *Loyal*—the loyalists also of course being the royalists—in the sample of names here was born in 1780, after some of the initial wartime fervor had worn off but before unreconstructed loyalists could be sure their fortunes would be in another country. Little Royal Manning, then, had a name that in 1776 might be widely read as associated with an unpopular, perhaps even obnoxious, cause, but not one so unpopular as to vanish altogether.

Other names that might have monarchical associations provide additional circumstantial evidence that people were conscious of name choices' political color. Several royalty-tinged names were similarly thrown off trend by the war, sometimes more permanently. Consider *Prince*: As the middle panel of figure 1.1 shows, it had withstood the nascent colonial grievances against Britain to attain new levels of popularity in the late 1760s and early 1770s, in line with the conventional wisdom that the colonists in the early stages of the divorce from Britain were more likely to blame Parliament and the prime minister than the monarchy for their grievances.[4] But the outbreak of war coincided with less usage of *Prince*, too, and it did not subsequently recover its prewar popularity, although as another name passed down from fathers or grandfathers, and a common New England surname to boot, it did not wholly disappear. The generally rarer *King* likewise mostly disappeared in the 1770s and 1780s before reappearing in the 1790s.

Not all names with aristocratic or monarchical overtones fared so poorly during the Revolution, though. One starchy hereditary title notably emerges as a name at that very moment: although it had not appeared in the New England birth records before 1779, *Marquis* is thereafter observed more years than not. *Marquis* may have been helped by lacking specific associations with the enemy monarchy given that the title does not directly exist in the peerages of England,[5] where the analogous title is marquess. The name might then have had general attractions for those who wanted a name with some of the sparkle of nobility and links to the colonies' French allies, yet less sullied by British ties. The more specific association with *Marquis*, however, was the Marquis de La Fayette,[6] General Washington's aide-de-camp and a stoutly pro-independence, anti-monarchical figure.[7] Any political signal sent by the newfound appeal of *Marquis*, then, likely differed from that sent by a name such as *Prince*.

In any case, disagreements with King George did not seem to sour the sometime colonists on royalty more generally. When the French Revolution kicked in a few years later, a handful of New England babies were named *Dauphin*, after the ill-fated young heir to the French throne, and the arrest (in 1789) and execution (in 1793) of Marie Antoinette marked the sudden arrival of hundreds of *Maria*s (the birth name by which the French queen was more commonly called in colonial newspapers) or *Marie*s, names previously very little used in New England. Other monarchies also had their attractions, as seen for example in the occasional if persistent use of *Czarina* across these decades as Russia was led by the Empress Elizabeth, followed soon after by Catherine the Great.[8]

At the dawn of their new country, then, Americans appeared quite willing to celebrate hereditary rulers, as long as those rulers ruled someone else, far away.

POLITICAL NAMES IN THE EMERGENT UNITED STATES

As these examples suggest, Americans using names that react to or comment on contemporary politics are as old as the republic—older, even. When the Dare family gave the name *Virginia* to their daughter, the first English baby born in the New World, they explicitly identified her with the reigning queen Elizabeth I and the colonial project. Similarly, old-timey Puritan names such as *Experience*, *Freelove*, or *Increase* ring as purely religious or just weird to today's ears,[9] but the distinction between civic and religious virtue was much blurrier at the time, especially in the quasi-theocratic Massachusetts Bay Colony, than it is now.[10]

By the time the thirteen colonies began moving toward independence, then, naming children after politically resonant people and concepts was deeply embedded in the incipient national culture. This could be seen, for example, in the use of the name *Liberty*, which was next to unknown as a personal name before emerging simultaneously in several colonies during the 1760s. (*Freedom* had a longer history, seeing rare but steady use back to the 1600s.) In New England, again selected only because it offers unusually complete eighteenth-century records, no *Liberty* appears in the birth registers before the Stamp Act crisis of 1765, and no more than two are born in any year before 1774. But then, in 1775, the year of the start of the Revolutionary War, ten *Liberty*s abruptly turn up, followed by another eight in 1776. These lurches into greater prominence in the 1760s and 1770s correspond neatly to when other symbols of liberty started appearing in American art and culture.[11] Although the name's uptake fell thereafter, parents continued to use it to commemorate civic occasions both trivial (Hezekiah and Lucy Palmer of Woodstock, Connecticut, had a baby boy on July 4, 1826, the fiftieth anniversary of the Declaration of Independence, and perhaps for that reason gave him the middle name *Liberty*) and momentous (World War I brought a major revival of the name, as chapter 4 further explores).

Nor was *Liberty* alone. Several names latched onto people, things, or ideas that were in the political air, reflecting the social preoccupations and preferences of their time. *John Hancock* erupted in use as a name in 1775 just as *Liberty* did, when its namesake became president of the Second Continental Congress and a prominent leader of the push for separation from the United Kingdom. *Independence* itself makes some of its rare appearances as a name in 1776 with (male) Independence Whitman born in Bridgewater, Massachusetts, and (female) Independence Booth born—on July 4, no less—in Enfield, Connecticut. Later on, the debate between Federalists supporting and anti-Federalists opposing the Constitution's ratification induced several parents to choose the name *Federal* from 1788 to 1790. Jonathan and Patience Sprague of Douglas, Massachusetts, threw subtlety entirely to the winds, naming their son *Federal Constitution*. And after 1800, the name *President* starts appearing with some regularity. For at least some name-givers, political ideas and debates of the moment were worth commemorating for the long haul. Although many of these names never took off and quickly faded from the record, others endured: *Jay*, for example, first saw widespread use in the 1790s, as John Jay achieved fame as a diplomat and judge, and has persisted as a common if never super-popular name ever since.

It was by no means given that society would adopt this expressive form of naming. Cultures vary wildly in how they handle names. Indeed, an individual person may not have a single or consistent name over time: Some people have multiple names of different categories (personal name, patronymic, religious name), which may change for various reasons over the life course.[12] At the extreme, some people lack anything like a personal name at all. For example, societies as disparate as the early Roman Republic and Korea at the dawn of the twentieth century did not always provide public names for daughters: in Rome, a woman often simply had the family surname as her only name (occasionally with a tag indicating birth order if the family had multiple daughters: *Quinta*, meaning *fifth*, would indicate the fifth-born sister).[13] In the Korean case, girls older than seven were said to only be referred to by the name of their male guardian.[14] Even in contexts where something akin to a given name appears, many societies have had quite restrictive norms about what makes for an appropriate given name. In some societies of West Africa, one important class of names primarily indicates the day of week of birth: *Kofi* might signify that the child is a boy born on Friday, as it did in the name of former UN Secretary-General Kofi Annan.[15] Some Inuit in the high Arctic instead maintain the traditional custom of naming children after recently deceased community members (of either sex) to signify that the memory and spirit of the namesake lives on.[16] Other societies have names strictly derived from birth order, use divination to choose children's names,[17] or include common generation markers among siblings.[18]

But the United States developed a tradition of quite free naming. Unlike various other societies, the country never established rosters of acceptable names from which parents were obliged to choose,[19] although some states have banned the use of obscenities, numerals, and other nonalphabetic characters in personal names.[20] The openness to creativity need not even respect traditional orthographic rules; a name-giver particularly drawn to the letter *Z* might experiment with names such as *Zreinu* and *Xzarweoasz*, to take the given names of two siblings from twenty-first century Connecticut.[21]

This freedom included the scope to offer comments, if very brief ones, on politics. Unfortunately, exploring systematic nationwide trends in the use of politically suggestive names is essentially impossible for the first decades of United States history. Although some towns and churches kept local records that would include personal names, recordkeeping was inconsistent and incomplete before the middle of the nineteenth century. The U.S. Census, notably, did not bother collecting the names of most enumerated people until 1850.[22] In earlier censuses, only heads of household were consistently identified, others merely being counted. Similarly, not all states required or maintained records of vital statistics such as births. Doing so would have required inordinate effort when state capacity was limited and other problems were more pressing, especially in remote reaches of the frontier. Only as technology developed and governments grew larger did records become more thorough. Massachusetts became in 1841 the first state with anything like a modern, systematic attempt to collect birth records, and other states followed suit at various points over the following decades.[23] From that mid-nineteenth-century era, it becomes possible to trace baby names across the country, so that is when this book's main account begins.

WHAT'S IN A NAME?

Analyzing names from before the mid-1800s would also have the drawback that, notwithstanding the occasional use of strikingly unusual names such as *Federal Constitution*, the set of names used in Revolutionary-era New

England was smaller than in most other parts of U.S. history. The more restrictive set of names in use reflects not just cultural conservatism but also the relative ethnic and geographic homogeneity of the observed names: Because Indigenous children often did not appear in the era's records, the population was overwhelmingly of British, especially English, ancestry. Indeed, amid the relatively small population of colonists, a high proportion were of interrelated families, the *Mayflower* descendants being only the most prominent example. This further concentrated the names in use. In consequence, the difficulty noted in the introduction in identifying the source of a name is particularly acute in this context—a difficulty that extends well beyond the example there of differentiating *George*s named for General Washington from those named for George III.

Consider the major uptick in the usage of *Warren* after 1775 (figure 1.2). That was the year Joseph Warren succeeded noted namesake John Hancock to lead the Massachusetts legislature and, subsequently, became a war hero by dying at the Battle of Bunker Hill. Joseph Warren thus seems a likely inspiration for the name of many post-1775 *Warren*s, especially, as a local, among the New England birth records available here. But then, many other prominent Warrens bestrode Revolutionary New England, including Joseph's own brother John Warren (who obtained a smaller measure of martyrdom in Joseph's wake when, as he looked for Joseph after the battle, a British sentry gratuitously though not fatally bayoneted him) or the author Mercy Otis Warren and her husband James Warren—the latter of whom succeeded the unrelated Joseph Warren in his legislative leadership role.

Warren might have had other contemporary sources, too; pro-British imperialists could conceivably have been celebrating Warren Hastings, the first governor-general of India, whose appointment began in 1773. Other possibilities include royal physician Richard Warren, model and courtesan Emily Warren, and newly elected parliamentarian John Borlase Warren, for three. These would, to be sure, seem less-probable namesakes—a courtesan?—than are the local newsmakers. But improbable things happen in any large set of observations such as that offered by names, and people clearly do choose possibly seemingly unlikely names such as *Xzarweoasz* or *Czarina*. No available evidence can then prove that all or some of the

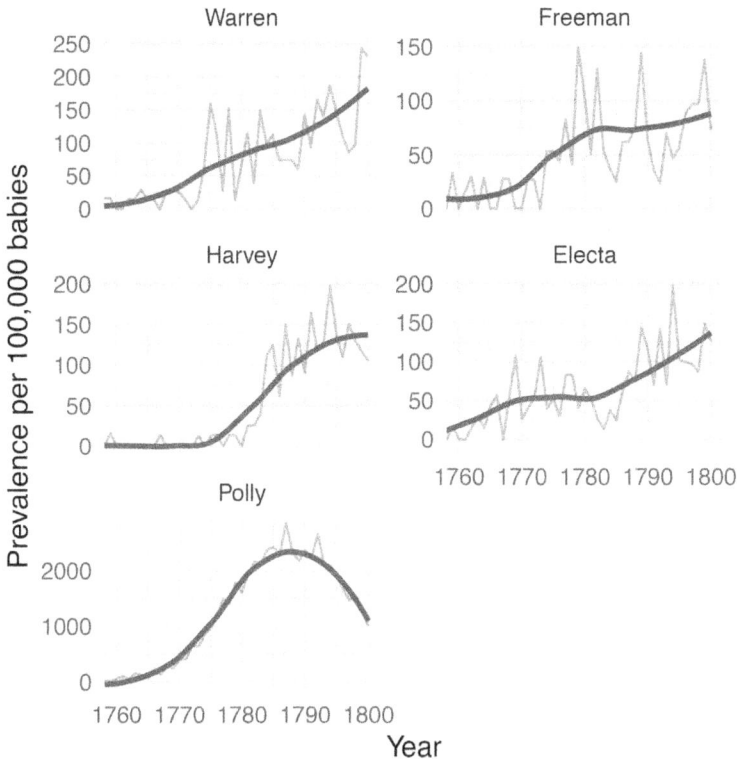

FIGURE 1.2 Trends in selected names in New England, 1760–1800.
Lighter lines show raw proportions; heavier lines show loess smoother.

newborn *Warren*s in 1775 were not named for less likely figures. Even if the name-givers could be interrogated, they might not be willing or able to articulate why they chose the names they did: Acknowledging the source would undercut plausible deniability for naming your child after a courtesan. And, as ever, names could have multiple antecedents, with the selectors consciously or unconsciously drawing on several sources, including those who were known only within the family or community.[24] Still, the names of this period do evoke newsmakers such as Joseph Warren often enough to suggest that he is the probable honoree of many of the *Warren*s of the mid-1770s: It would follow the same logic of renown or sympathy

23

that spurred the use of several names seen earlier in this chapter, from *John Hancock* to *Maria*. Or to, say, *Arnold* finding newfound heights of popularity after Benedict Arnold's triumph at the Battle of Saratoga, before largely disappearing when his later treachery became known.[25]

Freeman is another example whose trajectory is open to interpretation (figure 1.2). The name roughly triples in prevalence just at the time of the Revolution. This could be a variant of the *Liberty* arrival; the association with liberty parallels how one of the first people to sue for freedom from slavery under the Massachusetts state constitution chose the name *Freeman* after manumission.[26] Still, the name's surge could also be a simple shift toward a long-established name without political motivation.[27] Likewise, *Harvey* was barely present as a given name in the data before 1783, the year that the Irish merchant Reuben Harvey was commended by the Continental Congress for his efforts on behalf of the Revolutionary cause (figure 1.2).[28] Thereafter, it swiftly became established as a reasonably common name. But then, it had for more than a century been a family name in New England and throughout England's North American colonies, so other potential sources of the name were plentiful; it might just have happened to catch on at that moment, and could possibly have done so even without Reuben Harvey.[29]

The source of trends is even less clear in the more common case when a name's popularity changes more gradually or less starkly. For example, hundreds of babies in the New England records were named *Electa*, a name notionally appealing to the Calvinist sense that some of God's elect were a chosen people, predestined for salvation. But even if the original use was Calvinist, derivatives of *elect* also can easily be related to elections and the political process of democracy. *Electa* sees a marked rise in use in the years after independence, especially after the ratification of the Constitution (figure 1.2). But does this rise represent a response to the increased opportunity to participate in elections, especially at the federal level, or simply a happenstance movement?

Other names without any obvious current events hook shifted at least as dramatically in use as *Electa* did, after all. One quintessentially Revolutionary-era name was *Polly*, which defined the 1770s and 1780s as a trendy name in the same way that *Heather* or *Melissa* had vogues two centuries later, so that one would have a reliable if rough guess at the age of a woman named *Polly* even if one knew nothing about her except her name. Few names catch fire to the same extent, but such extreme cases show that the normal ebb and flow of names lacking political impetus can move much more markedly than *Electa* did.[30] A major shift in usage is consequently not enough evidence to show that names were driven by events, certainly not without some specific event that could plausibly have changed public views of a name. One might appeal to other evidence: *Electa* does, suggestively, seem to be somewhat more common in years with federal elections, but it is nevertheless hard to determine how much political elections affected that particular name choice.

When the meaning of the shifting popularity for a particular name is unclear like this, we can sometimes draw on the trajectories of analogous names to test theories about the source of the name's popularity. For example, *Isaac* had a brief surge in popularity in the middle of the 1770s in New England. This immediately follows Isaac Davis's achieving renown for his bravery in dying at the Battle of Concord in 1775; he was the first colonial officer to die in the war against Britain. That subsequent chapters see similar early hero figures who have similar arcs of naming popularity in other wars may help reinforce the conjecture that Davis is a relatively likely source of that flurry of *Isaac*s. Similarly, the fact that *Franklin* leaps in popularity in 1790, the year of Benjamin Franklin's death, and then rises from there, accords with a pattern seen on the demise of other famous political figures. However, that sort of comparison with like cases falters when, as with *Electa*, fewer obvious comparisons suggest themselves.

THE FUTURE IN THE INFANT

Despite such ambiguities, names can help trace political currents in the decades around and after independence. Although the specific elements of identity that most preoccupied society, and hence name-givers, changed over time, many of the patterns seen in these early political names fore-shadow the identities and features that would matter throughout the history of the United States and that animate later chapters of this book.

The invocation of abstract political concepts in the style of *Federal* or *Liberty* has been rare in the United States, but a few adventurous name-givers have always been bold enough to use them. More often, people would then and later name children directly after admired political figures; the war for independence saw newfound use of names such as *Washington*, which had previously not seen use as a given name in New England, and much greater uptake of names of other revolutionary figures such as *Franklin*. Or *Horatio* as in Horatio Gates, a prominent commander alongside Benedict Arnold at the Battle of Saratoga, which like *Washington* prefigures the powerful pull of military figures as namesakes for later generations, especially in wartime.

Even hints of partisan naming patterns appear, despite the well-defined party system having not yet formed. *Federal*, for one, took a side in the federalist versus anti-federalist debates over the constitution, but so might an example like *Jay*. *Jay*'s blossoming as a popular first or middle name (usually though not always following *John* in the latter case) started in 1794. In that year, John Jay served as lead U.S. negotiator for the agreement with Great Britain widely known as the Jay Treaty. That may be an unexpected launchpad for *Jay*'s popularity, given that most traditional historical accounts emphasize that public opinion in the newborn United States stridently opposed the treaty.[31] In fact, in the wake of the treaty, one Boston fence was chalked with the immortal graffiti "Damn John Jay! Damn everyone that won't damn John Jay!! Damn everyone that won't put lights in his windows and sit up all night damning John Jay!!!"[32] One might think association with such a derided agreement would make *Jay* less rather than more popular.[33] That the treaty appears to have inspired or at least not prevented namesakes suggests that, at least in some corners, it might not have been so reviled, especially given that Jay's career had previously been highly illustrious without inspiring the same number of namesakes: He had been president of Congress, secretary of foreign affairs (the office, before ratification of the Constitution, analogous to the later secretary of state), and chief justice of the United States, all positions that put him prominently in the public eye without seeming to lead to many baby *Jays*. Indeed, support for the Jay Treaty broke down on partisan lines: Expressing support for Jay during the treaty's ratification was expressing support for the Federalist Party's perspective.

As it would in many later eras, this partisanship had a regional dimension. The names looked at here being from New England, the base of the Federalists, likely emphasizes support for Jay. Notwithstanding the Jay-damning graffiti, regions farther south were more dominated by anti-Jay views, which might indirectly also create social pressures not to express support for the treaty in those regions even among those who genuinely believed it represented good policy. But records restricted to New England cannot directly show differences across the various regions of the country.

That blindness is unfortunate because differences between North and South over slavery and much else came to dominate politics in the decades after independence. So regional identities are a useful theme to begin exploring naming patterns. In jumping forward to the middle of the nineteenth century when nationwide naming information first becomes available, that issue of regionalism is accordingly where our story resumes.

2

REGIONAL IDENTITIES
(CA. 1850–1880)

The rise and fall of Savannah . . . *Regional names . . . Enduringly asymmetric sectionalism . . . State names . . . Military ranks . . . Battle sites and war heroes . . . John Wilkes Booth*

A 1982 children's film, *Savannah Smiles*, launched the name *Savannah* into a multidecade run as a popular name for girls. The name was not totally unknown before the movie's release—the writer of the movie named the title character after his own daughter, for example—but it had been quite rare, allowing it to seem fresh and new to 1980s audiences.

Yet *Savannah* was a name with a history.[1] Although somewhat less common than it would become in the 1990s, *Savannah* had been respectably popular in the nineteenth century before slowly languishing to near oblivion by the 1930s. This earlier run of *Savannah* differed from the revival, however, in its very particular geography. The nineteenth-century use of the name was disproportionately a phenomenon of the South: More than half the *Savannah*s in the 1880 Census listed their state of birth as Georgia or its neighboring states (see figure 2.1). The proportion of Southerners was

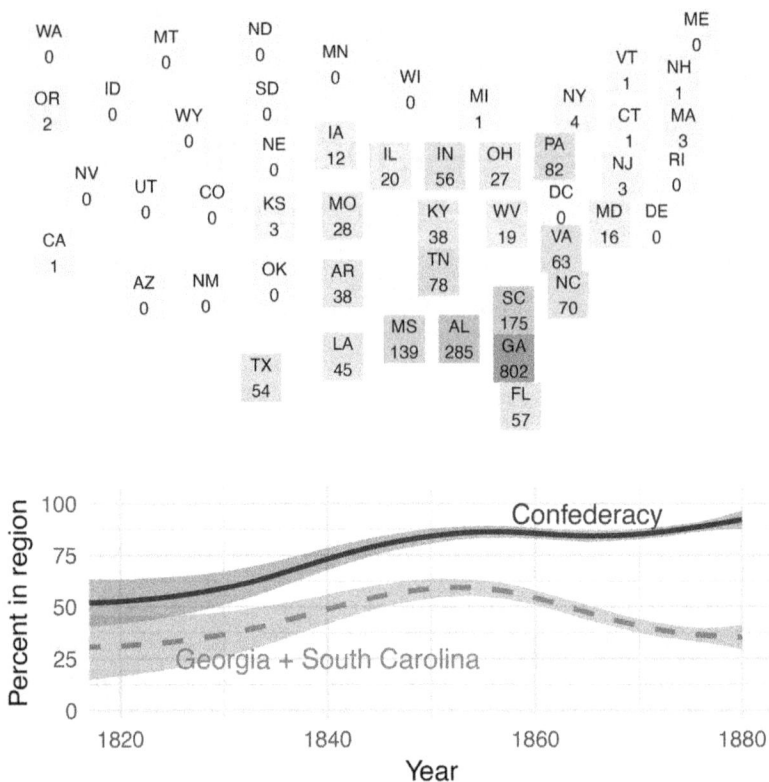

FIGURE 2.1 *Savannah* in the 1880 Census. Top panel shows the count by state of birth (darker shading indicates more locally born *Savannah*s); bottom panel shows the over-time smoothed trend in the proportion born in selected parts of the country (shading indicates 95 percent confidence intervals).

yet higher if one includes variant spellings (most commonly, in that era, *Savanah*).

Of course, *Savannah* has long had clear associations with Georgia. The city of Savannah, which had been the colonial and state capital, lies on the Savannah River, which forms most of the state's border with South Carolina. But as a given name, the regional connection intensified during the 1800s. Of *Savannah*s in the 1880 Census born before 1840, a mere

55 percent reported being born in states that would eventually become the Confederacy.[2] This proportion crept upward over time; by the 1870s, 89 percent of newborn *Savannah*s were Southern.[3] This shift is all the more impressive given that the Confederate states largely stagnated in population in the middle of the nineteenth century as the rest of the country grew: The South managed to increase its share of the *Savannah* births even as its share of babies overall dwindled, and the only sustained decline in the South's share of *Savannah*s occurred during the Civil War, when the region endured a particularly severe baby bust.

Even as the name became more specifically a Southern choice, it became more broadly dispersed through the South. Most Southern examples of *Savannah* from before the 1850s were from the states of the Savannah River valley, Georgia and South Carolina. But thereafter it rapidly gained popularity across virtually all parts of the Confederacy. True, Georgia and South Carolina saw particularly tepid population growth after the Civil War, but even accounting for this, their share of *Savannah*s fell. The name became less of an indicator of a specifically Savannah-region identity and more of a generic marker of being Southern, as people across the South adopted *Savannah* as their own and Northerners avoided it. Some of the diffusion across the South occurred as Georgia-born parents moved and then provided children with a name reminiscent of home; the name's preponderance in Alabama, for example, partly reflects the westward flow of nineteenth-century migrants.[4] Other Southern parents of *Savannah*s, though, do not claim in the census to have been born in a state near the Savannah River: The name seemed to gain a broader resonance in the region.

This fits with the period being a time of rising regional sentiment—what contemporaries would more often have called sectionalism, after the contending sections of the country.[5] Just as those living in the United States in the late twentieth century grappled with increasing polarization by partisan identities, their forebearers of the mid-nineteenth century witnessed an analogous rise in feeling based on where in the country they lived. And just as the latter-day polarization has been by many measures asymmetric between parties,[6] the sectionalist era may have been asymmetric as well,

Southerners feeling and flaunting an especially intense regional pride. Names such as *Savannah* would be one way to demonstrate such a regional sensibility.

To be sure, a name appearing mainly in one part of the country need not reflect any sectionalist attitude, let alone proto-secessionist truculence. Many names ended up with a regional patina because some cultural group tended, on migrating to the United States, to settle in a geographic cluster. *Yaro*, when seen in someone born in America, tends to suggest an origin in Ohio's Yugoslavian communities: It derived from *Jaroslav*. *Lumir* similarly shows up among the Czech-heritage populations of Nebraska and Iowa. Such echoes of regional ethnic heritage could even at times reflect history from before the United States claimed the relevant territory. People with Russian heritage were a far larger share of the population in Alaska than in most of the country, just as Hispanic origins were especially common in New Mexico, Japanese (and native Hawaiian) origins in Hawaii, and French origins in Louisiana. Hence *Nicholai* would likely come from Alaska, *Adelaida* from New Mexico, *Kiku* from Hawaii, and *Alcée* from Louisiana. Nor were regionally based cultural communities always knit together by ethnicity. Utah's Mormon history gave the state a wealth of *Rulon*s, *Hyrum*s, *Parley*s, *Orson*s, and *Lapreal*s (or *Laprele*s, or *Lapriel*s) mostly lacking elsewhere, and, much later, a prominent Catholic bishop of Pittsburgh, Regis Canevin, seems to have helped inspire a local appreciation for both *Regis* and *Nevin*. Similarly, because some parents use the mother's maiden name (or surname of a godparent or other family connection) as the child's given name, family names that happen to be widespread or prominent in a region can become locally common first names, such as *Estill* in Kentucky or *Bayard* in Delaware. All these types of names might acquire some geographic associations through their clustering, but they primarily reflect ethnic, religious, or family identities rather than regional ones.[7]

A name such as *Savannah* points more explicitly to regional pride in alluding to a specific place. Even if every widely used name mixes several sources of inspiration, the city's sheer importance meant that associations with the place would dominate. Savannah was a major regional center; for much of the nineteenth century, it was Georgia's largest city by population,

Atlanta surpassing it only in the 1870s. Not only that, Savannah's regional prominence held without any analogous Northern city sharing its name to muddy the Southern overtones, a notable contrast with *Augusta*, another major Georgia city and sometime capital whose name was more traditional as a personal name but also invoked the capital of Maine. Savannah's connections to the Southern cause were further cemented in 1864 by Sherman's March to the Sea, an important Civil War campaign ultimately targeting Savannah's capture.

That march of Sherman's had multiple legacies in the South. Some may have wanted to mourn the destruction of old Georgian society, but many others had cause to celebrate the social disruption. The march helped liberate the Black part of the local population, who might have wanted to commemorate that deliverance.[8] That potential connection complemented many Blacks' strong attachment to their home regions, with their neighbors and landscapes, despite the horrors of slavery those places had seen. For them, *Savannah* might appeal both through its association with a place but also with a campaign of deliverance. *Savannah*'s use thus rose not just among Whites, and its racial distribution changed over time. Around half of the 1880 Census's child *Savannah*s—that is, those born since the 1870 Census—were listed as Black (or Mulatto, a separate racial category in that census), whereas older cohorts of *Savannah*s were progressively likelier to be White. This age gradient owes something to racial minorities' shorter life expectancies, but earlier censuses point to the same pattern, with the *Savannah*s under age ten having an increasing proportion of Blacks (or Mulattos, though most of the rise was in the Black share) at each successive decade's count. By the last decades of the nineteenth century, *Savannah* was, especially in the South, disproportionately a name used by Blacks—a factor that may have contributed to the name's eventually slipping into decades of little use, given that Whites often flee from anything they fear might associate themselves, or their daughters, with Blacks.[9] Names can be as subject to this sort of White flight as neighborhoods are.

Although it reflected specific dynamics, *Savannah* was not unique in having a nineteenth-century regional origin that eventually dissipated. *Travis*, for instance, began as a Texas-specific name, after William B.

Travis, the martyred commander of the Alamo when it fell; it only later became common nationwide. But the pattern of strong regional cultures being flattened out into greater national homogeneity is also a tale of nationalizing political identities. The most notable regional identity countering this trend, for both its rebellious spirit and its racial diversity, is that of the South.

STATE YOUR NAME

The example of *Savannah* illustrates the possibility of geographic names to reveal regional attachments. It was by no means the only such example. *Memphis*, say, similarly had a run as a nineteenth-century name and a much later revival. But one of the more systematic ways to generate regional names in the 1800s was to draw on states. It was not just the long-standing names of *Virginia*, *Georgia*, and to a lesser extent *Carolina* that were used in this way. Using a state name for one's child expresses an identity with one's state in a very direct way: It specifically emphasizes an attachment to the state, pointedly underscoring that attachment rather than national identities. A politics or culture that emphasizes the role of states—a decentralized federalism, rather than a strong national government—might then use relatively more baby names derived from state names. This, of course, connects to a frequent rallying cry of the American South in the nineteenth century, the *States Rights* of baby names mentioned in chapter 1, as regional leaders sought to reframe arguments about slavery to being about principles of institutional design. Northern rhetoric, by contrast, tended to emphasize the federal union over the individual states.[10] One might expect that state names would accordingly be more common in the South.

Though the state name nearest at hand would be that of the baby's state of birth, it need not be the only choice. Cross-state migrants' nostalgia for their home might lead them to use the name of their former states of residence, and parents could also appreciate a state's culture from afar. Even then, patterns of migration and affinity suggest that Southerners would more likely draw on the names of other Southern states, and that Northerners would draw on other Northern states. That is, it seems likely not only that Southerners will have used more state names, but that the state names they used would especially tend to be the state of their child's birth and other Southern states, most emphatically from the mid-1800s on as North versus South sectionalism intensified.

This pattern would be colored by some state names being rather too over the top for directly inflicting on children. Very few babies were named *Mississippi*, the more popular *Magnolia* perhaps serving as a tribute to the Magnolia State. Wyoming and Utah also seemed to require reworking before being perceived as natural-sounding names, respectively tending to become *Wyoma* and *Utahna*. Delaware likewise turns into *Delema*, whether because that more closely resembles other common girls' names than *Delawa* would have or because of the pernicious influence of Maryland (other combinations such as *Mississouri* also crop up as well, suggesting use of a portmanteau might not be far-fetched though in some cases such combinations might reflect mistranscriptions). Such derived names can coexist with unsoftened originals. *Bama* and *Bamma* appear alongside *Alabama* as names, and *Okla*—often but not always with the middle name *Homa*—alongside *Oklahoma*.[11] Even so, most states with single-word names won at least a few direct namesakes, even when those single words are mouthfuls, such as *Connecticut*. For example, the mixed-race parents of Massachusetts Thompson of Alexandria, Virginia, perhaps were celebrating a state noted for abolitionist sentiment when they named their child in the mid-1850s.

Two-word names are harder to consistently observe; if your name were *Rhode Island*, would you take the time to insist that both names appeared in full on official documents?[12] It does happen; see Kansas Nebraska Stevens of Ashley County, Arkansas, a three-month-old in the 1860 Census whose parents were presumably true champions of the 1856 Kansas-Nebraska Act to give their child that name and report it in full. That said, both *Kansas* and *Nebraska* were quite widely used as names at the time, as many state names were when their associated territories joined the Union as new states; the formation of the new state of West Virginia likewise provoked several babies named *West Virginia* and so listed in the census. But those double-barreled names are less reliably detectable because most records omit middle names or reduce them to initials. To circumvent this, consider first names that match one-word state names—match being defined broadly to incorporate common misspellings and phonetic transcriptions.

As a starting point for examining the popularity of naming babies after states, figure 2.2 shows which states were the most common namesakes over this period, listing the ten nationally most popular state names for children born since the previous census the national censuses from 1850 to 1880. The figure also provides raw counts of totals for each name, not adjusted for the era's boom in national population. For consistency across the decades, states are defined broadly, including areas that would eventually become states. This choice may mislead in the case of *Washington*: Washington Territory did not obtain statehood until 1883—indeed, it was not even a named territory at the 1850 Census—and few parents outside the hardy pioneers of the Pacific Northwest were likely to primarily associate the name with the territory as such when George Washington himself loomed so large in public memory. But then, other state names also unavoidably have associations with things other than states: *Virginia* is a common girl's name in several languages dating back to ancient Rome and flourished even in English outside the context of the United States, perhaps most famously with Virginia Woolf. On the margins, however, the ebbs and flows of state names are likely to reflect connections to the states in question.

Census year

1850	1860	1870	1880
1. Virginia (11465)	1. Virginia (14126)	1. Virginia (16929)	1. Virginia (14989)
2. Washington (4720)	2. Missouri (3510)	2. Georgia (7121)	2. Georgia (11254)
3. Missouri (2370)	3. Washington (3367)	3. Washington (4708)	3. Washington (3769)
4. Indiana (1057)	4. Georgia (2502)	4. Missouri (3371)	4. Missouri (3270)
5. Georgia (1052)	5. Tennessee (1695)	5. Tennessee (1889)	5. Tennessee (1778)
6. Tennessee (938)	6. Indiana (1100)	6. Indiana (1147)	6. Indiana (1140)
7. Louisiana (857)	7. Louisiana (852)	7. Louisiana (870)	7. Florida (1074)
8. Florida (323)	8. Florida (523)	8. Florida (758)	8. Nevada (793)
9. Alabama (287)	9. Alabama (434)	9. Alabama (529)	9. Louisiana (788)
10. California (253)	10. California (392)	10. Nevada (513)	10. Alabama (698)

FIGURE 2.2 Ten most popular state names for children ten years of age or younger, 1850–1880. Number in parentheses is count of children with relevant name.

The set of top-ten state names holds steady across these decades, except that *California*, popular in the years following its gold rush and new statehood, is after the 1860 Census eclipsed by *Nevada*.[13] Notably, a majority of these most-used state names evoke states that seceded in the 1860s even though a relatively small proportion of states nationwide joined the Confederacy—and most of the seceding states had relatively small populations, with few residents to express home-state loyalty through naming choices. The Confederate states in fact have an average rank on the full listing of prevalence of state names some fifteen places higher than the average Union state's, a difference statistically distinguishable with high confidence: Those expressing state identities through their name choice predominately associated with Southern states.

Within this stability, the names do experience relative shifts in popularity. Although *Virginia* is consistently the most common name, its use expanded considerably through the 1850s and 1860s, as the country was breaking apart, before falling back in the 1870s. More remarkable was *Georgia*'s growth during these decades. It had long been a reasonably common girl's name, but its use spread phenomenally during the Civil War era. One benchmark is that *Georgia* was in the 1840s roughly as prevalent as *Indiana* but by the 1870s almost ten times as common. Few other state names could match that scorching pace of growth, but *Alabama* and *Florida* became substantially more popular. Conversely, *Indiana* was not alone in stagnating; *Louisiana* did too, as, after the 1840s, did *Tennessee* and *Missouri*—both of which were quite popular names for daughters through the nineteenth century, despite their later rarity.[14]

The commonness of these names does not just represent state pride. Indeed, commonness might indicate that the name associates less with the state rather than more. Being very common almost requires a name to geographically concentrate less in its home state, eroding the name's identification with the homonymous state.[15] The likes of *Virginia*, *Washington*, and *Georgia* could transcend regional associations for most Americans: When Georgia O'Keeffe was born near Madison, Wisconsin, in 1887, for instance, her parents named her after her maternal grandfather, without any obvious thought of the Southern state. Had O'Keeffe's parents instead named her *Wisconsin*, well, that might seem like a name that only a home-state loyalist could love. A name's overall prevalence, by this logic, would have a negative correlation with the name's specificity to a particular state. In that case, a state's name increasingly seeing use as a child name in other states would indicate less about home-state sentiment than about names' etymological origins becoming less relevant as they diffuse and become popular.

The upper panel of figure 2.3 checks for this potential negative relationship, showing the scatterplot of a name's prevalence against the proportion of its uses that occurred in the namesake state. (Note that the figure's x-axis has a logarithmic scale, so that moving a given distance to the right indicates a proportional increase in the name's popularity.) The potential negative relationship is not in evidence. If anything, the average trend has a slight upward slope, especially when weighting states by how many observations they have, which reduces the influence of the single *Oklahoma* in the data.[16] Aside from the *Oklahoma* anomaly, the names most concentrated in their home states, such as *Illinois*, *Kentucky*, and *Ohio*, are in the middle of the popularity distribution, whereas *Tennessee* manages to have nearly half its occurrences in Tennessee even though the state is not the sort of high-population state that easily could run up the numbers. Moreover, it would in fact have been out of the ordinary for Georgia O'Keeffe to have been named *Wisconsin*, a name that turns out to be less concentrated in its home state than most are: It appears to be a name of wistful outsiders, not Wisconsinites themselves.

Where those wistful outsiders lived may tell us something further about their regionalist politics. The importance of sectionalism might suggest that names would have some attraction elsewhere in their section but be disfavored outside their home sections as associating with an opposing, even adversarial, identity. On the other hand, the idea that state-oriented politics and identities focused particularly on the South, with the region's implacable insistence on states' rights (presumably for all states) suggests that Southerners might choose disproportionate shares of state names but be relatively indiscriminate about which states are the chosen namesakes. The two possibilities are not mutually exclusive; state names could generally be more common in the South, but Confederate-state names especially

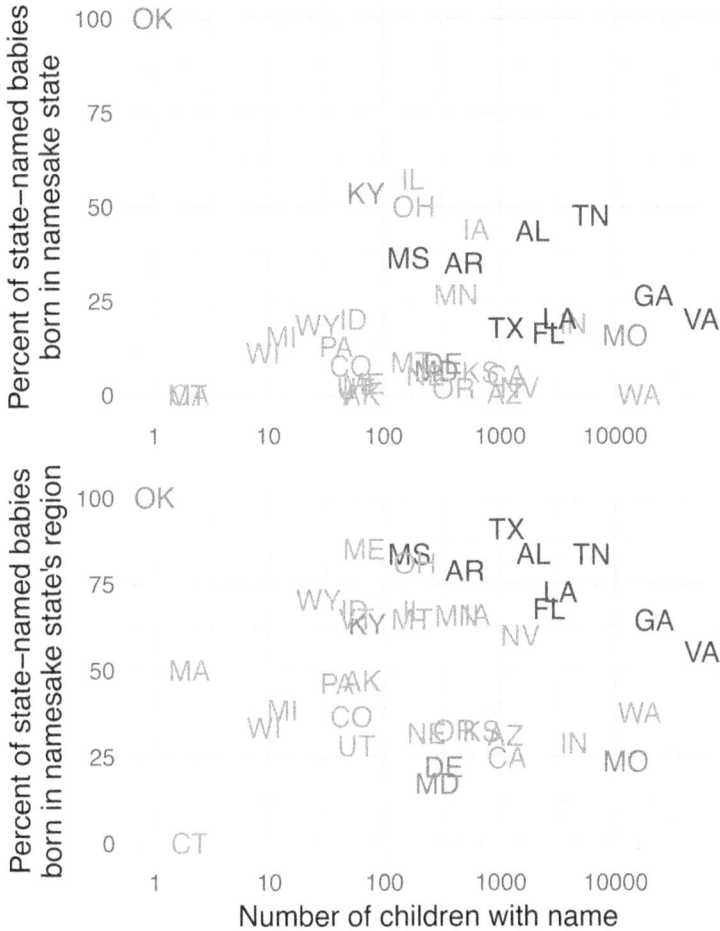

FIGURE 2.3 Share of babies named for U.S. states, 1840–1880, whose names match their state (top panel) or region (bottom panel) of birth. Observations are colored by Southernness of region.

so. Regardless, the regional pattern of the names may be as important as whether they were common in their home states. Figure 2.3's lower panel accordingly presents the share of children named for each state that were born within that namesake state's section: Confederacy, Border, or Union.[17] This includes those born within the namesake state itself, so the states in the lower panel will always be at least as high as their corresponding entries in the upper panel, and the vertical distance between a state's entries in the two panels indicates its share of namesake babies that were born in the state's section but outside the state.

Given that the South was less populous than the North and hence that a larger proportion of babies were born there, it is notable that most of the names toward the top of figure 2.3's lower panel—the anomalous single *Oklahoma* again excepted—are from Southern states. That is, Southerners managed to dominate the use of most Southern-state names even though they had fewer babies to name than the North did. (Contrast with the Border states, which see rises across the panels that are roughly comparable to their modest share of the overall population.) Although state names from all regions do appear appreciably higher in the lower panel, the tendency is especially marked in the South. For instance, the annexation of Texas was extremely newsy in national politics for a time, but the name *Texas*'s widespread use throughout the Confederacy was not seen elsewhere. Or maybe that regional slant was precisely because of the newsiness, given that Texas's slaveholding status was one of the central points of national contention over admitting it to the United States, a fact that intimately tied debates over Texas to the sectional divide.[18]

Texas was then not just place-specific as a political issue but also time-specific, and time specificity points to the possibility for state names to evolve in their use and meanings. Signaling attachment to state supremacy and to one's home region might have especially changed as sectional disputes spiraled into open conflict and war. Figure 2.4 thus complements figure 2.3 by showing changes over time. State-based names decline after 1865 in every region, according with the familiar ideas that, after the Civil War, people shifted away from individual states and toward the nation as a whole as the primary entity that they identified with.[19] This decline, though, played out differently in each region.

Fitting with the states-rights interpretation of emphasizing state identities, Southerners were likeliest to use state names, especially Confederate-state names, throughout these decades. Border states, intuitively, lay between the Confederacy and the rest of the country in this regard.[20] Despite this

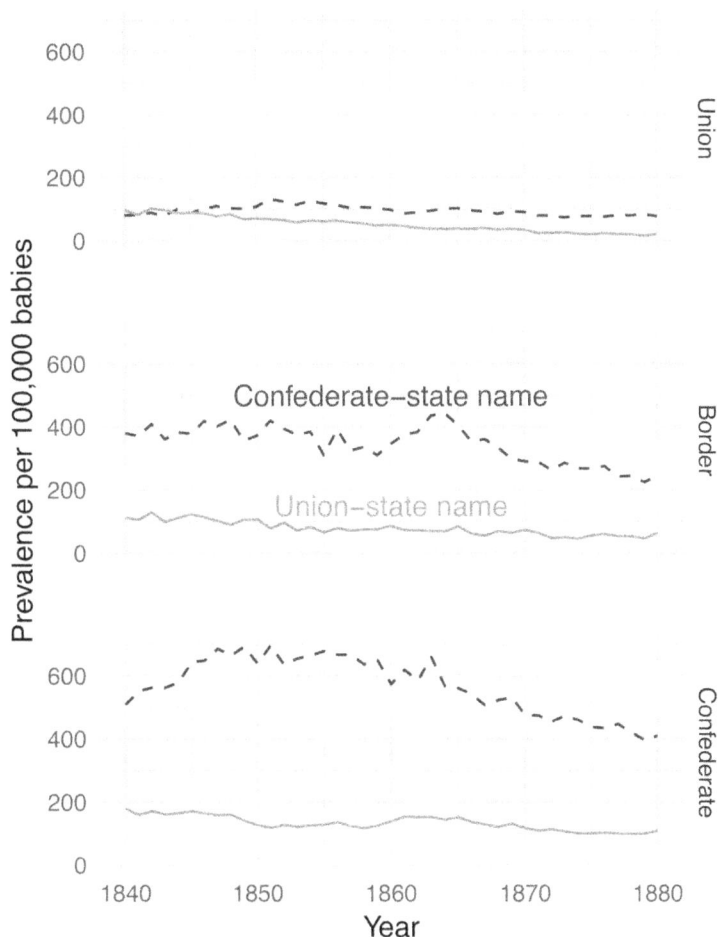

FIGURE 2.4 Prevalence of state names as given names, 1840–1880, by region of child's birth and state of namesake.

consistent link between Southernness and use of state names, the attraction of those names varied over time, Southern use of the names rising quickly in the 1840s, plateauing from then until the middle of the Civil War, then beginning a decades-long decline, most of this change involving names invoking Southern states. In the Border states, meanwhile, state-name prevalence was very slightly declining until an upswing in Southern-state names during the Civil War. After the war, the border region saw the same shrinking of state-name usage as the South did. In northern and western states, though, the slide in state names began somewhat earlier, around 1850, after they had held roughly constant over the previous decade. Even there, though, the distribution of names tended to shift to include a greater proportion of Southern states over time as state names other than *Virginia* and *Georgia* fell away.[21]

Given the thousands of babies involved, the 40 percent increase in the prevalence of Southern-state names in the South in the 1840s, or the comparable increase in Southern-state names in the border region during the Civil War, is unlikely to be a statistical fluke. And seeing such swings within particular regions reduces the odds that the difference reflects different regions having different naming cultures because of factors such as the different ethnic or national origins of their residents. Those differences were relatively constant in the period under consideration here, and so on their own could not spur within-region changes.

Aggregating across a whole region conflates multiple distinguishable processes, corresponding to the two panels of figure 2.3: Naming a child after the state of residence (or through which the child's mother happened to be passing at the time of birth) differs from expressing solidarity with other states in the region. The own-state name may indicate a purely local identity, whereas naming a child after another state in the region suggests that identity has at least partly transcended the specific state to encompass the broader section of the country. The diffusion of local names across their region, just as happened with *Savannah*, is one marker of identities consolidating from the kaleidoscope of distinct local cultures into the single main axis of North-South conflict. Figure 2.5 accordingly disaggregates the data, showing the percentage of each section's children named for any state for whom the namesake state was the state of birth (upper panel) or, instead, another state in the same section (lower panel).

As the figure's upper panel shows, the actual birth state tended to recede as a share of all state names over these decades; state-based names tended to become more cosmopolitan and outward looking. That trend held consistently across all three sections, except in the Union states in the 1840s and

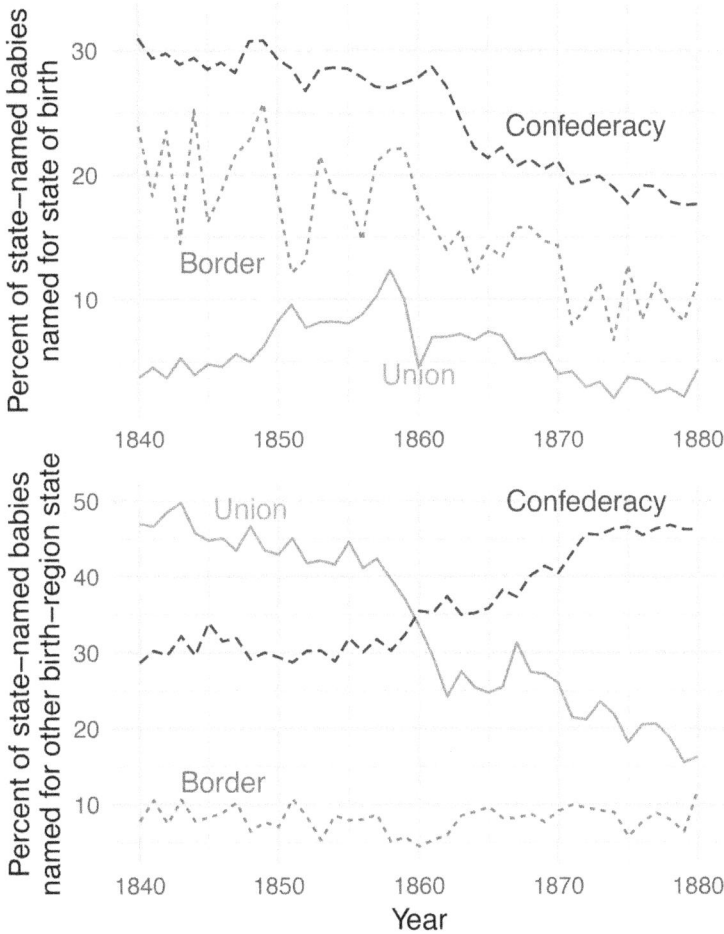

FIGURE 2.5 Names matching birth state (upper panel) or other state in region of birth (lower panel) as a share of all state-matching names, 1840–1880, by region of birth.

1850s. But the lower panel shows a divergence: Union parents who gave their children state names increasingly chose names from Border or Confederate states, with a particular lurch toward the names of other regions' states around 1860. In the Confederacy, the proportion of intraregional names was stable, except for a sustained rise from the mid-1850s to the mid-1870s.

Partly, to be sure, these patterns reflect factors unrelated to states. *Georgia*'s ascendancy over these decades (see figure 2.2) as it cast off many traces of expressing a state-related identity and instead became a generic name for girls was one dynamic. When *Georgia* becomes a national sensation, more people in the Confederacy will mechanically have a state name from within their region, whereas more people in the Union will have a state name from outside theirs. *Virginia*'s holding steady as a name as state names generally declined had a similar if smaller effect.

But *Virginia* and *Georgia* are only part of the story. Even as naming children after states fell out of the fashion during the last half of the 1800s and the Northern parents who still chose state names abandoned regional-pride motivations for their name choices, Southerners became more intensely regional in what state names they did use. They sustained a taste for expressing sectionalist culture even as their rival section to the North moved on after the Civil War—and, notably, the choice of state-based names in the South became increasingly sectional rather than specific to the birth state. The distribution of expressions of sectional identity between North and South, that is, appears to become much more asymmetrical.

MORE GENERAL REGIONAL DIVIDES

Sectional pride extends beyond mere incantation of local state names. Indeed, ways to express a regional identity proliferated in the 1800s as cultural and political divides widened between North and South. Even before the war, as the spiraling conflict over slavery (and, in its wake, a collection of irritant issues from national territorial expansion to the tariff level) produced repeated flashpoints of sharp disagreement between regions of the country. Many of these landmark events found their way into at least a few children's names.

In the 1860 Census, for example, a three-month-old free Black girl in Ocheesee, Florida, is named *Dred Scott* after the famous Black man who sued for his freedom but whose case—and entitlement to even basic civil rights—was brusquely rejected by the Supreme Court. The family name of the chief justice who authored that blistering opinion, *Taney*, also got a few subsequent uses. Roger Taney attracted very little other interest as a namesake, so it stands out that the *Dred Scott* opinion seems to have won him such admiration. In another example, John Brown tried in 1859 to capture weapons from the federal arsenal at Harper's Ferry, Virginia, for use in his fight against slavery. The effort failed, violently, leading to Brown's capture and execution. Suddenly, *John Brown* emerged as a name for several children from across the North, emphatically enough to have both first and middle name recorded in the census.

Even more widespread was the response to some notorious events of May 22, 1856, when South Carolina Representative Preston Brooks, an ardent slavery defender, beat Massachusetts's abolitionist Senator Charles Sumner unconscious on the floor of the Senate. This was not wholly unprecedented: Tiffs between legislators frequently erupted into physical violence during the nineteenth century.[22] But the ferocity of the attack, at a time of inflamed sectional passions, provoked strongly polarized reactions around the country, Northern politicians and newspapers predictably condemning the savagery and Southern elites just as predictably lauding Brooks as a defender of Southern honor.

The public, or at least those among the public who were choosing names, reacted similarly. *Preston*, *Brooks*, and *Sumner* all became substantially more widely used names in 1856 and 1857 than they had been in previous years (see figure 2.6). But their newfound popularity had a definite geographic cast: *Preston* and *Brooks* gained prevalence only in the South, *Sumner* only in the North. However, the relevant names did not noticeably retreat from the potentially hostile regions: Northerners did not suddenly reduce their use of *Preston* or *Brooks*, and Southerners did not avoid *Sumner* any more than before. Charles Sumner was prominent enough of an abolitionist that perhaps any Southern (White) antagonism to his name was already present, but prior to the attack Preston Brooks was a relatively obscure figure; the source of his newfound fame might be expected to have created new associations around his name. Of course, that the aggregate total of Northern *Preston*s and *Brooks*es did not change much in 1856 still allows that the

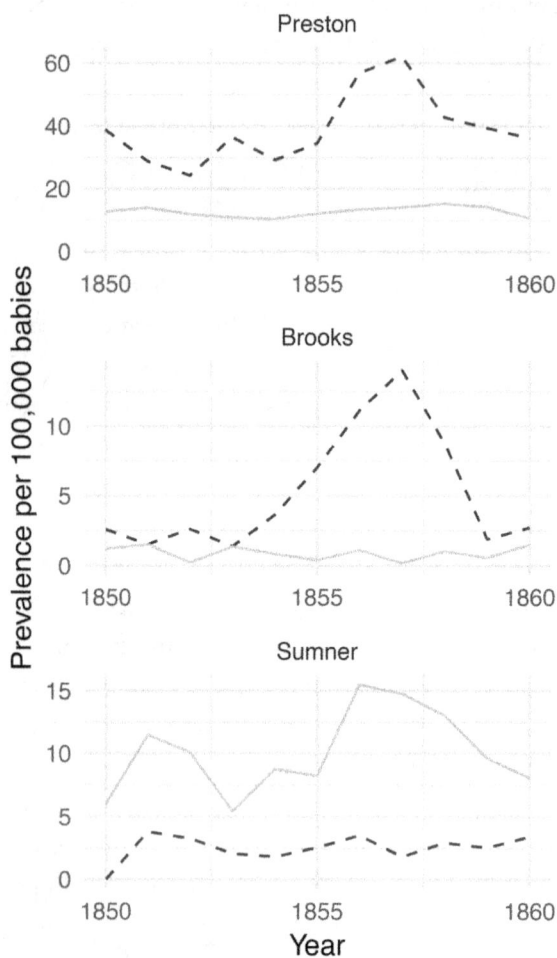

FIGURE 2.6 Popularity of names from the Brooks–Sumner confrontation, 1850–1860, in Union (solid line) and Confederate (dashed line) states, excluding the Border states, per the 1860 Census.

sorts of people within the North who used those names might have changed. It could be, in particular, that *Preston* was previously a neutral name that suddenly gained appeal for slavery defenders while losing it with antislavery Northerners. Circumstantial evidence argues against this: The names did not become poisonous in the generally antislavery New England states, for instance. But the nationwide birth data cannot more specifically show whether individual slavery apologists (or haters of Charles Sumner in particular) could have replaced others within their states as users of those names.

Regardless, the public's attentiveness to the story of the congressional violence soon receded from the baby-naming evidence. As measured by namesakes, the principals appear no more present in the public consciousness by the decade's end than they had been at its start. Some may complain about the overwhelming torrent of modern-day news shortening attention spans, but the rush of events as North-South conflict exploded was so all-consuming that even something as vivid as the public, incapacitating flogging of a well-known senator swiftly lost its currency. Well before Sumner was able to return to the Senate in 1859, the event had essentially disappeared from naming patterns. Notably, the event's fade into history occurred equally in both sections of the country: This example shows no sense that the South particularly held onto its prewar champions, even when their fame was rooted in defense of Southern and slaving interests.

A key word there, though, is *prewar*: The North-South divide culminated in the conflagration of the Civil War itself, which was harrowing enough to be a decisive cultural breakpoint. Moreover, the war itself offered many sources of names, creating a host of potential ways to mark regional identities. One venerable tradition named children after national military leaders, such as when the generations born during the American Revolution and subsequent decades saw many boys called *General Washington*. New parents naming children in the wake of the Civil War could thus readily use analogous names such as *General Lee* or *General Grant* or even *General Ulysses S. Grant*. Or, responding to the much-increased importance and visibility of military titles (or to memorialize multiple namesakes), parents could generically name their children not after specific commanders but instead after military titles such as *General*, *Major*, or *Captain*.[23] Such monikers sometimes reflected an underlying military spirit without reference to any particular conflict, or an interest in historical conflicts as with latter-day *General*s *Washington*. Most often, however, they grew out of feelings about the ongoing or recent war between North and South.

This genre of names has the advantage of capturing namesakes who relevant to supporters of either the Union or the Confederate cause. They thereby offer a relatively apples-to-apples gauge of sectional feeling—and of the relative degree to which the two sides continued to brood on the war over time. Military titles also incorporate some commemorations of the war that did not involve famous public figures: a veteran's former commanding officer, perhaps, or a neighbor whose exploits were only locally of note or may never have made any newspaper. Despite these many possible sources, such remembrances more likely refer to officers from the name-givers' side of the conflict, even when they celebrate personal comradeship rather than any of the war's high politics; that connection to one side's soldiery itself shows a measure of a kind of regional identity. As with the state-identity measures, the conventional presumption would be that the South and its Lost Cause would be more dominated by, and persistent in, its use of military-rank names.

Figure 2.7 plots the prevalence of such names for the principal army ranks—*Private, Corporal, Sergeant, Lieutenant, Captain, Major, Colonel,* and *General*—by region of child's birth. (Leaving out *Private* to focus on officers does not much affect outcomes: Almost no one was intrepid enough to use the name.) Per this book's normal procedures, the figures omit most variants of the relevant names, regrettable though it is to leave out the Alabamian named *Generalissimo* in 1857 or the Missourian whose parents adapted *Lieutenant* for a daughter by making her *Lieutenia*. These results also take no special note of first- and middle-name combinations such as *Major General*, which counts as a single *Major* here.

The names do plausibly trace Americans' attention to the military. As might be expected, the Mexican-American War (1846–1848) corresponded to an uptick in the use of relevant names, but this paled in comparison with the all-consuming onslaught of the 1860s. At that point, the Confederate states' greater use of military names soars, even though the South started from a higher base, having always by this measure tended to a greater militarism than the rest of the country did. Where the South previously had only used ranks as names only slightly more than the Border states did, though, the difference became far more marked amid the Civil War, the

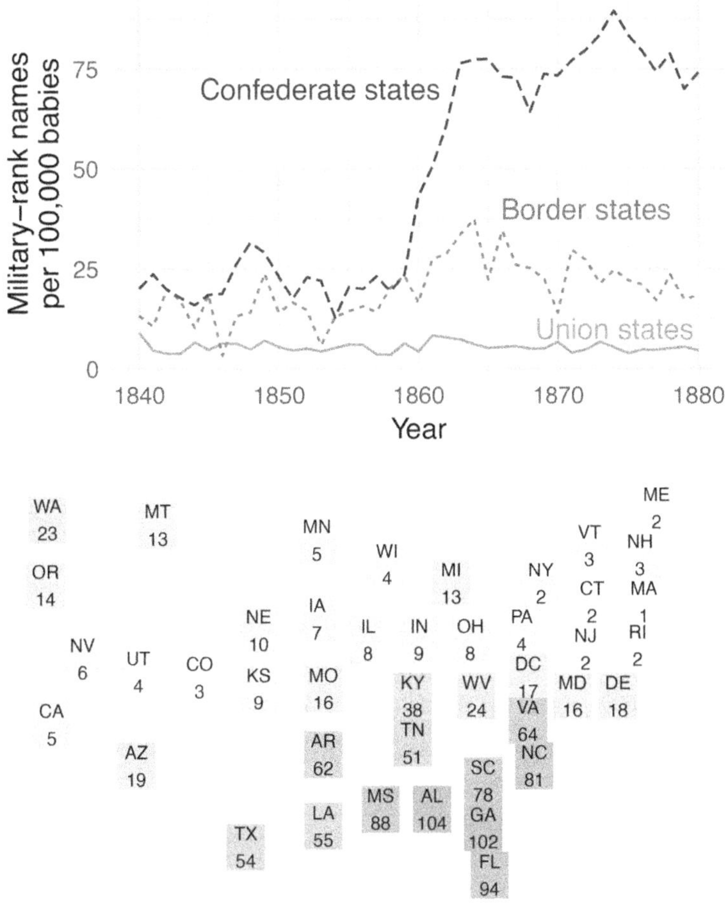

FIGURE 2.7 Army-rank names per hundred thousand children in the census: yearly rates by region, 1840–1880 (upper panel), and state-by-state overall rates, 1861–1880 (lower panel).

rate of such names in Confederate states double that in the Border states. This newfound Southern reverence for military ranks persisted after the war. Whereas the other regions' use of these names declined slowly but noticeably from the end of the war, roughly resuming antebellum levels by 1880, the South's use generally remained at wartime levels—even a bit higher in the mid-1870s. That is, although the South before the Civil War expressed somewhat more military interest through its child names than other regions did, the much starker difference in culture only opened with the war, and widened further as Reconstruction putatively knit the country back together.

Indeed, the use of these names in the years after the outbreak of the war, shown in the lower panel of figure 2.7, tidily distinguishes the regions. The seceding state with the lowest prevalence of army-rank names (Tennessee, with fifty-one per hundred thousand babies) easily outpaces the Border state with the highest prevalence (Kentucky, with thirty-eight). Likewise, only two non–Border Union states have prevalences higher than that of the lowest-prevalence Border state (Missouri, with sixteen)—and both those states, Washington and Arizona, had very small populations during this period, so that flukes involving a tiny number of babies can have outsized influence on the state's total numbers. Within the regions, too, predictable patterns emerge. Army-rank names were most popular in the Deep South, with the highest usage rates in Alabama (104 per hundred thousand babies), Georgia (102), Florida (94), and Mississippi (88). At the other end of the scale, all six New England states were, along with New York and New Jersey, the states with a prevalence rate below three per hundred thousand. The cultural gradient of Southern militarism ranged well beyond the interregional border.

THEM THAT LEFT A NAME BEHIND

It may seem natural that more seismic cultural shifts would persist concomitantly longer, as with the massive passion for the military in culturally Southern regions launched by the Civil War. Yet even war-connected fashions for names can turn out instead to be short, sharp shocks: flashes in the pan that may burn very brightly but fade just as quickly, like *Preston* and *Sumner* did.[24] This can be seen, for example, by moving away from the generic use of military signifiers like *Colonel* to more specific allusions to Civil War newsmakers.

Acknowledging a particular military leader did not require building the title into the name. If parents wanted to acknowledge General George McClellan, they could bypass *General* and simply call their child *George*. But if name-givers wanted to explicitly signal their side in the war, *McClellan* would most transparently celebrate the Union general. That would seem unlikely to be the choice of many Confederate sympathizers, even if McClellan's obstructive brand of military leadership did almost as much good for the Confederacy as for the Union.

Many names other than military leaders' could also invoke the war while being more natural for one or the other side in the conflict. The Civil War offered numerous possible sources of baby names from its very start. Consider battle sites: The first shots fired in the conflict famously occurred at Fort Sumter in Charleston Harbor. As a Confederate victory leading to the Union surrender of the fort, and one particularly resonant as the opening salvo in a hoped-for fight for independence, the site became a shrine to Confederate hopes. Thus *Sumter*—and even more commonly *Sumpter*, given the vagaries of the period's spelling and conflation with a now-obscure word for a pack animal—promptly gained popularity across the South, having previously been rather rare outside South Carolina. Some parents went further yet, removing any doubt about the namesake by reserving *Sumter* for the middle name while using *Fort* as the first name.

Battle sites were only erratically used as personal names, though, and are further complicated by regional differences in practices for referring to battles (was it Manassas or Bull Run? Antietam or Sharpsburg?).[25] As indicated by the widespread use of titles, military commanders were a more systematic name source. This preference for commanders over sites reflects that leaders' names were preestablished as personal names, even if nontraditional ones—though being nontraditional could be an advantage in more clearly conveying its namesake. *Stonewall*, for instance, was not an obvious name to choose before the Civil War. When it vaulted into popularity after 1860, one could reasonably expect that the name-givers were Southern adherents who wanted to celebrate the Confederate general Thomas Jackson by using one of his more prominent sobriquets. *Ellsworth*, though slightly more ambiguous in its source, often would serve to honor Elmer

Ellsworth, an acquaintance of Abraham Lincoln who gained a blazing celebrity in raising and leading a New York regiment of infantry before becoming the war's first Northern officer to die in action.[26] This association would make the name more obviously attractive as a name for Northern than for Southern parents.

Indeed, as figure 2.8 shows, the names follow the expected regional patterns. The figure contrasts dashed lines showing Confederate-state usage rates of the respective names against solid lines showing Union-state rate. *Sumter* and *Stonewall* were both far more common among Confederate-region babies than among their Union counterparts, whereas *Ellsworth*, by far the most popular of these, was conversely more popular in the Union states; as might be expected if the names really referenced the military figures, all the names had their major surges just as their war-related namesakes had their moments of greatest newsworthiness. (The figure excludes the Border states, which fall between the other regions in use of all the displayed names except for a period in the late 1860s and early 1870s when they showed even more enthusiasm about *Stonewall* than Confederate states did.) However, the interregional differences in the use of names are not quite parallel. *Ellsworth*'s increase in Confederate-state usage over its antebellum rates was smaller than *Stonewall*'s analogous increase in the Union, even though *Ellsworth* experienced a relatively larger vogue in the North than *Stonewall* did in the South. *Sumter*, similarly, had a detectable uptick in Northern usage at the same time as it gained its greatest popularity in the Confederacy. The asymmetry of Northern identity versus Southern continues, with more Northerners willing to celebrate the other side, whether because pro-Southern sentiment was relatively common in the North or because the social penalties for expressing pro-Northern views in the South were especially stringent.

Interpreting these differences more fully is difficult because each potential namesake has so many idiosyncrasies. Elmer Ellsworth's military achievements paled next to Stonewall Jackson's, but he had dash, charisma, and doomed youth whereas Jackson had a personality that even his apologists repeatedly conceded was "eccentric."[27] Ellsworth's death occurred mere weeks into the conflict, when it was still possible to see the war mainly as an arena

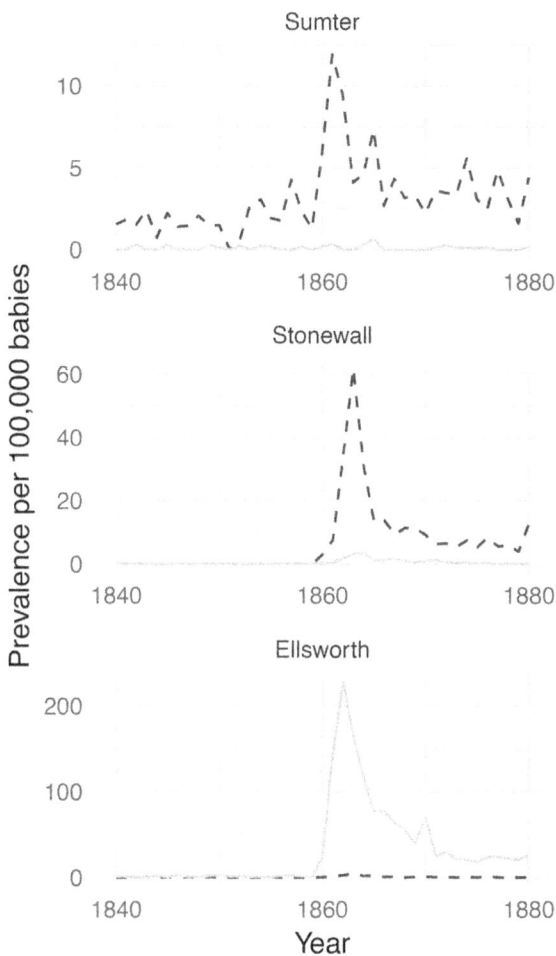

FIGURE 2.8 Popularity of selected Civil War–related names, 1840–1880, in Union (solid line) and Confederate (dashed line) states, excluding the Border States.

for pluck and heroics; Jackson's occurred after years of horrific slaughter had bloodily smashed any such illusions. Meanwhile, Fort Sumter was itself named for a notable Revolutionary War general and later congressman, memories of whose service might have been stirred by another war, and *Ellsworth* was a yet more common family name than *Sumter* (or its twin *Sumpter*).

Despite all these differences, all the names in figure 2.8 share a striking commonality that marks them out from the army-rank names of figure 2.7: their moments of popularity mostly dissipated quickly, roughly as quickly as those of the *Preston/Brooks/Sumner* examples had. To be sure, *Ellsworth* and *Stonewall* were more popular through the 1870s than they had been before the war—even *Sumter* was, after its less imposing wartime boom. But where the army-rank names retained virtually all their wartime popularity, at least in the South where they were most widespread, names tied to specific people and places that the war thrust into the spotlight often faded much faster regardless of their region of origin. The ex-Confederacy's persistent postwar homage to militarism did not always carry over to more personalized commemoration of the leaders and landmarks of the rebellion. Memorials to the war's specifics fell away but general valorizing of militarism and struggle endured.

To examine this point more systematically, we need more comparable war figures from the two battling sides. Some differences will of course arise in any comparison, but some roles were relatively analogous on both sides. In particular, the hierarchical nature of militaries mean that a few leaders were the special focus of attention in everyday news reports and discussions of the war. Just as the title *General* was common currency to both sides, so was the presence of notable or admired generals whose names could be passed on to another generation, though of course the specific generals likely to attract name-givers in the Union differed from those in the Confederacy.

Any definition of leading military leaders will be arbitrary; even something like the extent of newspaper coverage of a commander will struggle in the face of different levels of interest of enemy versus friendly armies, and in the different theaters of the war. To define a consistent sample, I rely here on the leaders who attained the top two military ranks of their respective armies during the Civil War, not counting brevet ranks or service with units of volunteers rather than with the regular, standing army. The Union (or Federal side) was considerably stingier than the Confederacy in doling out high military ranks, so for the Union side those top ranks are lieutenant general (one case, Ulysses Grant) and major general (nine cases), whereas for the Confederacy they are general (six cases) and lieutenant general (eighteen cases).[28]

This sample's arbitrariness shows up in a few ways. Some of the generals on the Federal side were to some extent has-beens by the start of the war: Winfield Scott as a great popular hero of the Mexican-American War had retained his iconic status, and John Ellis Wool served ably for the first years of the war but was thereafter forcibly retired, much to his chagrin, at the age of seventy-nine. (No level of gallantry could make the homely *Wool* catch on as a name, though: The census records do not show any examples in this era.) At the same time, some generals' names are so commonplace that it is never clear whether the associated general was a namesake. This applies above all to the Union's George Henry Thomas: *Thomas* was one of the most popular names for boys in the nineteenth century, and establishing how many parents primarily intended to honor General Thomas with the name *Thomas* is nigh on impossible.

This sample of names nevertheless shows detectable, predictable lurches during the war. Even names that were relatively common in the antebellum period, for which there were presumably a larger number of existing associations and less tendency to reflexively connect the name to the sectional conflict, saw stark shifts in their regional prevalence amidst the war if they were linked with a general. *Forrest* was predominantly a Northern name in the 1850s, with rates of use in the Union three to four times those in the incipient Confederacy. But that pattern abruptly flipped during the war, when Nathan Bedford Forrest became a celebrated figure in the South (and highly controversial in the North, presiding as he did over a massacre of Black soldiers at Fort Pillow and, after the war, over the Ku Klux Klan). *Anderson* followed a similar trajectory, with the Confederate general Richard Anderson perhaps assisted by the legacies of George Anderson (another of Robert E. Lee's high subordinates) and "Bloody Bill" Anderson, a Missouri Confederate-partisan guerrilla who attacked Federal loyalists. *Johnston, Smith,* and *Stewart* also became less typically Northern just as their namesake generals served the Confederacy, though all had been in decline in the North even before the war. Meanwhile, names like *Jackson*, *Lee*, and *Taylor* all became even more intensely concentrated in the South than they previously had been.

These changes collectively sketch various patterns, as figure 2.9 illustrates by showing the frequency of generals' names in the non-Border Union states (upper panel), Border states (center panel), and seceding states

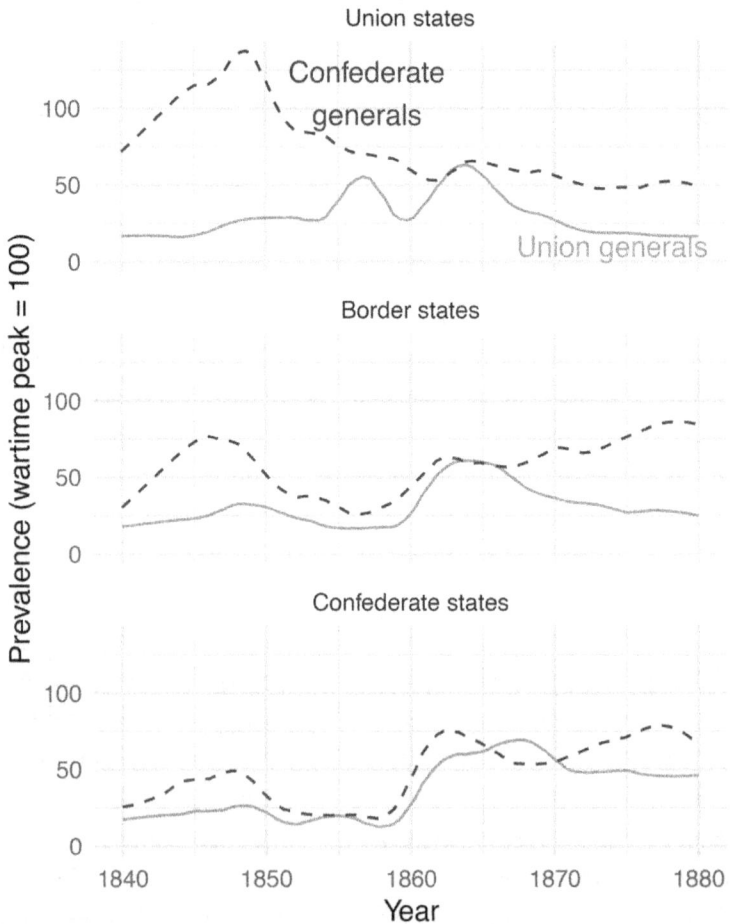

FIGURE 2.9 Smoothed average prevalence of generals' names compared to their 1861–1865 maximum, 1840–1880, by region of country and army of general.

(bottom panel). In each case, the figure averages the prevalence of names of Federal (solid lines) and Confederate (dashed line) generals, scaling each general's name so that the maximal annual prevalence observed during the Civil War years of 1861 to 1865 is defined as one hundred.[29] Two key trends highlight the postwar asymmetry in attention to sectional conflict. First, the Confederate generals' names mostly outshone the Federal generals' during the decades after the war (in the 1840s, Confederate generals look more popular as *Jackson* and *Taylor* had vogues unrelated to the Confederate generals with those names; the North's late-1850s boom in *Fremont* reflects the future general's nomination as presidential candidate for the Republicans, anticipating chapter 3). To the extent the names reflected attachment to war-related symbols, partisans of the Confederate cause expressed that attachment relatively enduringly regardless of where in the country they lived.

The second notable trend relates to the first: Although Union generals' names mostly did not have the staying power of Confederate generals', the Southern states defied this pattern. In the South, even Union names held on to unusually large proportions of their wartime use. This Confederate-state persistence is largely the act of Black and Mulatto populations. Just as their White neighbors kept the names of their wartime leaders current, the newly emancipated peoples preserved memories of Union military figures. As with their adoption of *Savannah*, Southern Blacks created a distinctive naming culture, one that reflected attachments not only to place but also to the political movement of liberation. Indeed, wartime protagonists remaining so prominent in the cultural vocabulary of the emancipated may in part reflect the constant celebrations from the surrounding Confederate culture of the conflict's slaveholding side—and may in turn have stimulated more emphatic Confederate symbolism in response. Such a dynamic could have helped perpetuate the prominence of the Civil War in Southern culture.

The averages in figure 2.9 gloss over differences across the names and might raise questions about whether they are driven by the influence of a few outliers. To show more detail, figures 2.10 and 2.11 show the over-time trajectories of names of some of the more prominent generals who fought for the North and for the South. As figure 2.10 shows, when the Federal

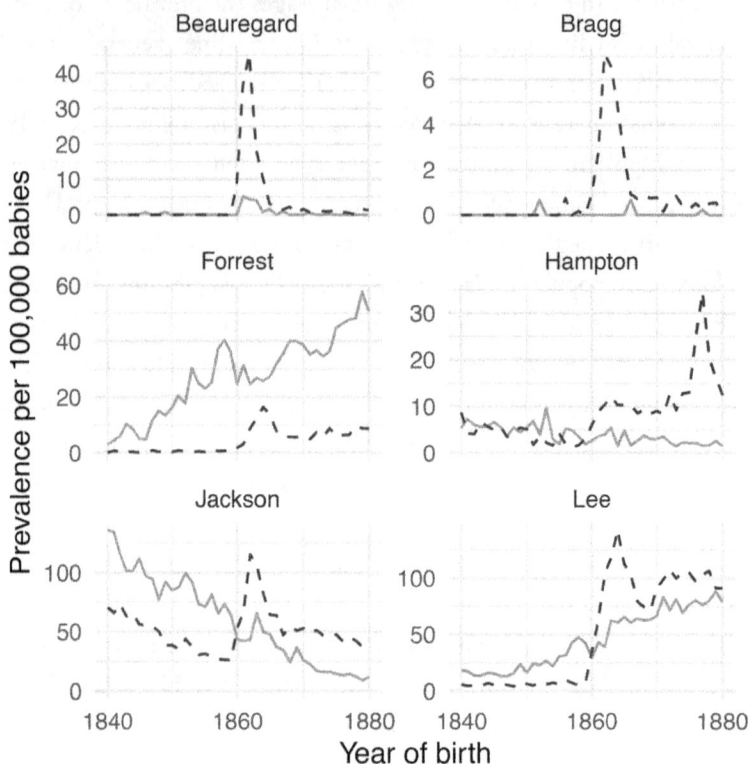

FIGURE 2.10 Trajectories of names of selected Civil War Confederate generals, 1840–1880. Solid line shows prevalence of names in (non-Border) Union states; dotted line, in Confederate states.

generals have commands, their names often surge in popularity, but the surges largely die off within a few years, with names returning to their prewar trends. True, *Grant* subsequently received additional fillips of popularity from the general's presidential campaigns, but other Federal generals' cultural currency passed very quickly. Even *Sherman*, which at its peak exceeded *Grant* in popularity (helped by having been more familiar as a given name before the war), was by the second half of the 1870s no more popular than it had been twenty years earlier. The evanescence of Federal generals' names does not simply reflect that the Union cycled through

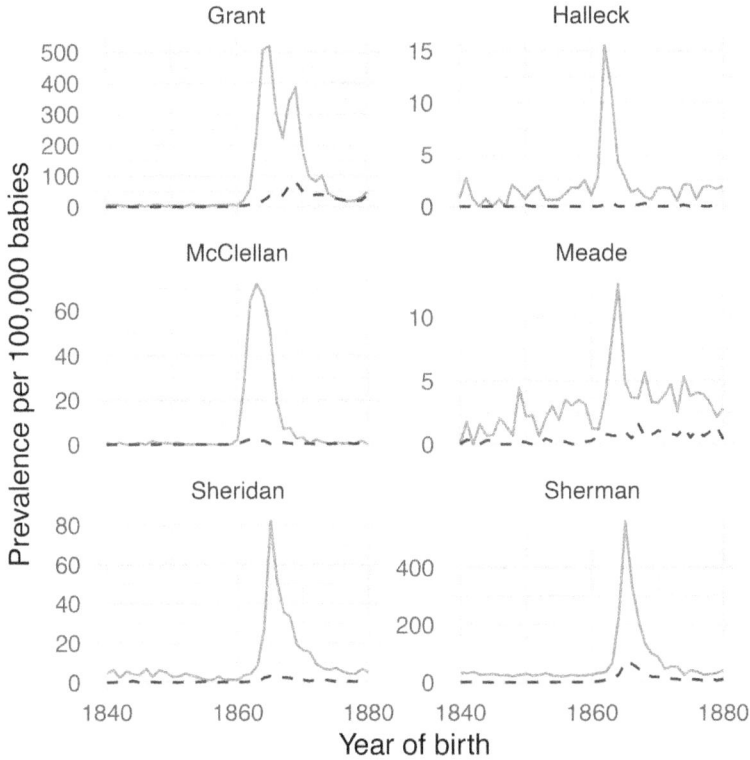

FIGURE 2.11 Trajectories of names of selected Civil War Federal generals, 1840–1880. Solid line shows prevalence of names in (non-Border) Union states; dotted line, in Confederate states.

several incompetent generals who quickly (or not so quickly, in McClellan's case) flamed out after the initial popular enthusiasm: The names of successful generals also withered quickly.

To be sure, some Confederate generals enjoyed a similarly brief, intense burst of prominence as a namesake: *Beauregard* and *Bragg* both shot to reasonably widespread use but then almost disappeared, use dropping from their high points by 90 percent within a few years.[30] Most of the Southern generals' names had considerably longer half-lives, however. Although names such as *Forrest*, *Hampton*, and *Lee* all did become less common in the immediate postwar years than they had been during the fighting, these lulls were not the near-total collapse of the Federal generals' names—and thereafter the names did more than stabilize; they actually rose above their prevalences of the late 1860s. Even *Jackson* saw its rate of decline slow after the war despite the disappearance of Andrew Jackson from most name-givers' living memories. Southerners tended to hold on to more of their cultural memory of the war, showing the same lingering attachment to sectional symbols that arose with state-derived names. Conversely, association with a Confederate general could only briefly depress Northern interest in names; *Forrest, Jackson,* and *Lee* did all dip below their trend lines at the start of the war but already by its second half mostly recovered, whether from active Confederate sympathizers or those who simply no longer had Confederate generals at the forefront of their minds.

This war's longer hold in the South also appears with Federal generals' names, just as it did in figure 2.9. Consider the trajectory of *Grant*. Even though the maximum prevalence of the name in the Union states was several times as high as that in the Confederacy, by the later 1870s the name was just as common in the two regions; its retreat from the North was so much faster that just a few years after the war it was not even recognizable as a Northern name. This, again, was largely a phenomenon of Southern Blacks, and *Grant* may stand out because it commemorated not only the triumphant general but also the president who had overseen the brief window of Reconstruction when civil and political rights were far more available than they were before or after. But Blacks also showed relative loyalty to names such as *Sherman*, allowing the name to maintain a larger share of its wartime success in the South than it did in the North.

ASSASSIN NATION

The Black population's adoption of state-based names such as *Alabama* or military titles and generals' names (even if *General* was more likely to accompany a middle name of *Sherman* than it would have been among White

Southerners) illustrates that names celebrating the South need not have any hint of favoring slavery or insurrection. Some other names more pointedly embraced the violent side of the Confederate cause, though. They, too, remained in circulation even after Northerners seemed to have mostly moved on, in naming if not in mourning, from the Civil War.

This appears quite pointedly with the names *Wilkes* and *Booth* and their connection to Lincoln's assassin John Wilkes Booth. At the time of the assassination, *Wilkes* was an uncommon name, though not unheard of; it was the name Booth himself usually went by. The eighteenth-century British radical John Wilkes, after whom Booth had himself been named, had mostly slipped from public memory, and though *Wilkes* turned up as an occasional name running in families, it showed few signs of wider adoption. One localized exception surrounded the city of Wilkes-Barre, Pennsylvania, which quintupled in population in the twenty years after 1860: Its local mines prospered as the national railroad network expanded and voraciously demanded coal, leading to an outbreak of local pride expressed through children named *Wilkes Barre*.[31] Potential association with a notorious assassin was clearly not enough to overcome this local association, in another bit of evidence that Northerners were no longer consumed by associations with sectional conflict. *Booth* had more ongoing sources of use—if nothing else, Wilkes Booth's own brothers, also very prominent actors— but was never a particularly popular name selection, either. Even for the author Booth Tarkington, perhaps *Booth*'s most famous exponent, it was a middle name: His given first name was *Newton*, as he was named after his uncle Newton Booth, a governor of California.

Naming a child *Wilkes Booth* in the 1860s after President Lincoln's murder is therefore a strong signal. The signal is especially potent because, as the assassin himself bitterly bemoaned, his deed had earned him widespread opprobrium even in the South, not the accolades he had hoped for: Many Southerners reviled him for the blowback to be expected from a vengeful North and from the combustible new President Andrew Johnson, or for the perceived dishonor of shooting an unarmed man in the back of his head (in the presence of the victim's wife, no less). That revulsion was not universal, but it was very widespread, at least among the elites such as politicians and writers of newspaper editorials.[32] Thus, choosing to publicly celebrate Booth in a child's name would seem to risk a negative reaction. Yet the more ground-level view of public opinion through child names shows a small but significant sprinkling of otherwise ordinary-seeming people disregarding the odium and openly celebrating the assassin. And the naming was fairly clearly tied to the assassination, given that John Wilkes Booth's celebrity as a matinee-idol heartthrob did not lead to namesakes observable in the records before April 1865.

Wilkes and *Booth* did however become relatively more prevalent in the South after 1865.[33] Like most surname-derived given names, they were even beforehand more common in the South than in the North: From 1840 to 1864, the states that had joined the Confederacy or were soon to do so saw an average of 0.6 children named *Wilkes* or *Booth* per hundred thousand, and the non-Border Union states saw an average of only 0.2. But this North-South gap widened considerably after the assassination. From 1865 to 1880, the analogous rates were 1.5 in the Confederacy and 0.3 in the Union.[34] That is, the names went from being three-and-a-half times as common in the South to being more than five times as common. This increasing gap is even more striking in light of the cluster of postwar Pennsylvania *Wilkes*es mentioned, the primary source of the rise of assassination-adjacent names in the North. That happenstance made any findings of the South seeing a relative increase in the use of *Wilkes* less likely; the gap would have been even larger when looking at unambiguous *Wilkes Booth* name combinations, which overwhelmingly hailed from the defeated Confederate regions.

That the distribution of these names skewed Southern is less notable in some sense than that parents were using the name at all. Although the overarching regional pattern is clear, exceptions when Northern parents decided to name their children after John Wilkes Booth can also be revealing. Support for the assassination, it seems, could pop up anywhere. Wilkes Booth Hanna was born in 1875 in Illinois, the very Land of Lincoln—in Pope County, at the state's southern extremity, but Illinois nonetheless. And Wilkes Booth Peel was born in the town of Madrid in central Iowa barely a week after the assassination,[35] when the manhunt for the killer was still ongoing. What might the neighbors have thought of that bold gesture, especially in a state marked by particularly assertive support for the Union cause?[36] (The Peels did leave Madrid soon after Wilkes's birth, though that may be a coincidence given that their place of residence was often unstable.) Conversely, the assassination continued to be a live enough issue to inspire namesakes for decades, even discounting *Wilkes Booth*s Junior who were presumably named after their fathers rather than the assassin directly. Wilkes Booth Violett, for example, was born in 1919 in Kentucky; he lived into the 1980s, keeping Booth's name alive more than a century after the assassination. Lincoln's reputation might eventually have risen to the point where it was no longer seen as socially acceptable to celebrate his murderer, but any such development was—if it ever occurred in all the country's subcultures—a long time coming.

This folk memory of John Wilkes Booth seems to have been bound up in its sectional spirit. Later assassins, after all, did not arouse such evident parental enthusiasm. Part of that may be down to the familiarity of *Wilkes* and *Booth* versus the impenetrable names of future presidential killers such as *Czolgosz*. (In December 1883, two years after Charles Guiteau shot President Garfield, Frank and Minnie Powell of Oneida, New York, did choose to call their son *Guiteau*, but that had been Minnie's maiden name: She was Charles Guiteau's second cousin through their shared great-grandfather Francis Guiteau. The name probably did not specifically honor the assassin, who was not personally well liked among his family, or for that matter among pretty much anyone else.) But the bitter, divisive politics of the Civil War era surely encouraged more parents to want to name their child in such a way. Being able to signal affinity, even or especially spiteful affinity, with the large and tenacious Confederate team—and implacable opposition to the other side—apparently had substantial social value. That politically prominent and controversial figures would be at the center of naming patterns, though, would continue long after the war and Reconstruction ended.

3

POLITICAL CELEBRITY
(CA. 1860–1940)

The power of Frances Cleveland ... Politics versus popular culture ...
Presidential names ... Campaigns and also-rans ... Drivers of endur-
ing public esteem ... The rise and fall of Garfield ... Senators, gover-
nors, and nonelected political leaders

On September 9, 1893, through little fault of her own, Esther Cleveland became the only presidential child born in the White House.
If that were not enough to put her in the public eye, Esther's mother
Frances Folsom Cleveland was a formidable tastemaker. In one indication
of her public position, Frances Cleveland would become, as "the most
popular and beloved woman in America," the lead-off subject of a series of
biographical profiles in *Ladies' Home Journal*, displacing the sitting
president to the series' second entry.[1] And that was during the McKinley
administration, after her stint as First Lady had ended. At Esther's birth,
Frances was still First Lady and so even more of a publicity magnet.

Esther was already a name on the rise before Esther Cleveland's birth; it
is perhaps unsurprising that someone as stylish as Frances Cleveland would

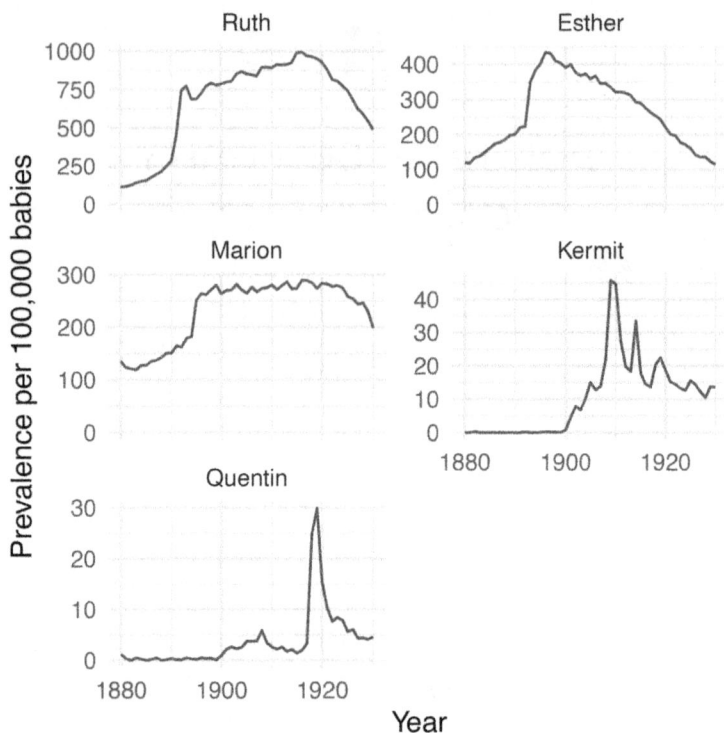

FIGURE 3.1 Popularity of names of selected presidential children, 1880–1930.

be in tune with the tastes of her time. But the Clevelands' choice of name turbocharged *Esther*'s popularity (see figure 3.1). The popularity of the name rose by around a third just between babies born in August 1893 and those born in September of that year—and, as the era's openness to delayed baby-naming meaning that some children born in August could be named after Esther, the August prevalence was itself around a quarter higher than that for babies born in July. *Esther* had never before been so popular in the United States and as yet has never regained the popularity it had in the months after Esther Cleveland's birth.

But *Esther* was not even the Clevelands' biggest naming splash. The birth of their first child, Ruth, was enough of a media sensation for the purveyor of the Baby Ruth candy bar to be able to claim decades later with a semi-straight face that he had named the candy after her rather than the base-ball player Babe Ruth,[2] and it sparked that sensation even though Ruth Cleveland was born in 1891, during the interregnum between Grover Cleveland's terms as president. *Ruth* was, like *Esther*, already becoming popular before the Clevelands chose it: They built on a gathering trend rather than singlehandedly launched it. Still, the naming of Ruth Cleveland corresponded with a spectacularly rapid acceleration in the name's popularity, which persisted much longer than *Esther*'s moment in the sun. And the Clevelands' powers extended beyond the names of biblical heroines. When their third child *Marion* was born in 1895, an abrupt but enduring swell of namesakes immediately followed in her wake as well.

Even though the Clevelands were in a league of their own, they were not the only young and fashionable presidential couple of the U.S. Belle Époque. Theodore and Edith Roosevelt also managed to bring multiple names into prominence, and with the further handicap of selecting names that had previously been obscure rather than up-and-comers such as *Ruth* and *Esther*. *Kermit*, though an established Manx name, was little known in the United States outside Edith Roosevelt's family—it was her middle name, and the surname of her great-uncle—but emerged in popularity when Roosevelt assumed the presidency, peaking when Roosevelt's teenage son Kermit joined his postpresidential father on the Smithsonian's well-publicized African Expedition of 1909–1910.[3] Kermit's youngest brother also had what was at the time a relatively little-used name: *Quentin*. But he increasingly gained namesakes both during the senior Roosevelt's presidency and especially after Quentin's own greatest moment of national prominence, when he died in 1918, age twenty, in aerial combat over France during World War I.

The attention surrounding such presidential progeny reflected the particularly strong aura of celebrity surrounding politicians during the late nineteenth and early twentieth centuries. Celebrity is often an important driver of baby names. The emergence of a famous and, with luck, admirable person or fictional character often stirs parents; many pop songs and actors have launched waves of namesakes. But widespread adoption of names based on popular culture requires a widespread popular culture, which could only occasionally come together in the fragmented media environment in and before the nineteenth century.[4] This absence shows up most clearly by comparing what happens to names after movies start making their presence felt as a national phenomenon in the leadup to World War I. *Vivien* saw a miniature fad as early as 1911 after the release of cinematic recounting of the Arthurian Lady of the Lake legend, and the "Adventures of Kathlyn" and "Zudora" serials sparked similar increases for their eponymous heroines' names in 1913 and 1915. Lead characters in hits continued to inspire names—*Jeannine* burst onto the scene in 1928 and 1929 with the movie *Lilac Time* and its featured song "Jeannine, I Dream of Lilac Time"—but once actors started being credited on their films, actresses became as important as characters as a source of names. *Theda* (after Theda Bara)[5] surged in 1916 and 1917 and was perhaps the first screen actress name to have a major moment of naming fashion. In the 1920s, *Gloria* (Swanson), *Colleen* (Moore), and *Leatrice* (Joy) did as well. By the 1930s, names such as *Carole* (Lombard) and *Claudette* (Colbert) and *Marlene* (Dietrich) and *Shirley* (Temple) and *Sonja* (Henie) took off with metronomic regularity as their namesakes became stars.[6]

Hollywood was neither the first nor the only notable source for pop-culture names. *Marvel*, the title character of a bestselling 1888 novel, briefly became a somewhat popular girl's name, and *Trilby* followed suit in 1895. Boys' names, though perhaps regarded as too serious a matter to be as widely derived from the performing arts, had a notable tendency to derive from sports figures: *Corbett*, *Willard*, and *Dempsey* saw some popularity as boys' names when their namesakes were world heavyweight boxing champions, and *Sherburn* enjoyed a brief 1906 fashion from its link to the football hero Sherburne Wightman. It was not just sports. Both *Delphin* and *Delmas*, of all things, managed to have small fads in 1907 when Delphin Delmas served as a defense attorney in one of the sensational tabloid scandals of the day, the trial of Harry Thaw. But the rise of mass media such as movies and, slightly later, radio heralded a move toward a broader national popular culture that would vie with politics as a source of news and names. They also expanded the range of celebrities available, so that people not intrinsically interested in national or world affairs could more easily ignore political events to focus on their actual interests.[7]

Before the age of such media, then, political figures faced less competition for the public's mental real estate as figures of prominence and esteem. Indeed, in the absence of movies, some celebrities emerged from political roles that would today be thoroughly unlikely to be known to the public, such as the entourages of foreign ambassadors.[8] Still, politics' greater place in celebrity discourse does not necessarily mean that it spurred naming choices. People could just have ignored momentary celebrity altogether and found names in other sources, such as family or religious figures, absent an appealing popular culture. But to the extent that politics was avidly followed because people esteemed and identified with candidates and officeholders, one might expect politicians to have been particularly common sources of baby names in the nineteenth century and early twentieth century relative to later eras—and potentially a larger role than in earlier eras, too, as the expansion of the role of the government with the Civil War, Reconstruction, and the rise of national markets made politics a larger part of life and society. Any uptick in politics-themed names would tie into the long-standing view among historians that politics garnered wider, deeper public interest in the nineteenth century than it subsequently did.[9] Indeed, baby names bear out this idea.

THE RISE AND FALL OF PRESIDENTIAL NAMES

The easiest place to see this is through the presidency. U.S. presidents have a national office, with quasi-national elections, depending on how one thinks the Electoral College operates, and unique institutional power. They also serve more readily as a single, personalistic protagonist of a narrative than most members of legislative or judicial branches, given their officially collective decision-making, usually can. All of those forces attract relatively intense media attention to the executive, so the presidential pulpit is indeed a bully one, and previous studies of names have often looked at

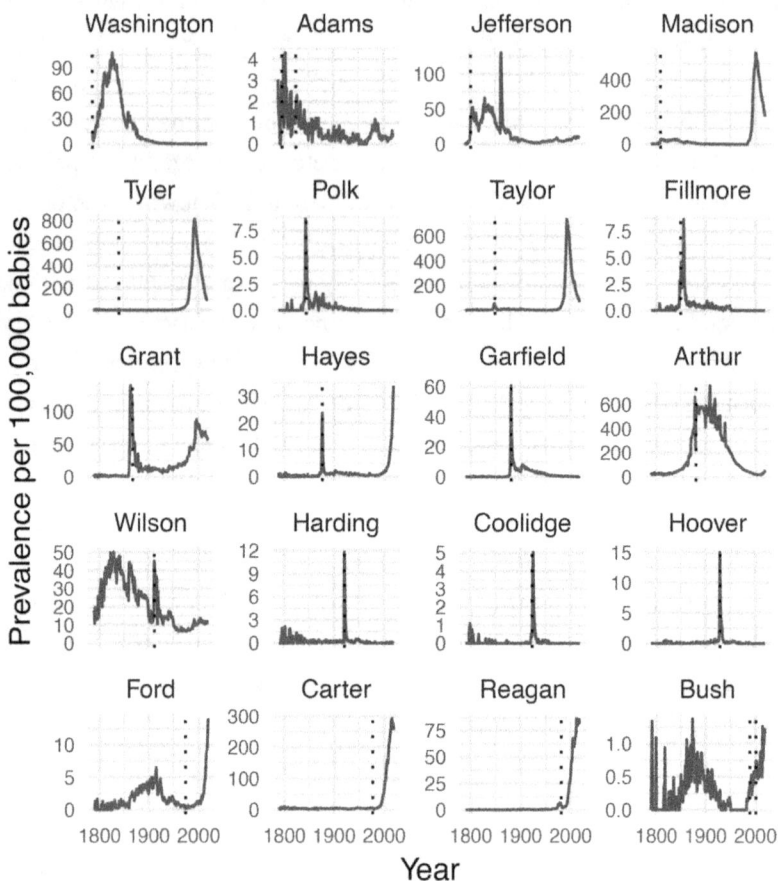

FIGURE 3.2 Prevalence of presidential surnames as baby names, 1789–2020; dotted vertical lines mark year when associated president or presidents assumed office.

presidential namesakes.[10] Figure 3.2 shows how frequently each presidential surname—the family name, setting aside for the moment adoption of the president's given name or names—arises as a newborn's name from Washington's inauguration until 2020. Every occasion on which someone with the given surname assumed office is marked with vertical dots (this does not include reinaugurations of incumbent presidents).

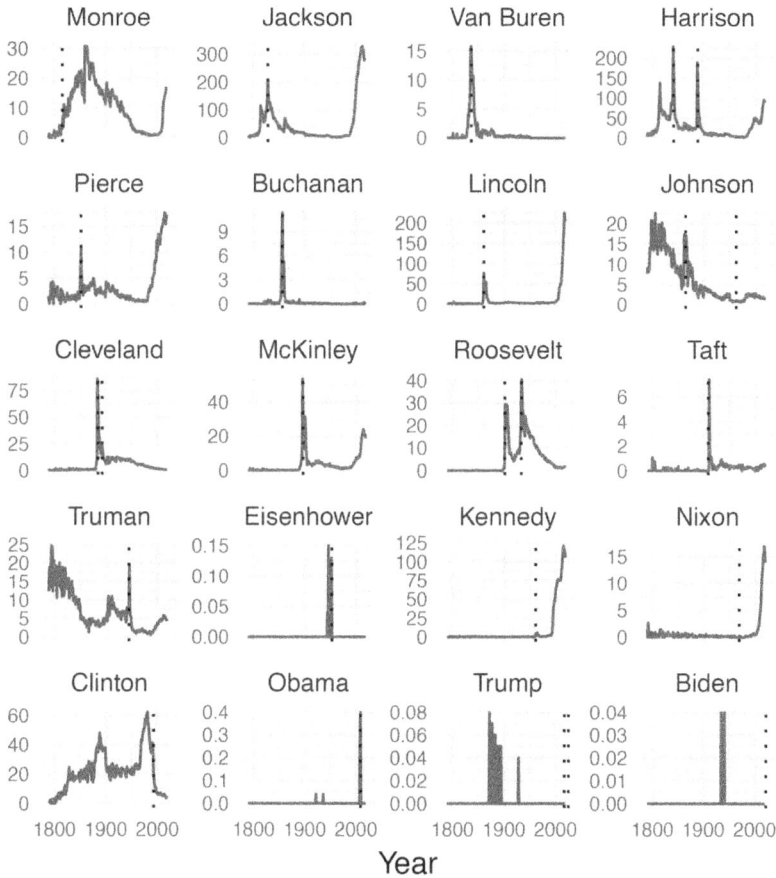

FIGURE 3.2 (*continued*)

Over and over, new presidencies see a sharp increase in the commonality of the associated baby name. Several names that were essentially unknown as given names, or restricted to a small number of people for whom it was a family name, burst into widespread use around the time of their namesake's election and inauguration. Names such as *Grant* that latterly became unremarkable, and may even have lost their original association with a president in the public mind, first became prominent in tandem with their associated president. Even names that already had wide-spread use, such as *Wilson*, saw spectacular increases in incidence.

The usual caveat applies that presidents are not the only sources of names,[11] especially names that are common Anglo-Saxon surnames, as most presidents' are. Much of the variation seen in figure 3.2 does not directly stem from presidential goings-on: Few people who named their children *Taylor* during its 1990s prime were likely to be intentionally commemorating Zachary Taylor in any way (but my regards to anyone who was). It is nonetheless unlikely to be a coincidence that names so often rise dramatically in popularity exactly alongside their namesakes' political success, and a formal statistical test rejects the hypothesis that the pattern in the figure arose from chance alone. The logic that politics had an especially tight grip on public attention historically, however, would suggest not merely that names become more common when their presidents assumed office, but also that the presidents who assumed office during the nineteenth century would have seen larger increases in the use of their names than earlier or later presidents would.

Several examples in the figure do fit this pattern. The presidents Harrison may be semi-forgotten today, coming up mostly as smugly dismissive trivia about the elder Harrison's brief tenure in office, but each inspired an enormous rise in the use of the name *Harrison*, with thousands upon thousands of babies seemingly named after them. The rises outpaced the names of subsequently more revered (and reelected) presidents such as the Roosevelts. Of course, *Harrison* had the advantage of already being a reasonably common name when the Harrisons took office, and also was of the familiar form "common male name plus -son." It probably felt like a natural potential name to more English-speaking Americans than *Van Buren* or *Roosevelt* did, let alone something like *Eisenhower* or *Obama*.[12] But more linguistically atypical given names from the decades around 1890, such as *Garfield* and *Cleveland* and *McKinley*, also managed to break out alongside their presidents.

Contrast this with the pattern in the decades after 1950. Richard Nixon also had a surname derived from a familiar name plus the -son suffix, but *Nixon* could not emerge as a widespread baby name—at least, not until several decades after President Nixon himself resigned in scandal: The name did start picking up hundreds of newborn adherents each year after 2000. Only ten babies are recorded as being named *Nixon* in the 1969 inauguration year, however, not even matching the peak of thirteen Nixons born in 1905 among a much smaller cohort of births. *Clinton* actually experienced a massive drop in popularity as Bill Clinton took office, its prevalence falling by almost exactly half between 1991 (in October of which Clinton announced his candidacy) and 1993 (when he was inaugurated), dramatically hastening the name's longer-term decline. *Reagan*, similarly, had been gathering steam as a popular name in the 1970s but fell back considerably on Ronald Reagan's inauguration, not to resume its upward trend until just as Reagan left office, and *Carter* fell to its lowest prevalence in decades when Jimmy Carter took office. Even when the figure shows visible popularity bumps for incoming presidents' names around more recent inaugurations, those bumps are numerically tiny: Only a handful of people named their children *Obama* in 2008 or 2009, when even such unloved nineteenth-century figures as Martin Van Buren or James Buchanan easily reaped hundreds of namesakes during their respective rises to power. One clean contrast across the centuries holds the name constant between *Johnson* at Andrew Johnson's 1865 inauguration and at Lyndon Johnson's ninety-eight years later as each succeeded an assassinated predecessor. Andrew Johnson's drawing power as a namesake thoroughly overshadows Lyndon Johnson's, despite the earlier Johnson's antics raising widespread suspicion of drunkenness at his vice presidential swearing-in, not the sort of behavior that traditionally enticed name-givers.

Do these individual anecdotes fairly build to a common pattern? More systematically comparing the size of spikes in presidential name usage requires a consistent baseline. Establishing one is somewhat tricky, in that the first trickles of an onrushing wave of names sometimes arise years in advance as a politician edges toward the presidency. Indeed, presidents such as Andrew Jackson and Ulysses Grant had established fame before becoming chief executive. Many of those who bestowed the names *Jackson* or *Grant* shortly before the respective presidencies were naming their children after the soon-to-be president, sometimes in explicit hopes of encouraging the associated politician to seek higher office. Measuring the increase in incidence of names from this elevated baseline may then somewhat understate the effects of presidential candidacy on name-giving. Nevertheless, consider the difference in the prevalence of a name between the time of each inauguration marked with dots on figure 3.2 and the point two years before. Two years is a short enough time frame to limit the scope for swings in a name's fashionability unrelated to the incoming president, but skips over the election year, when campaign effects are likely to affect use of a name. For *Washington*, then, this measure subtracts the prevalence of the name in 1787 from its prevalence in 1789; for *Adams*, the prevalence in 1795 from that in 1797 (and, as a separate observation, the prevalence in 1823 from that in 1825); and so on. Positive values indicate an increase in the name's popularity at the time of the inauguration relative to the baseline, and negative values indicate a decrease. The upper panel of figure 3.3 shows the smoothed trajectory of this difference over time (along with a 95 percent confidence interval on that smoother); the figure looks very similar if one instead takes the same two-year difference but uses the election year rather than the inauguration year as the endpoint of the two-year period for those presidents who took office by being elected in their own right, rather than rising to the presidency on the death or resignation of their immediate predecessor.

Presidents' names had a relatively slight tendency to become more popular on their inauguration in the early years of the republic, at least from the very spotty data available for that period. However, the effect grew over the 1800s, cresting at around thirty extra babies per hundred thousand sharing the presidential name toward the end of the century. The tendency to name babies after the president then shrank again over the first half of the twentieth century before settling around zero for the years since.[13] If baby names reflect public attention to and interest in the presidency, then, they comport with the historical consensus that politics was previously more central to American social life than it has become in more recent decades.

To be sure, presidential politics still appears in names: Chapter 5 explores how other partisan names, including those associated with presidential

POLITICAL CELEBRITY (CA. 1860–1940)

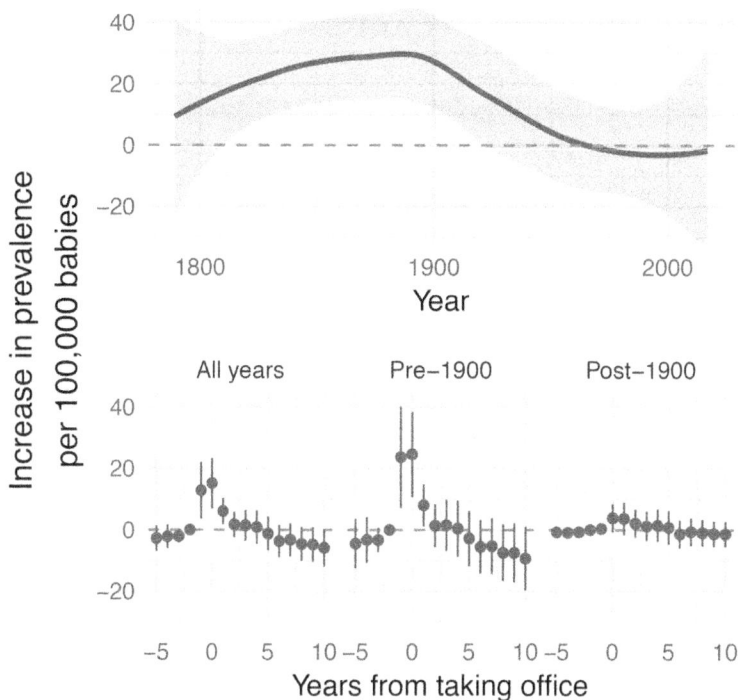

FIGURE 3.3 Increase in presidential names, with 95 percent confidence interval shaded, in the two years leading up to the inauguration (upper panel); change in prevalence of president's name relative to two years before entering office; vertical bars indicate 95 percent confidence intervals (bottom panels).

races, continued to prosper into the twenty-first century. It is specifically using the name of the incoming or current president that has declined. So, figure 3.3 may also reflect not only the decline in political interest but also the increasing unfashionability of earnest appreciation of traditional national symbols—or for that matter state symbols, given the simultaneous fading of state names such as *Missouri* and *Tennessee* discussed in chapter 2—and declining trust in major governmental institutions.[14] Political organizations and leaders seemed to lose their earlier cachet.

75

THE GLORY AND THE POWER

The wide use of expressly political names in the late nineteenth and early twentieth century allows for the exploration of several questions about politics. Seeing the contexts when political names were relatively popular allows insight about public opinion, cultural geography, and related fields.

One obvious question to start with might concern why, exactly, people would choose the name *Harding* for a child they purported to care about. That is, which of the multiple potential motivations lead to naming a child after the president? Parents could be expressing partisan support for the president, showing that they are on a particular political team or, perhaps, emphatically not on the opposing team. Greater prevalence of presidential names might then reflect national intensity of partisanship. Alternatively, presidential names could be expressing respect for the presidential office. Or they could simply represent surrender to a name being constantly in the air through continual public discussion of presidential activities, so that the higher use of presidential names might show when larger portions of the reported news concerned politics and the presidency.[15] These different motivations would not be mutually exclusive, but interpreting more precisely what presidential baby names have communicated about public engagement with politics involves disentangling these various potential rationales for choosing a presidential name.

One source of insight that can help distinguish the processes is the timing of babies receiving presidential names. To the extent that a president's name heavily concentrates around the election campaign and inauguration rather than during the term of office, the partisan competition is a more obvious explanation of baby-name recognition. Soon-to-be presidents at this electoral point do not have the authority of the office; for much of United States history, including the period of most widespread presidential naming, the campaign trail was indeed seen as thoroughly undignified. Nor do nonincumbent office-seekers have presidential accomplishments to earn naming plaudits, which suggests that names during an incipient presidency come from name-givers' expressing in longer-lasting life choices their in-the-moment identities regarding electoral politics.

On the other hand, when a president's name sustains elevated use over the years of the term or even gains popularity after inauguration, it might suggest that policy achievements or cumulative exposure more substantially drive naming patterns. At these later, postinauguration dates, name-givers have more distance from the straight-up partisan contest of the campaign (though partisan feuding does, for better or worse, occur during as well as before presidential terms). Attention to elections and to postelection governments can, again, coexist and both separately motivate name choices. But the two processes are conceptually distinct and would differ in their likely timing relative to elections.

The bottom panels of figure 3.3 present the average changes in presidential-surname results along with the uncertainty around those averages, using the same baseline point as in the figure's upper panel of two years before assuming office. The figure does show a swift fall from the heights immediately surrounding the inauguration. The spasms of enthusiasm for presidential names shown in the upper panel of figure 3.3 typically lose around 80 percent of their height by the year after inauguration, dissipating more quickly than, say, the surge in popularity of an actress name such as *Theda* or *Leatrice*—a pointed comparison, given how swiftly Hollywood has historically discarded actresses. Notwithstanding these transient waves of popularity around the election, a new presidential name nevertheless tends to settle for a few years into a prevalence slightly higher than that seen before its namesake's presidency. These shifts appear even though the figure includes the presidents from the more recent era when, per figure 3.3, being the president's surname did not raise a name's popularity. Thus it may understate the popularity of presidential names around elections in the nineteenth century—and, in fact, the size of the surge is approximately 50 percent larger than that across all years if the analysis looks only at presidents inaugurated before 1900. The rightmost two panels of the bottom row in figure 3.3 show this by subdividing the data into the two time periods.

Additional evidence of the greater public attention to electoral than to policy prominence appears, as so many things do, in the life of Millard Fillmore. *Fillmore*, in figure 3.2, sees the accustomed upwelling in 1850, when Fillmore assumed office after the death of his predecessor Zachary Taylor: Fillmore had not headed the presidential ticket in 1848. Nor would he head one in 1852, given that his Whig Party, after a protracted stalemate at their national convention, snubbed him to nominate the war hero Winfield Scott instead.[16] However, in 1856, Fillmore *was* the presidential nominee, albeit for the American Party, otherwise known as the Know-Nothings.[17] Only around this 1856 election did *Fillmore* reach its zenith of popularity as a baby name: a third-place candidacy that won only one, middling state provided more naming leverage than years of actually serving as president did,[18] both 1856 and 1857 handily seeing more *Fillmore*s born than did any years of Fillmore's presidential incumbency. This neglect is not entirely because his presidency was undistinguished. Fillmore's administration may not have been the most accomplished, but it did among other things oversee the passage of the landmark Compromise of 1850, hailed at the time by many for averting a much-dreaded civil war and the sort of success that presidents often take credit for even if it was in reality primarily a congressional initiative. Nevertheless, that sort of achievement paired with any residual sympathy for the presidency from Taylor's death still lacked the name-giving pull of a modestly successful third-party presidential campaign.

An additional way of showing how much public attention to politics revolves around partisanship and elections might examine presidential candidates, people who ran for the office but failed to secure it. Such literal also-rans provide the partisan hook for publicly declaring support for a candidate without the potential spillover of respect for the office. And, as might be expected given how many parents named their children for presidential candidates who eventually won the election, losing candidates' names frequently emerged as notable fads during the period when politicians were more generally namesakes for babies. After an election, when everyone knows who the winner is, names skew more heavily toward the winning candidate, whether in celebration or because parents no longer fear the risk of embarrassment from not picking a winner.[19] Before the election, though, some people will mispredict the election winner, especially if strong partisan blinders cause them to interpret evidence optimistically for their preferred candidate—a wrong-footing even likelier before systematic polling was available as a benchmark for expectations, and when cross-country communication was more limited than it later became so people might presume local favorites were more universally popular than they really were.[20]

Figure 3.4 highlights some of the more dramatic swells of prevalence for losing-candidate names, those surrounding James G. Blaine (who ran against Grover Cleveland in 1884), William Jennings Bryan (the Democrats' nominee in 1896, 1900, and 1908), Alton Parker (Theodore Roosevelt's 1904 opponent) and Charles Evans Hughes (Woodrow Wilson's 1916 rival).

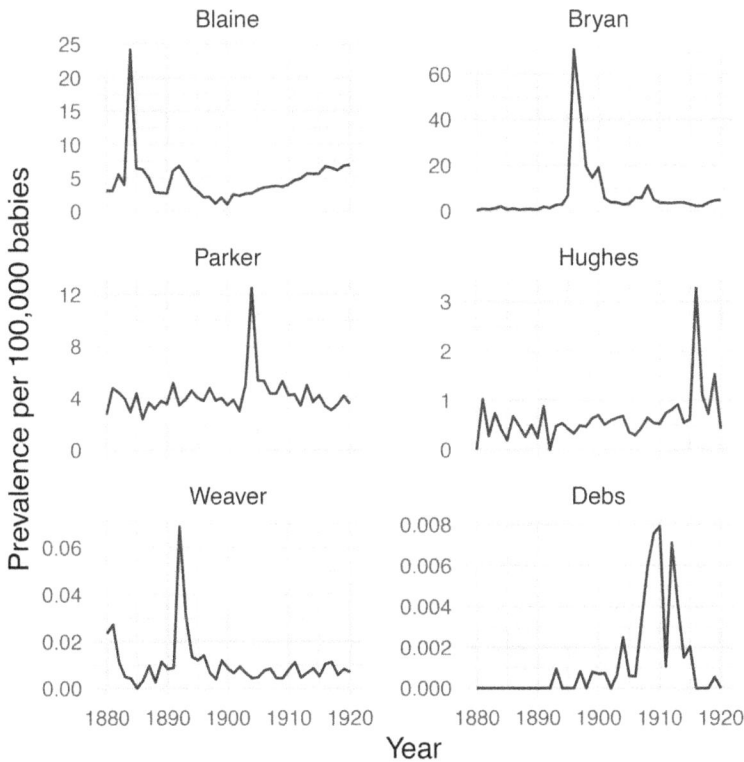

FIGURE 3.4 Popularity of names of selected losing presidential candidates, 1880–1920.

These are, to be clear, somewhat unrepresentative cases in seeing particularly large leaps in popularity. Still, none of these candidates' surnames were at the time particularly common names, and the enthusiasm for all of them ebbed almost immediately after their election losses. Bryan's case is especially notable as a repeated candidate: Each of his successive candidacies eked out a smaller increase in children named *Bryan* than the one before did. By the third run, in 1908, the uptick hardly exceeded the name's typical year-to-year variation. The biggest shrinkage in the election-year surge, though, arose between Bryan's first two candidacies, despite them resulting in virtually identical popular-vote distributions: Something of the freshness of the 1896 candidacy seems to have worn off in the mind of name-givers, which may point to fatigue with a given newsmaker as another factor provoking the decline in number of new presidential namesakes as their terms progress.[21] (The second peak for *Blaine*, in 1892, also corresponds to an occasion when James Blaine was rumored to be seeking the presidential nomination. He ultimately placed second at the year's Republican convention, despite making few formal moves to campaign.) In any case, the willingness to name babies after losing presidential candidates largely faded. Latter-day losing-candidate names such as *Dole* or *Gore* or *Romney*, like the names of their respective vanquishers, did not have even the fleeting popularity of their analogues of a century earlier.

Not all naming choices reflect misguided faith that a candidate would win. Even minor-party candidates (such as Fillmore in his American Party campaign) could see baby-name support, presumably not because their parents expected an upset victory but to voice support for a party or candidate they believed in. Other than Theodore Roosevelt's 1912 attempt to regain the presidency, the two most notable third-party candidates between the Civil War and World War II were James Weaver, who ran in 1880 for the Greenback Party and again, more successfully from the perspective of attracting votes, in 1892 for the Populists, and Eugene Debs of the Socialist Party, who ran in every election from 1900 to 1912 and again in 1920. Both of these candidates prompted small but detectable shifts in baby names, as shown in the two rightmost panels of figure 3.4's bottom row. The third-party candidates' numbers of namesakes are in absolute terms very small, especially for *Debs*.[22] *Eugene* had bigger boosts than *Debs* did during Debs's campaigns as might be expected given how unlike most given names *Debs* is, but for consistency figure 3.4 focuses only on surnames.

Weaver shows the prototypical brief jolts of popular interest, with short, sharp increases in uptake of his name corresponding to his two campaigns. The relative size of the two bouts of popularity neatly corresponds to Weaver's share of the vote in his two presidential runs, breaking the *Bryan* pattern of diminishing returns. *Debs*, on the other hand, was roughly as popular as a name source outside election years as he was when running for office—fittingly, given that Debs himself judged his work organizing unions as more important than his political campaigns. Radical union leaders could attract their own namesakes in this era: witness *Haywood*, the popularity of which waxed and waned in synchrony with the newspaper coverage of the radical leader of the Industrial Workers of the World, Bill Haywood. Even *Debs*, though, tended to tick upward in the years of Eugene Debs's presidential runs, especially 1904, 1908, and 1912. Regardless of the year, naming children after him showed a powerful commitment to leftist politics.

Elections, then, are powerful drivers of naming trends. But politics moves name-givers, even those who are not hardcore Eugene Debs fans, outside campaigns as well. One notable phenomenon indicating that names signal broader respect for the presidential office is the frequency of siblings getting the names of successive presidents. Siblings in this instance were almost always brothers, given that presidential surnames were until recently overwhelmingly boys' rather than girls' names. A younger brother of a boy named *McKinley* in the first years of the twentieth century was disproportionately likely to be called *Roosevelt*, for example. Some families managed considerably more exotic combinations: The Dillards of Green Hill, Alabama, had boys in the 1850s named both *Fillmore* and *Buchanan*, not even honoring politicians from the same party or ones that were notably popular name sources. These recurrences seldom involve children born during the heat of presidential campaigns, moreover; they instead look more like conscious choices to celebrate prominent national leaders. The era's tendency toward large families may of course have sometimes made the presidential names desperation moves when needing to contrive several names in succession. Yet some of the presidential-name sibling sequences appear to begin with parents' firstborns, and the choice to resort to presidents instead of, say, biblical figures suggests something about the civic culture's outlook on politics.

In any case, over the course of a term baby names appear to track the public attention to the presidency. Figure 3.3, in averaging across all presidents, obscures any individual surges of presidential names responding to specific events. To examine events in finer detail, figure 3.5 focuses on the example of James A. Garfield's presidency, presenting in its top panel the counts of month-by-month *Garfield* births provided by the 1900 Census.[23] The figure marks for reference some of the major events of Garfield's campaign and brief tenure in office. For comparison of newsworthiness, the figure's bottom panel shows how many *New York Times* articles in the given month included the word *Garfield*. Garfield was a surprise nominee, emerging from the Republicans' June 1880 convention only after a protracted stalemate among the three frontrunners Ulysses Grant, James G. Blaine, and Garfield's own preference, Ohio Senator John Sherman. Garfield in fact was not one of the six contenders who received votes in the convention's initial balloting, and at one point found himself ignored at the convention when he formally objected to receiving votes. But his personal popularity and charisma—how else to describe a politician with the ability

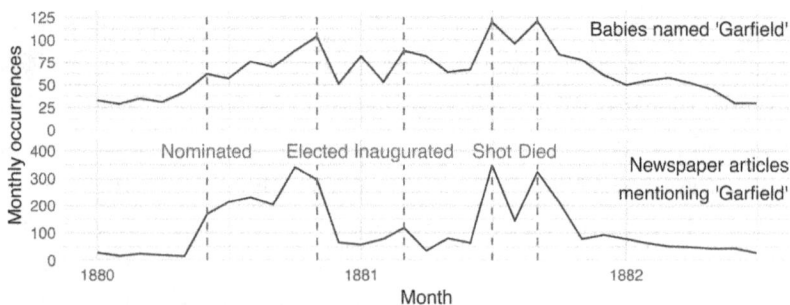

FIGURE 3.5 Frequency of *Garfield* in 1900 Census names and news coverage compared to key events in James A. Garfield's presidency.

to formulate a new proof of the Pythagorean theorem,[24] or to simultaneously write in Greek with one hand and Latin with the other?—led dele-
gates to stampede to his support as a way out of their deadlock. These
events catapulted him to new national prominence from prior relative
obscurity. In May, he had been mentioned, often glancingly, in a total of
thirteen *New York Times* articles, mostly about the somewhat unprepos-
sessing topic of tariffs on wood-pulp products. In June, he was suddenly the
subject of more than 150 articles, including some on spicier subjects such as
his attitudes toward polygamy. (He was opposed.[25]) The convention happened early enough in June that use of the name *Garfield* jumped that
month by approximately half from where it had idled for the first few
months of the year. From there, it steadily grew in use through the campaign, culminating in more than a hundred *Garfield*s in the month of
Election Day, roughly triple its prevalence in a typical month at the start
of the year.[26]

After the election, *Garfield* became less prominent, the number of
namesakes falling by around half from the November peak. This drop
again echoed news coverage; the count of relevant *New York Times* articles
fell by roughly three-quarters between November and December and
remained flat until the March 1881 inauguration. At that point, coverage
briefly and moderately increased, before plateauing until the July atrocity
of Garfield's shooting. Then, news coverage poured in at a rate not seen
since the height of the election the previous November, and the number of
babies named *Garfield* surged even beyond the election-time level. President Garfield lingered for weeks, enduring both breathless media coverage and a wavering prognosis as incompetent medical treatment wracked
his body with infection.[27] During this prolonged crisis, he received attention in the form of both newspaper articles and especially baby names at
rates consistently higher than they had been in the months of his administration before the shooting. Both measures spiked once again in September when Garfield finally succumbed to his wounds.

The match between news and naming in figure 3.5 is not perfect, in
telling ways. Besides having generally lower levels of month-to-month
volatility than news coverage did, baby names tended to slightly lag the

news. This delay is not just because information takes some time to dis-
seminate to the public, or because parents may settle on baby name choices
before the date of birth, but also because the emotional hangover of an
event can persist even after that event has concluded. An election campaign may end early in November (in 1880, Election Day was November 2,
its earliest possible occurrence in the American calendar) and thereafter
become old news as far as the media is concerned, but celebrations of the
result, including in baby names, continue for some time thereafter. Similarly, relevant news coverage quickly abated after Garfield's death—
although discussion of his assassin or surviving family was possible, little
new could be said about the president himself—but naming of children
after him dwindled more gradually as name-givers continued to express
the national grief.

News-tied names linger only so long after events, though. Even if the
election-related surge in naming lasted much further into November 1880
than election coverage did, it had largely run its course by December.
The public moves on as other events arise, just as they did from the
Brooks-Sumner fracas or wartime namesakes discussed in chapter 2. Even
something as arrestingly unexpected and emotionally fraught as an assassination held attention only temporarily; by January 1882, six months after
the shooting and four months after Garfield's death, fewer people named
Garfield appear in the census than at any point since Garfield's nomination. By a year after the assassination, *Garfield* was roughly as common a
name as it had been at the start of 1880, and its appeal to parents only
continued to decline thereafter. This is in line with how other emotional
shocks tend to play out: An event such as a terrorist attack may be perceived at the time to have changed everything permanently, but the emotional state of those not directly affected typically returns to the status quo
ante within a few months.[28]

Besides being delayed relative to news reports, child names respond to
somewhat different events. The emotional depth of a news item strongly
shapes its propensity to feed into baby names. Those wood-pulp stories, eco-
nomically and socially important as they might be, were unlikely to

capture wide attention or to make their subject seem worthy of a baby-name tribute. By contrast, the plight of a hearty young president stoically enduring pain as his children, some not yet teenagers, watched him slowly die, more naturally inspired parents even if it provided little new for journalists to write about day to day. The steeper fall in Garfield-related news coverage than in *Garfield*s in August 1881, the month between his shooting and death, may stem not only from people responding belatedly to the shooting, but also from the continuing emotional punch of what stories did emerge, fewer though they might have been.

Looking just at the use of *Garfield*, or of any presidential surname, likely understates the prevalence of naming after the president. The results all concern only names that exactly match presidents' surnames. Inadvertent misspellings, wordplay (several girls named *Rose*, *Rosa*, or *Rosie* got middle names resembling *Velt*), and variants-cum-nicknames (*Cleve* became much more common in the data whenever Grover Cleveland was in the news) all may veil parental efforts to pay homage. Parents could and do draw on the presidents' given names, too, as the example of *Debs* versus *Eugene* illustrates; although such names are usually less distinctively associated with the president and so less distinct signals of political influence—calling your child *James* after President James A. Garfield blends in with all the other biblical, historical, and social sources of the name, though *James Garfield* as a first-and-middle combination discards some of the ambiguity when the middle name appears too—presidential first and middle names also tended to gain popularity in parallel with surnames when their holders were elected or inaugurated. This is clearest when those given names were not generic boys' names. Mildly uncommon names such as *Chester* (Arthur) or *Grover* (Cleveland), or, later, *Woodrow* (Wilson) or *Warren* (Harding) or *Calvin* (Coolidge),[29] stand out in becoming popular alongside their presidents. Middle names such as Franklin Roosevelt's *Delano* or nicknames such as Dwight Eisenhower's *Ike* can also get traction when their holders are popular, and all this logic applies to also-ran candidates as well (*Jennings* popped along with *Bryan* during William Jennings Bryan's runs). Yet even looking narrowly at the use of presidential surnames, emphatic and high-cost signals of political affinity that they are, illustrates just how much sway politics can have on people's mental landscape—or, at least, how much it could in the past.

WHAT CHARACTERISTICS MADE PRESIDENTS ATTRACTIVE NAMESAKES?

Not all presidents are created equal, however, and differences in how popular presidents' names become are not simply a matter of when they served. Figure 3.2 shows some presidents spurring much larger naming spikes than others do on taking office. The peak prevalence of *Hoover* is more than twice that of *Taft*, for example, even though Taft assumed power closer to the time when new presidents' names were most apt to take off. The figure also shows some presidents' names entering the pantheon relatively permanently but others withering quickly into obscurity. Before the 1870s, when Hayes rose to power, no more than six babies in the sample were named *Hayes* in any year and the average year saw only one; after Hayes left office, no year's tally was ever so low again, and the average year saw more than twenty newborn *Hayes*es even before the post-1990 fad for the name. *Coolidge*, by contrast, burned relatively brightly in the 1920s, more than four hundred children age nine or younger listed in the 1930 census as having the name, but had already sunk back into obscurity by the end of the 1930s. To the extent that baby names reflect broad public sentiment articulating both the parents' personal preferences and their expectations of what is acceptable in their community, these variations in popularity and persistence can shed light on otherwise murky corners of public opinion. Finding that light requires considering what factors might make a president likelier to stimulate the public imagination, or to do so more enduringly.

Several hypotheses suggest themselves. One suggestive strand of past analyses, foreshadowing chapter 4's discussion of war, finds that military celebrities receive particularly enthusiastic public support in the political arena.[30] Historical lore, similarly, emphasizes popular adulation of sometime military leaders: the heroes of the battles of Tippecanoe (William Henry Harrison, 1811), New Orleans (Andrew Jackson, 1815), Monterrey (Zachary Taylor, 1846), and so on won honor quite separate from their political careers, and the historical image of the soldier as a master of toughness, masculinity, and patriotic sacrifice might enhance the political mystique of military veterans. Those whose pathways to the presidency involved high military commands might then produce a larger or more lasting shift in naming from their presidential service. Conversely, the soldiers' having already been popular namesakes through their war-related popularity might limit the upside of a political run for their names' prevalence; the incremental number of people wanting to draw on a widely used name may be more limited.

Any definition of what constitutes a position of military leadership is somewhat arbitrary. For a straightforward rule, the basic measure here is whether someone achieved the rank of colonel or higher during active, wartime service. This excludes many notable presidential veterans. William McKinley rose through the ranks to become a (brevet) major in the Civil War, for example, and John F. Kennedy's service as a lieutenant on PT-109 during World War II was a fixture of his campaign narrative, but neither of these count by the simple rule here. Similarly, Harry Truman and Richard Nixon became colonel and commander, respectively, in the reserves after their wartime service, but these are also excluded, whereas some figures not necessarily remembered today for their military valor, such as Franklin Pierce and Benjamin Harrison, do count. (Military service was prominent in Pierce's and Harrison's campaigns for office; the famous jibe that the alcoholic Pierce was "hero of many a well-fought bottle" played on his publicity touting his service during the Mexican-American War.[31]) Fortunately, the average effect of military leadership on name prevalence does not change much when choosing ways of coding of these marginal cases.

Military glory is not the only form of success parents might want to celebrate in their children. A president who was elected might appear to have achieved more than someone who took over because of the midterm departure of the actually elected predecessor. This would suggest that elected presidents might inspire relatively more names. Conversely, most unelected

presidents have assumed office on the death of the incumbent, the newsiness and emotion of an unexpected change in presidency might instead
attract more namesakes.

The role of popularity might also imply that name-givers would shun of
the name of a failed president, or of one perceived as having failed. One
measure of success is reelection; insofar as baby-naming patterns pick up
the same sorts of popularity that elections measure, one might expect
reelected presidents to have larger or more enduring effects on baby names,
the size of the original peak (as distinct from its persistence) contingent on
how well the public can correctly anticipate who will win reelection. The
use of reelection as an indicator of public sentiment is slightly complicated
by some presidents who did not clearly seek reelection. James Polk and
Rutherford Hayes both promised before becoming president to only serve
one term, and so their longer-term electoral durability was never actively
tested in the same ways as was that of other presidents. Of course, history
is littered with politicians who backtrack on pledges about their own term
limits; had Polk's and Hayes's reelection chances looked different, they
might have run again, in which case their single-term tenures are in fact
indicative of worse electoral performance. Grover Cleveland raises a ver-
sion of that issue in his second administration, too,[32] posing the conundrum
of having in 1888 lost reelection while winning the popular vote, which
could plausibly be treated either as having electoral popularity or as not; he
is counted in the results as having lost reelection, to parallel Rutherford
Hayes's being treated as a winner in 1876 despite losing the popular vote.[33]

A more widespread and potentially conceptually distinct reason that
presidents failed to win reelection is that they were dead. A tragic ending
may be good for the reputation: Having been shot to death, or expiring from
illness while seemingly in the prime of life, might distract from a politician's flaws. Dying in office might therefore change the course of a name's
popularity, as the *Garfield* example illustrated. Even more than with future
reelection prospects, presumably few people can foresee at the time of most
inaugurations that the president will die in office.[34] Anyone who can has
more important things to do than name babies, so subsequent death in
office is likely to be a factor less relevant for how sharp a rise the president's

name gets at the start of the term than it is to how enduring the popularity of the name might be in ensuing years.

Finally, a president's support base may also matter for naming prevalence. Some populations may be more culturally receptive to the use of surnames as given names; this has historically been particularly noted in the South. At the same time, chapter 2 notes that Southerners for much of American history emphasized state-based identities at the expense of national ones, which may taint a name associated with the current national president in Southern eyes. These sorts of factors suggest that a president who drew electoral support in the South might accrue more namesakes, because the people inclined to draw on surnames also tend to support the president—or fewer, because the people inclined to support the president avoid the unionist overtones of a presidential name. Southern support is measured here by whether a president captured a majority of the electoral votes from the states that made up the Confederacy.[35]

Figure 3.6 shows the predictions of a model that brings these variables together to predict how much of a start-of-term upsurge a president's surname will see in the naming statistics, and how quickly that upsurge will fade.[36] Because each variable is a yes or no condition, the panel associated

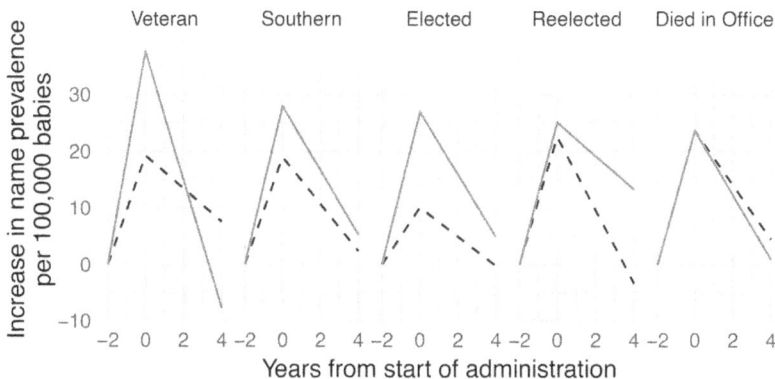

FIGURE 3.6 Effect of presidential characteristics on course of name prevalence. Solid lines show average trajectory for those with the characteristic; dashed lines the average for those without.

with it shows the average trajectory of names for presidents with the given characteristic with a solid line, and that for presidents without the characteristic with a dashed line. For example, the solid line in the veteran panel shows how much the typical president coded as having been a military leader spiked from the preelection baseline and how much that spike petered out over the course of the term. The dashed line in the panel shows the analogous results for the typical president coded as not having been a military leader, holding all the variables from the other panels constant. (In the background, the models also account for the over-time trend shown in figure 3.3, where presidents in the late nineteenth century had larger start-of-term bursts of naming. No similar over-time pattern is evident in how long the president's name persisted as a popular choice.)

A past of military leadership proves the most consequential of these factors for the naming patterns here, leading to a particularly frenzied rise in the frequency of the president's name around the time of inauguration, followed by a relatively steep fall: Veterans' names burn brightly before crashing. To be sure, the models imply that the higher the start-of-term peak, the steeper its subsequent fall is, on average. Even accounting for that general pattern, however, naming after those who come to office on a past of military heroics seems to decline faster than would otherwise be expected. Having won office in one's own right, illustrated in the figure's middle panel, also leads to a statistically appreciable increase in the initial name burst, reaffirming the earlier discussion about how the partisan combat of a campaign seems to compel more name-giving than actual administration achievements, general newsiness, or the wave of attention one might expect an unexpected change of leader might produce. Still, in absolute terms, a president's being elected attracts substantially fewer parents to the surname than the military career does. Conversely, going on to win reelection does not associate with an original burst of popularity—name-givers, reasonably, do not anticipate who will still be popular years later—but it does associate with the presidential name's popularity holding up better after the election.

The other variables tend to have smaller or less certain effects, with one partial exception: Dying in office does not seem to lead to a name's having a longer run of popularity, though that result is somewhat sensitive to how things are measured. It turns out that being assassinated (or more generally dropping dead in office) is an effective short-run play for getting one's name out there, but the swift decline of *Garfield* was no fluke. American baby-namers are a fickle public, and, after the shock of the death has passed, the (ex-)presidential name tends to decline even more quickly than names do at the start of presidential terms. This means that the projected trend for a name's endurance depends on when the president in question died. Those who pull a William Henry Harrison and keel over immediately get a dazzlingly sharp peak—seriously, look at all those 1841 *Harrison*s in figure 3.2—that collapses almost as suddenly as it emerged. The summit was particularly impressive for *Garfield*, in that it had not historically been a very common name at all and was dissimilar from most common names given to people (though to be sure *Winfield* with its -field suffix was more familiar in the nineteenth century than it would later be). When the president's death, and the resultant outpouring of sympathy, arises later on in the term, so does the quick rise and fall of names. This second peak befuddles statistical models trying to predict how long the name of someone who dies in office sticks around as a common choice, increasing the uncertainty of estimated effects.

OTHER POLITICAL FIGURES

The presidency as a locus of power has a natural draw for popular attention. Really appreciating the depth of public attention focused on political figures during the political-celebrity era requires looking at an office without any of the purpose or dignity. Fortunately, the United States has the vice presidency.

In fact the name-givers have at many points in history named their children after the vice president, just as they might have named children after the president.[37] As might be expected from the discussion of politics in public life, this paralleled in miniature the tendency to name children after

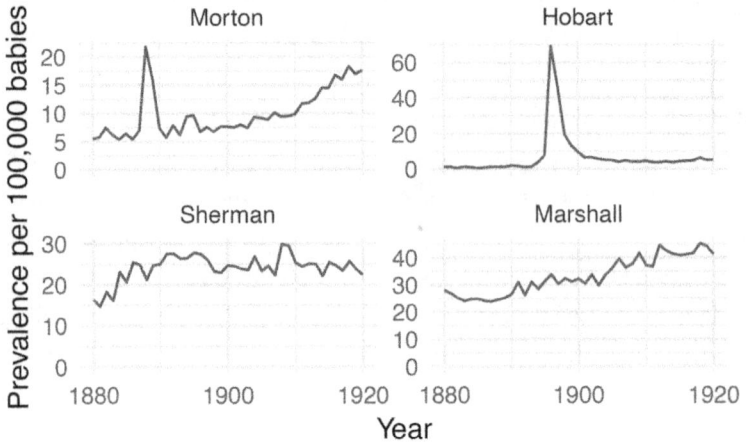

FIGURE 3.7 Popularity of names of selected vice presidents, 1880–1920.

the president: Such names were more frequent in the past than today, the crest of the trend toward vice presidential names arising in the late 1800s and early 1900s. Figure 3.7 shows some notable examples of that era's vice president–related names, focusing on Levi Parsons Morton (Benjamin Harrison's vice president, elected in 1888), Garret Hobart (William McKinley's first vice president, 1896), James Schoolcraft Sherman (Taft's vice president, 1908) and Thomas Riley Marshall (Woodrow Wilson's vice president, 1912 and 1916).

All four names do become more common the years their holders were elected, but they show distinct patterns. *Hobart* ties quite precisely to its holder's election, coming from almost complete disuse to brief but intense prominence. It quickly dropped off again after the inauguration and Hobart's 1899 death in office, though it retained modestly greater prevalence after its flash in the pan than it had had beforehand. *Morton* similarly leaps in use at the 1888 election before falling back to slightly above where it started, though that starting baseline was much higher than *Hobart*'s. *Morton* later enjoyed a much slower resurgence, especially among Jewish communities. Although this use was not directly related to the vice president, the name's second act allegedly reflects uptake as a familiar

English-language name, ideally reminiscent of the upper classes, whose sound somewhat resembled that of *Mordechai* and its diminutive *Mortke* and so could also invoke those ancestral Jewish names.[38] The name's greater familiarity among Gentile communities from a previous vice presidential vogue and association with a prominent, wealthy political leader might have encouraged this repurposing. The growth of *Sherman* and *Marshall* when they became the vice presidential names, and their subsequent fall, were rather more muted, in part because those names had already been in wide use, which among other things made them less effective for anyone striving to flaunt vice presidential love. Despite this, each did manage a statistically appreciable increase in frequency on their namesakes' election. That they did not become as popular at their respective peaks as *Hobart* did at its may hint at something about public impressions of Garret Hobart as a person or a politician, but it could equally reflect that the sound of *Hobart* happened to catch the tastes of the moment. It does meet the usual criteria for being a hit name of being novel but similar to something already familiar, such as *Bart* (a common though not top-rank name in the 1800s).

Public attention to secondary offices expressed through baby names was not just a phenomenon of the vice presidency, either. Other political figures in relatively obscure offices could also find themselves commemorated in baby names, if they were making the news (see figure 3.8). In 1910, the head of the U.S. Forest Service, the conservation-minded Gifford Pinchot, found himself at odds with the secretary of the interior, who pushed for Western development and exploiting natural resources. Pinchot was fired after he publicly raised questions about the impropriety or even corruption of the secretary's dealings, but he could console himself in having been commemorated in a burst of baby names: *Gifford* suddenly became unwontedly popular that year, with dozens more occurrences than in any other year. Even without any formal position of power, political commentary could launch a name into wide circulation. In the wake of the success of Booker T. Washington's books *The Story of My Life and Work* and *Up from Slavery*, the previously obscure name *Booker* was given to hundreds of children a year, especially by Black parents, for decades from 1901 on—perhaps further aided by a political furor when Washington that year became the first African

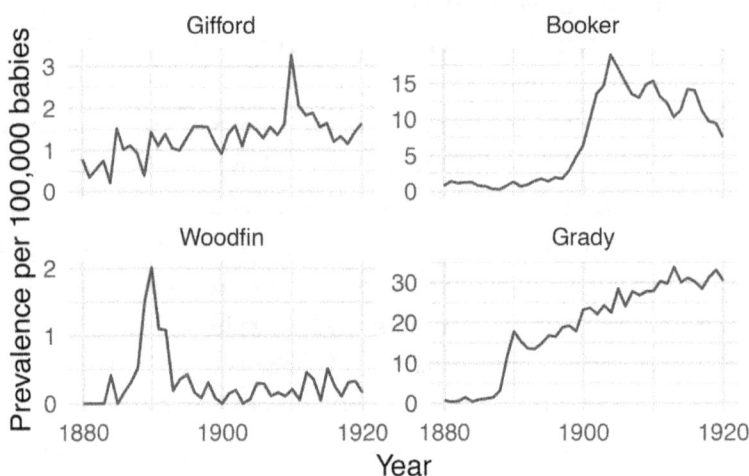

FIGURE 3.8 Names of selected public figures other than elected officials, 1880–1920.

American to dine at the White House as a social equal of the president (rather than as a servant). Nor was this naming for unelected but politicized figures unique to minority ethnic communities marking group members' success. An analogous example might be someone like Henry Woodfin Grady, a political journalist who zealously promoted Atlanta, Georgia, and the idea of the New South, and whose death at age thirty-nine in late 1889 was mourned through naming practices. Both *Woodfin* and *Grady* promptly became more popular name choices, though, perhaps because *Woodfin* is *Woodfin*, only *Grady* permanently became a widely used name.

As Grady's example and chapter 2 suggest, regional identities were still quite strong in the late nineteenth century and beyond, particularly in the American South. In consequence, one might expect subnational politicians to also supply popular baby names, again particularly in the South. The most visible such subnational politicians are typically governors. Figure 3.9 shows a parallel test to that of the bottom-row panels of figure 3.3, looking at the prevalence of names of states' governors among babies born in that state. A slight complication is that states vary in whether governors assume

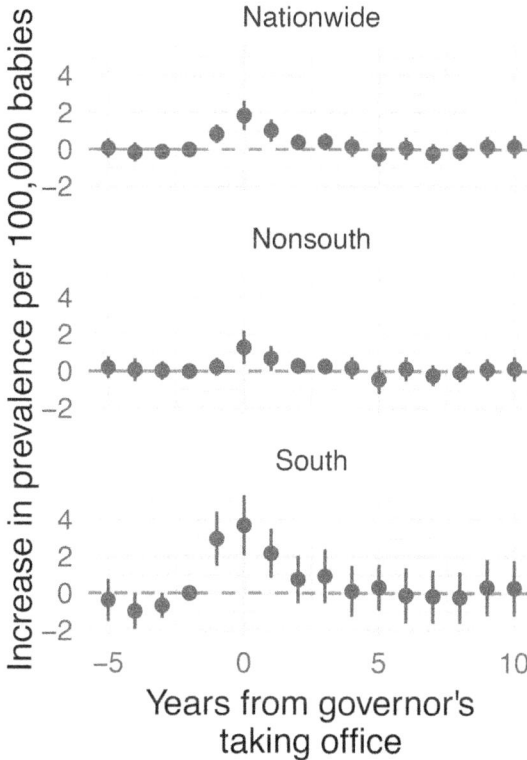

FIGURE 3.9 Change in prevalence of governor's name relative to its average prevalence in the state two years pre-inauguration, 1880–1940; vertical bars indicate 95 percent confidence intervals.

office in the same calendar year as the election, so the relationship between election year and inauguration year is less clear-cut than it was at the national level, but the baseline for the figure remains two years before the inauguration for consistency with figure 3.3. In figure 3.9, the top panel shows the overall national picture; the other panels break those national figures down according to whether a state was in the Confederacy.

Everywhere, gubernatorial surnames had noticeable increases in popularity during the usual election and inauguration period, even if those increases were small on average. But the figure affirms that this national average contains regional variation. In the South, on the other hand, the installation of a new governor typically associated with a larger and more enduring boom in related baby names than it did in the rest of the country.

Of course, Southern culture did not stop cleanly at the borders of the Confederacy. Bluntly dividing the states by Confederate status conceals details of cultural geography. Several other states vie with the seceding states in their use of gubernatorial names—and such states themselves have a marked tendency to have been on the cultural or geographic fringes of the South. Notably, the two non-Confederate states that by most measures seem to use the names of their newly inaugurated governors are Kentucky and Oklahoma. This matches many other existing indices of state South-ernness, which also often find that Kentucky and Oklahoma are the most culturally Southern of the non-Confederate states and perhaps even more Southern than some parts of the Confederacy were.[39] Kentucky and Okla-homa are, in fact, the most common states for analysts to combine with the Confederacy in definitions of the political South,[40] and their affinity for gubernatorial names may speak to another dimension of the states' cultural Southernness.

For more concrete examples of gubernatorial naming, figure 3.10 shows the distribution of children in the 1910 Census with the names of a few selected governors who had been prominent in the preceding decade. These governors are today rather obscure, and their names did not spread into broad or permanent use. Yet, even without knowing the politicians involved, and without the figure adjusting for the small population size of states such as Florida in this era before air conditioning, a glance allows a confident guess as to each governor's home state. Take *Beckham* in the figure's upper left. J. C. W. Beckham became Kentucky's governor in particularly arrest-ing circumstances. His predecessor, William Goebel, is to this day the only sitting governor of a state to be assassinated, dying three days after being sworn in and one day after having been shot amid continued feuding with his predecessor over who really won the election. (Hundreds of Kentucky parents also chose the baby name *Goebel*, variously spelled: Just as for pres-idents, death and assassination were good for the gubernatorial naming brand.) The sensational events made national news for months as a case

Beckham

WA 0, MT 0, ND 0, MN 0, WI 0, MI 0, NY 0, VT 0, ME 0, NH 0, OR 0, ID 0, WY 0, SD 0, IA 0, IL 0, IN 0, OH 0, PA 0, CT 0, MA 0, NJ 0, RI 0, NV 0, UT 0, CO 0, NE 0, KS 0, MO 0, KY 205, WV 0, DC 0, MD 0, DE 0, CA 0, AZ 0, NM 0, OK 0, AR 0, TN 0, VA 0, NC 0, SC 0, MS 0, AL 2, GA 1, FL 0, LA 0, TX 1

Comer

WA 0, MT 0, ND 0, MN 0, WI 0, MI 0, NY 0, VT 0, ME 0, NH 0, OR 0, ID 0, WY 0, SD 1, IA 0, IL 0, IN 0, OH 0, PA 1, CT 0, MA 0, NJ 0, RI 0, NV 0, UT 0, CO 0, NE 1, KS 0, MO 4, KY 7, WV 0, DC 3, MD 0, DE 0, CA 2, AZ 0, NM 0, OK 6, AR 5, TN 32, VA 0, NC 3, SC 2, MS 3, AL 144, GA 55, FL 3, LA 1, TX 11

Heyward

WA 1, MT 0, ND 1, MN 0, WI 0, MI 0, NY 1, VT 0, ME 0, NH 0, OR 0, ID 0, WY 0, SD 0, IA 0, IL 0, IN 1, OH 3, PA 2, CT 2, MA 0, NJ 0, RI 0, NV 0, UT 0, CO 1, NE 0, KS 0, MO 1, KY 1, WV 1, DC 1, MD 2, DE 0, CA 0, AZ 0, NM 0, OK 0, AR 0, TN 1, VA 2, NC 3, SC 230, MS 0, AL 5, GA 28, FL 4, LA 5, TX 2

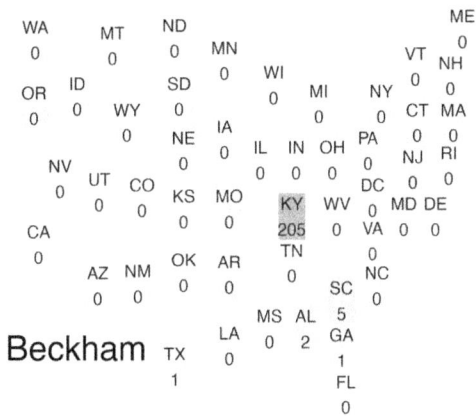

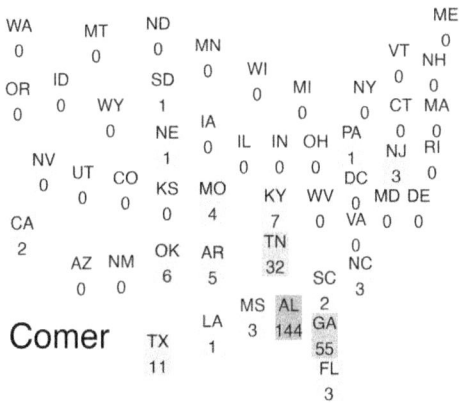

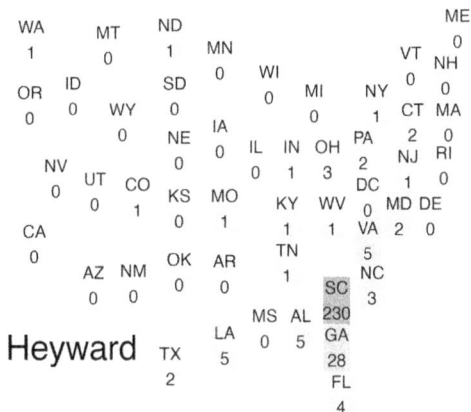

FIGURE 3.10 Newborns given selected gubernatorial names, 1901–1910, by state of birth. Darker background color indicates higher frequency of name in the state.

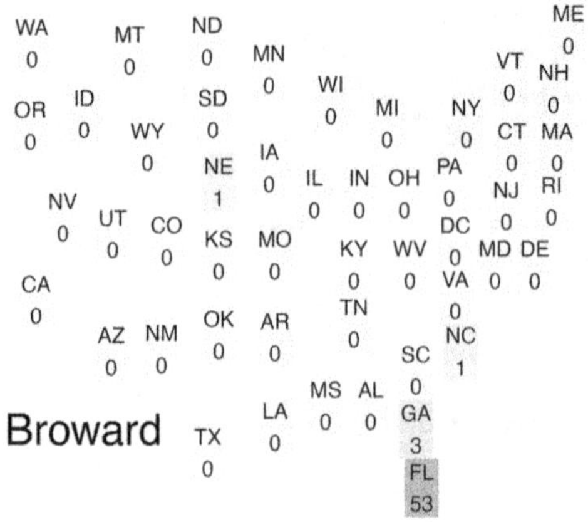

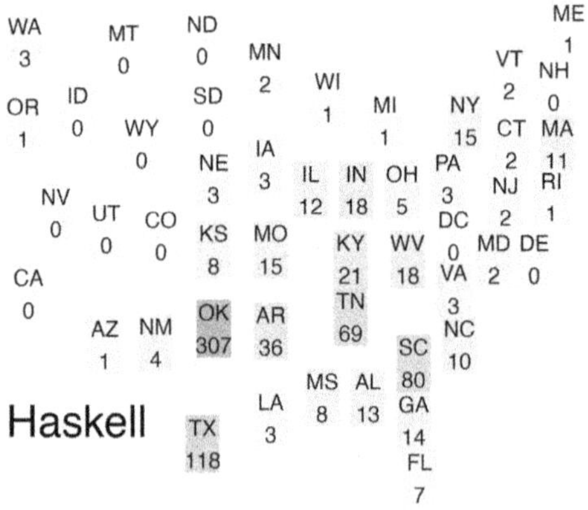

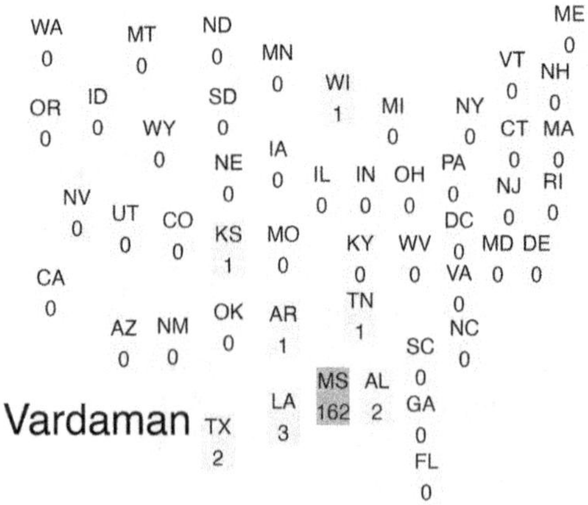

WA 0   MT 0   ND 0   MN 0   ME 0

WI 0   VT 0   NH 0

OR 0   ID 0   SD 0   MI 0   NY 0   CT 0   MA 0

WY 0

NE 1   IA 0   IL 0   IN 0   OH 0   PA 0   NJ 0   RI 0

NV 0   UT 0   CO 0   DC 0

KS 0   MO 0   KY 0   WV 0   MD 0   DE 0   VA 0

CA 0

AZ 0   NM 0   OK 0   AR 0   TN 0   NC 1

SC 0

MS 0   AL 0   GA 3

Broward   TX 0   LA 0   FL 53

WA 3   MT 0   ND 0   MN 2   ME 1

WI 1   VT 2   NH 0

OR 1   ID 0   SD 0   MI 1   NY 15   CT 2   MA 11

WY 0

NE 3   IA 3   IL 12   IN 18   OH 5   PA 3   NJ 2   RI 1

NV 0   UT 0   CO 0   DC 0

KS 8   MO 15   KY 21   WV 18   MD 2   DE 0   VA 3

CA 0

AZ 1   NM 4   OK 307   AR 36   TN 69   NC 10

SC 80

MS 8   AL 13   GA 14

Haskell   TX 118   LA 3   FL 7

WA 0   MT 0   ND 0   MN 0   ME 0

WI 1   VT 0   NH 0

OR 0   ID 0   SD 0   MI 0   NY 0   CT 0   MA 0

WY 0

NE 0   IA 0   IL 0   IN 0   OH 0   PA 0   NJ 0   RI 0

NV 0   UT 0   CO 0   DC 0

KS 1   MO 0   KY 0   WV 0   MD 0   DE 0   VA 0

CA 0

AZ 0   NM 0   OK 0   AR 1   TN 0   NC 0

SC 0

MS 162   AL 2   GA 0

Vardaman   TX 2   LA 3   FL 0

FIGURE 3.10 (*continued*)

about the election made it all the way to the federal Supreme Court. Despite this attention, though, *Beckham* made virtually no inroads outside Kentucky: More than 96 percent of the decade's *Beckham*s nationwide were born in the state.

It seems that the cultural power of governors, however famous or infamous, to affect names did not extend far geographically. To be sure, some examples in the figure have clear regional spillovers, with a popular name seeing its home-state popularity echo in adjacent states: Both *Comer* and *Heyward* picked up appreciable namesakes in Georgia, for example, despite the associated governors respectively having led Alabama and South Carolina. (Besides prospering in adjoining states, several of these governors' names see a few adoptees in Texas, perhaps reflecting the state's history of immigration from across the South, suggesting the immigrants' continued connections to their native states.) But spilling over even into next-door states was not guaranteed. *Beckham* did not have any such regional nature, and none of the sprinkling of out-of-Kentucky Beckhams arose in the state's neighbors.

This localism is true even when the governors themselves moved on a broader stage. Charles Haskell of Oklahoma, the protagonist of the center-right panel of figure 3.10, was prominent in national Democratic politics, serving in multiple leadership roles at the party's 1908 national convention and publicly sparring with President (Theodore) Roosevelt about several issues. Yet although the rate of naming Oklahoma babies *Haskell* went up tenfold when he became the state's first governor in 1907, it saw notable parallel increases only in adjoining parts of Arkansas and Texas at the time, and Haskell's subsequent service in various national roles with the Democratic Party did nothing to push his name further outside Oklahoma. Other states where *Haskell* was a reasonably common name, such as Tennessee and South Carolina, had seen similar rates of its use long before Haskell's inauguration. Indeed, the Haskells had been a prominent political family in South Carolina through the late 1800s, which may have contributed to some of the use of the name there.[41] Even though people may have paid more attention to politics during this era, baby names suggest the attention—or at least admiration for the figures involved—most often stopped with those who held some measure of power locally.

As the various far-flung groups of *Haskell*s suggest, governors often come from locally prominent families that relatives and neighbors might honor in a newborn's name even without the added fillip of a gubernatorial connection. One might then wonder whether these geographically concentrated patterns really relate to the governor as opposed to the broader famous family. Just as shown in the previous figures, though, most of the births occur when the governor is in office, particularly at the beginning of the term. Nothing particularly distinguishes the 1901–1910 decade in this regard, either. Although it is roughly the height of the tendency for children to be named for governors, fashions for naming children after the sitting governor reappear frequently, especially in the South, from the *Houston*s of Texas and *Quitman*s of Mississippi before the Civil War, to the *Talmadge*s of Georgia in the 1930s and 1940s. It may be relevant that many of these examples of popular namesakes were rabid segregationists (and other, nongubernatorial examples of ardent Jim Crow politicians becoming notable namesakes, such as *Bilbo* after Mississippi's Theodore Bilbo, are not difficult to find). The implied endorsement of governors in baby names may not be specifically focused on those governors' racial politics rather than, say, their populism or their personal charisma, to be clear. Avid support for Jim Crow was nearly universal among post-Reconstruction Southern governors, so in the absence of a clear measure of the intensity of politicians' support for racial policies, any link between popular uptake of a name and staunch segregationism is speculative.

Just as with presidents, it is rare after 1945 for a new governor's surname to become more common as a baby name than it previously had been in the state. Occasionally the governor-elect's surname was already gathering popularity, as with Bob Graham (who became Florida governor in 1979) or Jim Edgar (Illinois, 1991). Those cases do not see any evident acceleration of the name's growth like *Ruth* did around the time of Ruth Cleveland's birth, however. That is, the rise in *Graham* or *Edgar* coincident with their respective namesakes entering the gubernatorial office remains roughly in line with the longer-term diffusion of the name, without any obvious statistical deviation from the ongoing trend. Only two of the hundreds of governors in the postwar period appear to have a surname enjoy a discernable step up in popularity around the time they took up the governorship: *Thurmond* (as in Strom, though his given first name was James) in South Carolina in 1947, and *Carey* (as in Hugh) in New York in 1975. When only two examples pop up in a large sample, the possibility that those exceptions were random, meaningless flukes looms large. That possibility advises especial caution in the Thurmond case, given that only a handful of *Thurmonds* were born each year in South Carolina even at the name's peak uptake, and the enthusiasm for his name may (à la figure 3.3) have tied as much to his 1948 presidential run as to his gubernatorial service. As the name of a Southerner with retrograde racial attitudes, though, it was an apposite case to help bring down the curtain on the age of newborns getting their governor's family name.

Of course, by focusing exclusively on gubernatorial surnames, this discussion again sets aside given names such as *Hoke* (M. Hoke Smith, a Georgia governor) or *Huey* (Huey Long, a Louisiana governor) that similarly experienced regional waves of popularity. It also neglects the potential for other regional politicians, such as those serving in Congress, to arouse popular enthusiasm in the form of names. Still, the evidence again points to prominent elected policymakers as having declined in the consciousness and regard of the public since 1900. Politics may however sneak into names by other, less literal ways than directly naming a child after an elected official, such as via several of the foreign affairs associations to which the next chapter turns.

4

FOREIGN AFFAIRS (CA. 1898–1990)

Colin Kelly . . . Dewey *wins a war* . . . *Commanders and others* . . . *The Great War* . . . *The many names of power in war* . . . *Attention to international news* . . . *Unpopular ethnic associations* . . . *Anticolonialism and Black Power*

T he Gaelic boy's name *Colin* has an eminent past, but it nevertheless remained relatively obscure in the United States for most of the country's history. In 1850, the whole country contained only around three hundred Colins of any age, including among immigrants, although related names such as *Collin* and *Cullen* would add to the total. When *Colin* did pop up among American newborns, the children tended to have Scottish ancestors or to descend from Northern Irish Protestants who themselves had Scottish connections.

Another such Colin was born in Florida in 1915: a scion of the Kelly clan, with a great-great-grandfather from Kintyre in western Scotland. Young Colin went to West Point, joined the Air Corps, and started a family, his life proceeding apace but unremarked by the wider world. Then came World War II.

Two days after the attack on Pearl Harbor, Captain Kelly, in command of a B-17C bomber, took off from the northern Philippines in search of Japanese naval vessels. The bomber found its target, striking two enemy ships. It was attacked by Japanese fighter aircraft while returning from the bombing run, though, leaving the plane heavily damaged and on fire. Kelly remained at the controls as he ordered the crew to bail out, trying to keep the plane stable. In this he was largely successful, and a half dozen of those on board escaped the aircraft. Kelly himself, however, died in the plane's crash landing.

Kelly's heroic actions created a sensation in a country aflame with patriotism as it reeled from the shock of the Pearl Harbor bombing. Tributes to his gallantry appeared in popular songs, in street names across the country, and from President Roosevelt. And, of course, in the names of newborns.[1] In much of the country, the newspapers reported Kelly's name and exploits on December 13, and already on that day multiple newborn boys were given the name *Colin Kelly*: Colin Kelly Moffitt in Tennessee, Colin Kelly Main in Virginia, Colin Kelly Brock in Texas, and so on. It even reshaped the names of children already born. Kelly had pronounced the first syllable of *Colin* with a Southern twang, more *coal* than *caul* or *call*. Colin Powell, later secretary of state, had at birth been named with a short o in his name; his name retained that pronunciation within his family, but everyone else began to pronounce his name like Kelly's.[2]

The name eventually took off from these roots. Nor was *Colin* the only name whose fortunes were shaped by America's entry into World War II. Figure 4.1 complements *Colin* with some examples showing the range of names whose prevalence swiftly veered from previous patterns at the start of the war, illustrating some of the typical American naming responses this chapter observes in response to foreign policy shocks.

Pearl directly commemorates the bombed naval base at Pearl Harbor. Along with other gemstone names (such as *Beryl*, *Opal*, *Ruby*, or *Jewel*), it had been quite popular as a girl's name in the late 1800s and early 1900s,[3] but its popularity waned almost every year for decades thereafter. It had

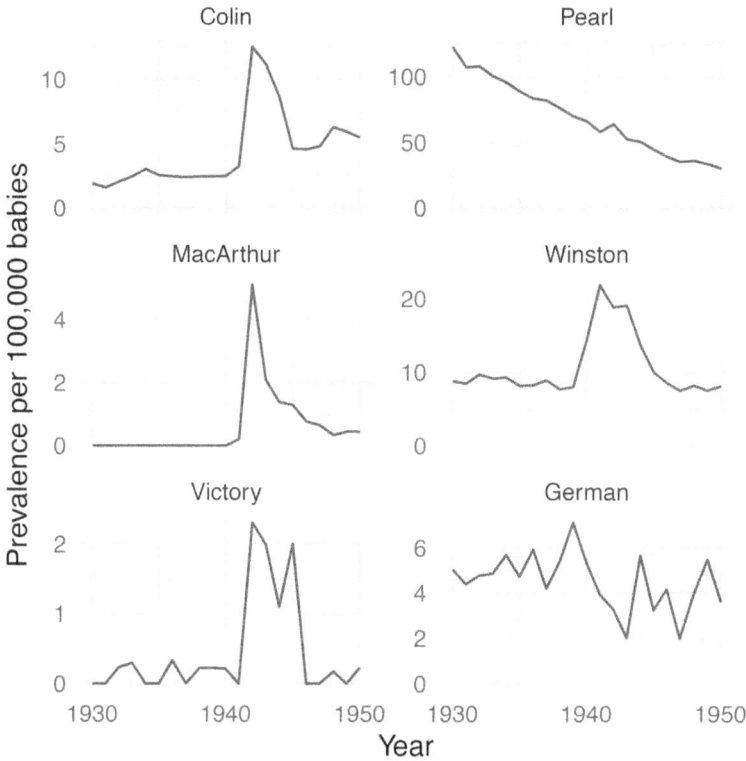

FIGURE 4.1 Prevalence, 1930–1950, of selected names associated with World War II.

thus been in long decline by the 1940s. *Pearl*'s fortunes abruptly reversed in the first year after the United States' entry into the war,[4] however, with the yearning to mark the trauma of the surprise attack able to partly outweigh, at least for a moment, the increasing perception that the name was passé. Although the blip may not appear dramatic against the course of the name's slide into disuse, it represents hundreds more babies named *Pearl* than would have arisen had the previous trajectory continued. Even after the fall in prevalence resumed, it did so from the somewhat higher baseline established in 1942; *Pearl* remained more common for years afterward than its prewar trend would otherwise have suggested.

Other names, like *Colin*, celebrate figures relating to the war effort. Douglas MacArthur, the head of the U.S. Army Forces in the Far East and already a well-known public figure from his time as chief of staff of the Army, was on the front lines of the response to the attack: a classic wartime general as instant military icon, even if the first few months of the war involved much defeat and retreat for American forces. (*McArthur* and *Mac* actually saw even bigger start-of-war increases than *MacArthur*, but figure 4.1 maintains the general's spelling for clarity.) Nor was the public's attention restricted to purely domestic or military figures. For example, Winston Churchill, the prime minister of the United Kingdom, also garnered wartime namesakes as a symbol of steadfast defiance against the Axis threat.

Acknowledgment of the war also moved beyond directly transcribing current events to embrace abstract concepts, the hopes and ideals that war brought to the fore. Representative of this genre is *Victory*, a chronic dream of peoples at war. Although *Victory* was barely used as a name throughout the 1930s, it rapidly gained use once war broke out, only to disappear after the war's end almost as rapidly as it had appeared.[5] Indeed, as we shall see, thematic names in the style of *Victory* recurrently become more popular naming choices when the country is embroiled in international conflict. Conversely, conflict can make other concepts less popular, to the cost of associated names. *German* invoked an enemy country once the Axis powers declared war; even though the name was thoroughly innocent of any relationship to Germany (*Germanus*, a name of multiple ancient Roman saints, evolved into the Spanish *Germán*; *German* can also derive from a Russian transliteration of *Herman*), its popularity, though volatile from year to year, did drop at the outset of the war. Its average prevalence, moreover, underwent a long-term drop just as the United States went to war with Germany.[6]

These examples show that important touchstones of public feeling, and luminaries, too, can arise from foreign policy and international events. This is notable, because these topics are not normally seen as a hotbed of mass interest or acclaim: Scholars of international relations have long bemoaned how little most people in the United States know or care about the world abroad.[7] Yet examples such as *Winston* show that people respond to global events so profoundly as to embed their response in the enduring form of children's names. Of course, World War II was an abnormal time in American history; it may not be much of a surprise that some names danced to the rhythm of the fighting between 1941 and 1945, when foreign affairs were so dominant, even existential. Yet any international crisis is apt to create attachment to country at its keenest, centering a nationalist or patriotic sentiment that names can express.[8] This attachment, no less than the partisan or regional attachments that the last two chapters focused on, has been crucially important to many people in the United States: tens of thousands of babies have been straightforwardly called *America* over the centuries.

But in subtler ways, too, the course of America's international relations shapes the country's choices of names: As *Pearl* and *Victory* show, war heroes are not the only foreign affairs sources of baby names. And, as it turns out, Americans do not require a crisis to key on foreign affairs—names often permanently commemorate something as small as the passing of a foreign potentate through a newborn's hometown, scarcely noticed anywhere else. Americans, in fact, draw on a variety of sources in reaction to international relations. This was always true, as the *Czarina*s of chapter 1 could attest, but became especially evident from the late nineteenth century, when America's new role as a world power entangled the country more often with issues abroad. The gradual national emergence from the preoccupation with the internal affairs of Civil War and Reconstruction found a parallel expression in a wide range of names connecting to the international scene.

That mention of *gradual* deserves emphasis: No dramatic overnight switch led Americans to start paying attention to the world: The change, like most social processes, was subtler than that. It resulted from the convergence of several forces moving in the direction of greater overseas engagement—from technological advances that made it easier to learn about overseas events to the country's growing position on the international stage—that themselves progressed over time and did not all happen at precisely the same moment. The upshot, however, was an increasing number of baby names reacting to various features of foreign affairs.

THE SPLENDID LITTLE WAR

One great swell of names reflecting overseas events occurred amid the Spanish-American War. Compared with the later American conflicts of the twentieth century, the war's fighting ended relatively quickly, and the lack of mass mobilization or conscription might be expected to limit public attention. Yet, from start to finish, the war was a matter of intense public attention, stoked by journalistic coverage.[9] Indeed, the conflict's brevity likely limited disillusionment, making it easier for the fire of public interest to remain stoked throughout. And, as true of any war, the fighting provided several potential avenues for affecting baby names.

One expectation, following readily from chapter 2's discussion of naming after Civil War generals and chapter 3's emphasis on leaders as namesakes, is that the war's military leaders would be a major focus for naming attention. Many such leaders took part in the conflict, especially given that both the Army and the Navy were heavily involved in the war's operations. This raises possibilities of exploring what makes the public more or less attentive to particular leaders: What characteristics make some of them more important or attractive sources of names than others? Naturally, some differences have little to do with the actions or qualities of the leaders themselves: *Sigsbee*, the family name of the captain of the USS *Maine* when it famously blew up in Havana and thus a prominent figure during the war, may have been unlikely to see wide use simply as a matter of sound, given that relatively few given names include three consecutive consonants, such as *gsb*. Other things that encourage naming patterns may have to do with personal charisma: Being good-looking, charming, or flamboyant may attract parents, for instance.

But—pathbreaking though it might be to assess the relative hotness of Spanish-American War generals, a subject on which the scholarly literature is disappointingly thin—hypotheses about the would-be namesakes' substantive achievements also suggest themselves. The public could at least in rough terms distinguish the size of many military successes: Disabling a single enemy ship is typically less impressive than sinking an entire enemy fleet, and capturing a town is under most circumstances less dazzling than conquering an entire province. The cost side of the ledger can similarly matter, in that an achievement gained at the cost of fewer casualties has obvious advantages in motivating public celebration (although particularly hard-fought, costly triumphs could also conceivably win acclaim). Even when the military actions had similar characteristics, their timing is likely to influence public interest and therefore conversion into a name. Because people often find novel events especially exciting and memorable but lose interest over repetitions—witness in chapter 3 the diminishing interest in William Jennings Bryan—popular heroism might have a first-mover advantage: Those who stake a position in the public consciousness early may prevent the spotlight from moving in full intensity to later triumphs.

One war leader's name towered over all others. *Dewey* saw an extraordinary surge in fashion in 1898 even though it had been nearly unknown before the war (see figure 4.2). It did, to be sure, have a head start in being used as a potential name by dint of rhyming with recognizable, established first names such as *Louie* (or the French pronunciation of *Louis*). That is no small advantage; as mentioned, new fashions most often prosper when they combine familiarity with a small innovation, making them comfortably familiar while also appealingly new.[10] *Dewey* was the opposite of *Sigsbee* in this regard. But Admiral Dewey's victory at Manila was so total that it was always likely to earn particular public attention, especially given that it happened early in the conflict before other leaders had had a chance to establish themselves as the conflict's preeminent hero. Even after the main frenzy of *Dewey* fever wore off, the name settled for decades as a much more common name than it had been before American conquest of the Philippines: Into the early 1980s, triple-digit numbers of *Dewey*s were born each year in the United States.

Despite *Dewey*'s dominance, several other commanders' names also became appreciably more common during the war.[11] Such tributes honored leaders from across the services (figure 4.2), with naval leaders such as William *Sampson* as well as army leaders such as William *Shafter*, and across theaters, from Wesley *Merritt* in the Philippines to Nelson *Miles* in Cuba and Puerto Rico. (As in chapter 3, those whose surnames were being adopted

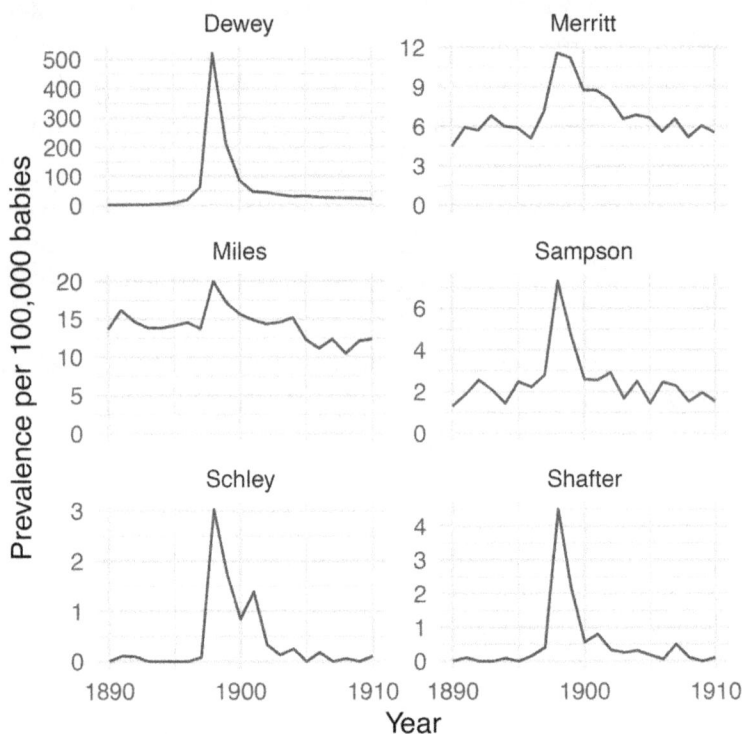

FIGURE 4.2 Prevalence, 1890–1910, of names of selected United States military commanders of the Spanish-American War.

by name-givers also received first-name namesakes. The most distinctive example in the Spanish-American War was *Elwell* after Elwell Otis, Wesley Merritt's successor in several leadership roles in the Philippines.) But the wartime increases in prevalence for these names was orders of magnitude smaller than for *Dewey*. Admiral Dewey's fame thoroughly eclipsed that of other military figures, even though they did get new luster of their own.

Those who command whole armies and navies naturally draw attention. Their position means that they and their achievements are most widely known. Yet, as Colin Kelly proved, circumstance can also launch less-exalted fighters to public acclaim, especially with displays of valor. The prime example in the Spanish-American War was Theodore Roosevelt's gathering of the Rough Riders cavalry unit and leading it in the Battle of San Juan Hill: Roosevelt's social connections in New York ensured that his bravado attracted thorough press coverage in high-visibility outlets, and *Roosevelt* duly started circulating as a popular name choice. Roosevelt soon went on to still greater things in both politics and namesakery,[12] but his name's initial ascent during the war reflects the public affection that proved decisive to his political career.

At the time, however, Roosevelt had competition within public enthusiasm for lower-rank fighters (see figure 4.3). The naval officer Richmond Hobson in June 1898 valiantly led a group of volunteers to sink the coalship *Merrimac* at the entrance to the harbor of Santiago, Cuba, hoping to entrap the Spanish naval vessels within. The *Merrimac* did sink under Spanish fire, but without blocking the harbor—and with its crew becoming prisoners of war, if comfortably treated ones. As their leader, Hobson became a sensation, so enrapturing the public that an alarm was raised that he could be spreading disease through all the women who were kissing him,

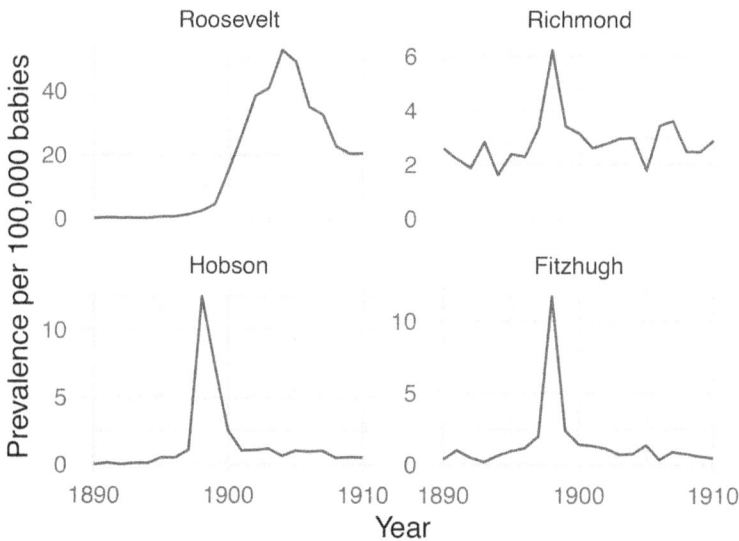

FIGURE 4.3 Prevalence, 1890–1910, of names of celebrated figures of the Spanish-American War other than commanders.

or trying to.[13] (This despite Hobson's being something of a prig, a ferocious campaigner for decades afterward against alcohol, marijuana, and other intoxicating substances, including during several terms of service in Congress.) Indeed, both *Richmond* and *Hobson* became dramatically more popular names in 1898. Even his middle name, *Pearson*, briefly quadrupled in popularity relative to its previous baseline.

Other such honorees demonstrate the range of people and characteristics that the public can latch on to. Fitzhugh Lee, for example, was the United States consul general in Havana, the country's most senior diplomat in Cuba. This put him in the spotlight in trying to defuse the tensions around the USS *Maine*, the American warship whose explosion in Havana's harbor killed much of its crew and accelerated the rush toward war despite little conclusive evidence that the Spanish had any role in its sinking. *Fitzhugh* accordingly became roughly as popular as *Hobson* did, even though Fitzhugh Lee did not take part in fighting heroics in the fashion of Theodore Roosevelt or Richmond Hobson (figure 4.3). He did, it is true, resign his diplomatic post to join the Army, but because he was in his sixties—he had decades earlier during the American Civil War served along with his uncle, Robert E. Lee—his primary military role was as a governor during Cuba's occupation by the United States. Simply being at the center of international events of intense public focus in his case was enough to inspire namesakes.

As with *Pearl* and *Victory* during World War II or the army ranks that became common Southern names during the Civil War, conflicts do not only make names of people (figure 4.4). Places and things can also see wartime surges in use as names. The boundary between those categories can be fuzzy: A small proportion of people choosing to honor George Dewey or other naval figures did not use their names directly, but instead their title or office. In the case of Dewey, this might mean *Commodore*, as he started the war, or *Admiral*, the title to which he was promoted soon after his triumph at Manila Bay. Many of the *Admiral*s and *Commodore*s in fact had *Dewey* as their middle names.

Battle sites also continued to see notable commemoration in names: One could honor the fallen, or take national pride in a victory, by repurposing

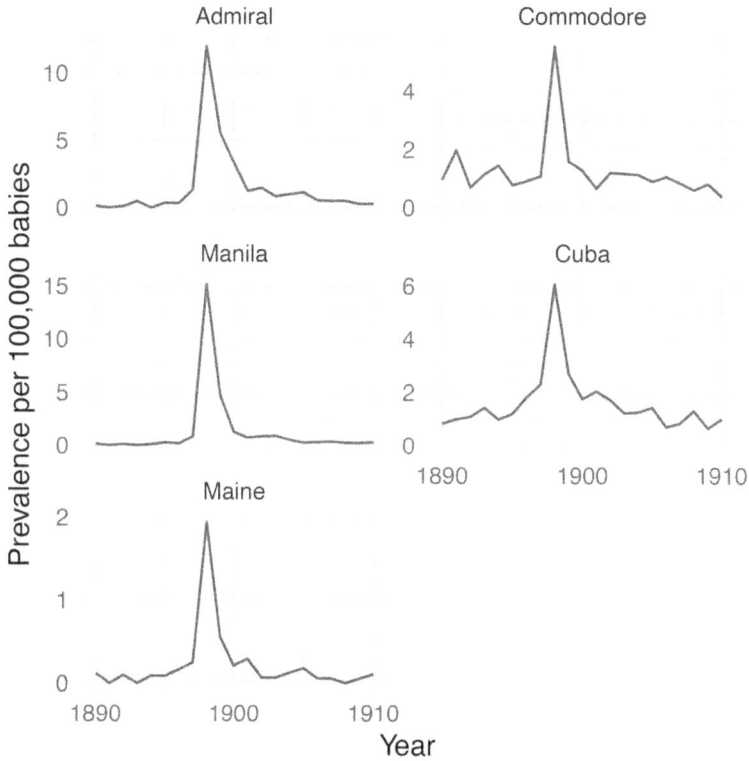

FIGURE 4.4 Prevalence, 1890–1910, of names involving concepts associated with the Spanish-American War.

the name of its place as a child's name. Just as *Dewey* was the champion of leaders, the location of his most famous victory, *Manila*, saw particularly broad use as a namesake, especially as a variant spelling, in this case *Manilla*, was once more only slightly less popular than the standard spelling through-out the same trajectory of brief but intense faddishness. The Pacific was not the only theater of the war whose places showed up in names, however. Important war locations in the Caribbean, such as *Cuba* (and to a lesser extent *Havana*), also saw wartime use: Victories and conquests were often enshrined in children's names. So were more solemn tokens of the war. If people today remember anything about the Spanish-American War, it is the *Maine*. At the time, too, people felt a need to preserve the memory of the lives lost, and *Maine* duly became a much more common name than it has been before or since. Of course, even victories have casualties, so even some of the uses of other battle sites could, as with the later *Pearl*, appear more in commemoration of the lives lost rather than as celebration of the locale's events.

ENTRENCHING NEW NAMES

These examples show how even a brief, less-than-total conflict can rivet attention to the extent that parents draw on a variety of its events to serve as baby names—especially if the war is marked by triumph and derring-do, as from the American perspective the fight against Spain was. *Dewey* outclassed almost anything from the Civil War for uptake, despite the much larger role the earlier war had in the nation's lore. Similarly, after the United States claimed the Philippines as a spoil of war and saw a much grimmer face of conflict, with the slow, brutal struggle of a counterinsurgency campaign, which may be why the Philippine War fails to show up in names in the same multifarious way as the Spanish-American War did. But longer or deadlier conflict can also inspire names. Indeed, many sources of Spanish-American War names appeared in analogous ways during World War I, a larger war in almost every way. For example, just as Admiral Dewey had been the standout hero and runaway favorite as a namesake during the earlier war, World War I had John Pershing, the head of the American Expeditionary Force in France (figure 4.5). *Pershing* had not previously been a common name choice, and would not be after the war, either, but it leapt to brief prominence in 1918 as American involvement in the fighting took hold. Despite or because of the greater intensity of the fighting, though, *Pershing* was even at its peak far less common than *Dewey* had been.

The world wars did differ from the Spanish-American War in that the United States fought alongside a set of allies. This opens the possibility for an even more internationalized perspective than was seen in the

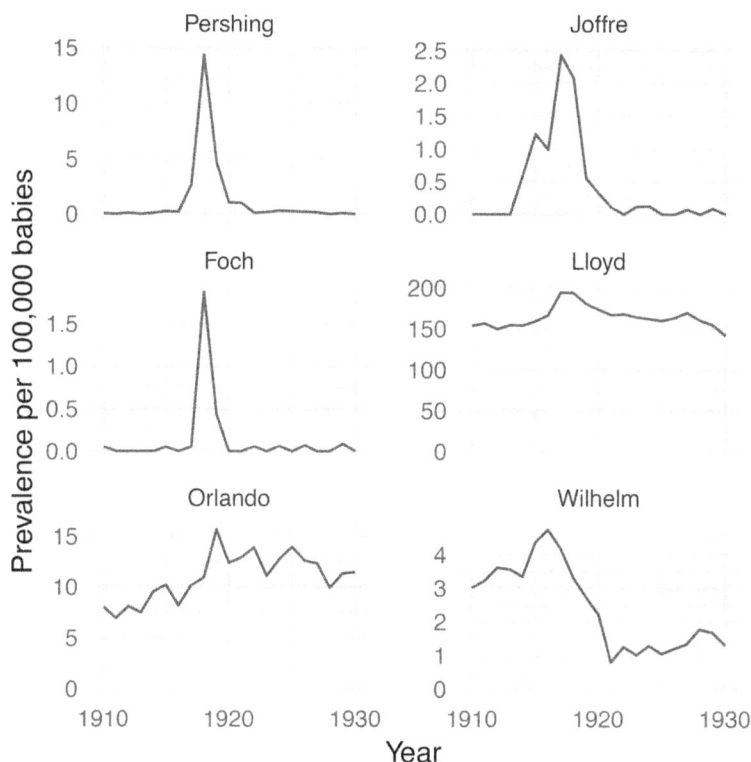

FIGURE 4.5 Prevalence, 1910–1930, of names of leaders connected to World War I.

Spanish-American War, given the fellow feeling of comradeship and shared struggle. This was seen in the example of *Winston* in World War II. Yet it was not restricted to British names, despite the extra cultural and linguistic affinities that connect the United States to the United Kingdom and hence to British names; name-givers were also drawn to other allies.

In World War I, France was a particularly prominent non-British ally, both as a key player in the fighting and as the site of deployment of most American troops. The United States, moreover, had deep cultural ties with the French going back to the American Revolution and because French was the nineteenth century's premier language of diplomacy and culture. All of this could make French names speak comfortably to most Americans in ways that Serbian names, for example, were unlikely to no matter how pluckily Serbia resisted the Central Powers.[14] Several French leaders duly appeared as namesakes in the United States. *Joffre* and *Foch*, for example, the surnames of two of the most famous French generals in the war, both saw some use during and immediately following the war (figure 4.5).

Indeed, an emotional connection with France was strong enough to get *Clemenceau*, the family name of France's prime minister for most of the United States' time as a party to the war, bestowed on several children despite its length.[15] The names of President Wilson's other political partners among the Big Four at the war-ending Paris Peace Conference, prime ministers Lloyd George of Britain and Orlando of Italy, were more familiar, common names, which may have contributed to their seeing much larger surges of use at the time of the conference—though Clemenceau's exasperated sparring with Wilson about how harshly to treat Germany in the postwar settlement may also have tempered American attitudes toward him and his name.

The Big Four were sufficiently esteemed that their more-official designation as the Council of Four turned up in a double-digit number of babies named *Council* in 1919, a higher-than-usual number although *Council* was used a name intermittently throughout the late nineteenth and early twentieth centuries. Conversely, just as *German* might have potentially unpalatable associations with the enemy during a war against Germany, so did the name of the German Kaiser, *Wilhelm*, become sharply less popular after the U.S. entry into the war, after having somewhat risen in popularity, especially among German American communities, during the earlier part of the conflict.

But Americans did not turn only to leaders as cues about potential baby names relating to World War I. As they had in other wars, battle sites gained popularity as name sources (see figure 4.6). Consider examples such as *Verdun* and *Marne*, the locations of vicious clashes on the Western Front.[16] Parents could also memorialize the entire theater of war, and the sufferings of an allied nation, by choosing a name such as *France*—or a region such as *Alsace*, whose wartime sufferings were the focus of French

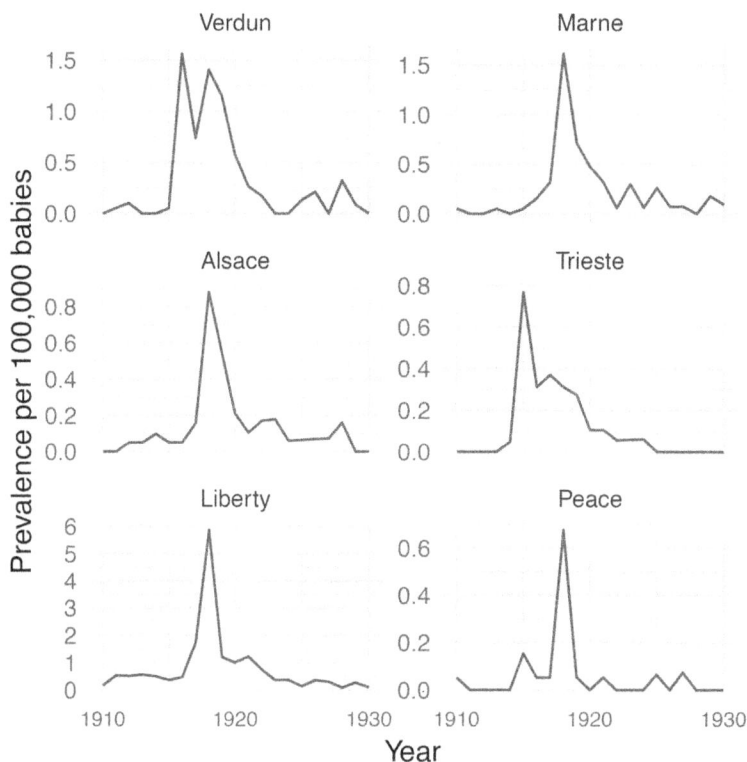

FIGURE 4.6 Prevalence, 1910–1930, of names involving places or concepts associated with World War I.

propaganda efforts to assert a territorial claim (*Lorraine*, already a widely used name, also shot up in popularity, becoming almost twice as common in 1918 as it had been in 1917).[17]

Asserting this territorial claim on behalf of an ally was not unique to the Western Front. Notably, the Austro-Hungarian city of Trieste was a key claim of Italy as it entered the war against the Central Powers. *Trieste* accordingly became a substantially more popular name during the war, if still a rare one. This new popularity was distinctive in multiple ways. First, the family names of babies named *Trieste*, and the census records of their parents' birthplaces, suggest that the name was almost entirely a phenomenon among Italian Americans. Second, although *Trieste*'s popularity was elevated throughout the war years, its greatest prevalence came in 1915, the year Italy declared war on Austria-Hungary but well before the United States joined the belligerents. *Trieste*, that is, shows another case, like *Wilhelm*, when the attention to wartime events illustrates less a rallying 'round the American flag than Americans asserting their affinity with their ancestral homeland: war could provoke sympathy for other countries' nationality as well as traditional American patriotism.[18] (*Joffre* had similarly become more popular before the United States entered the war, though that popularity rose further upon American entry.)

Also echoing patterns seen in the Spanish-American War and World War II, some abstract concepts became more common during World War I. One of the words most associated with the war effort was *Liberty*. Government fundraising hawked liberty bonds, sauerkraut was called liberty cabbage to avoid the stigma of a German name, and so on; the association was strong enough that the eventual official national museum to the war was originally called the Liberty Memorial. Accordingly, *Liberty* also saw sudden, widespread take-up as a name during the war, and for a few years afterward. (It would see a similar burst of popularity during World War II, again echoing its use in such wartime argot as liberty ships.) In 1918, it was joined as a reasonably common name by *Peace*, reflecting the relief that the shooting had stopped, though that proved a less enduring name choice.[19] Not that name-choosers quit paying attention to news about peacemaking efforts; other names reflecting the peace negotiations emerged, for example with dozens of babies named *Dardanell* or *Dardanella* in 1920, when the Treaty of Sèvres demilitarized the Turkish strait known as the Dardanelles.

DOMINANT NAMES OF WARTIME

The common patterns of parents turning to commanders, battlegrounds, and terms such as *victory* as sources of names suggest some of the qualities that people particularly yearn for during international conflict. But these examples, however evocative, may not be representative. It would be helpful to see whether the discussed trends generalize to systematic patterns.

One way to do so is to look at the everyday nouns, verbs, adjectives, and other words that people use as names. Those words have meanings that are naturally brought to mind when thinking about the names—indeed, baby-name books often heavily emphasize the meanings of names in their source languages, and the importance and obviousness of the meaning is all the stronger when the word is in the dominant language spoken in the country. Think of the Puritans of chapter 1 naming their children after cherished virtues, for example, or the common tendency for African Americans in the decades after emancipation to give their children aspirational professional names such as *Doctor*, or the examples of *Victory* and *Peace* earlier this chapter.[20] Even if the word is used as a name not because of its meaning but because of other associations (as when being named *Doctor* after one's uncle of that name, or being called *River* because it was the mother's maiden name), name-givers are likely to consciously or unconsciously realize it carries with it some overtones of the word's common meaning. Hence words are essentially never used as names if their meanings are dire enough, no matter how euphonious they sound or how aptly they describe a particular infant: Who would name their child *Murderous* or *Diarrhea*?

The popularity of names with any particular plain-language meaning would naturally wax or wane as the linked concept became more or less culturally attractive. One hypothesis is that the contest for dominance inherent in war might increase the attention and interest in being able to express power, so words with meanings that did so would become more prevalent during wartime. Conversely, meekness might be valued at other times, but is less attuned to a martial zeitgeist, so that words connoting it would be less appealing when the country was fighting.

Assessing whether names suggest the quality of making others surrender is a formidable task. But linguists, psychologists, and others who use text as data have already thought at length about how to measure words' emotional color, and provided lists of words that speak to this very question. One of the longest-established systems of analyzing the sentiment of text along these lines is the General Inquirer,[21] which among other things provides dictionaries coding which words that usually indicate power as well as words connoting its opposite, submissiveness. Examples of high-power words are *sovereign*, *enforce*, and *egotistical*. Presumably, if war prompts a systematic tendency for people to want more symbolic power, high-power words will become relatively more attractive and common as names when the country is fighting, while submissiveness-cuing words such as *homage*, *react*, and *imitation* will become less common.[22]

Just as the selection of words raises potentially thorny question of measurement, so does determining what a war year is—with complications arising both from war and from year. The United States famously has not declared formal war against another country by its constitutionally mandated procedure since the declarations of 1941 and 1942 against various Axis countries in World War II. Yet it has obviously fought many bloody military conflicts since then. Consistently coding war is an enduring struggle in international relations, but analysts have established some conventions for counting wars; the analysis here draws on one of the more prominent such rules, counting as wartime any calendar year in which the United States suffered a thousand or more deaths in battle.[23] Both world wars, the Korea conflict, and several years of American fighting in Vietnam meet this criterion, but other American conflicts of the 1898 to 1990 period under examination, notably including the Spanish-American War, do not. Having to rely on calendar years adds further noise to the measurements because it obscures any patterns about when within the year the war was active. Pearl Harbor and all the American battle deaths in 1941 occurred in December: For more than 90 percent of the year, parents selected names without certainty that 1941 would be a wartime year for the United States. Even in World War I, when the United States formally declared war in April 1917, the time needed for mobilizing troops and transporting them across the ocean meant that the American Expeditionary Force saw little combat before the fighting at Cambrai starting in late November of that year.

Figure 4.7 shows when power-invoking names became more common relative to their long-term trend. That is, it looks at how much more

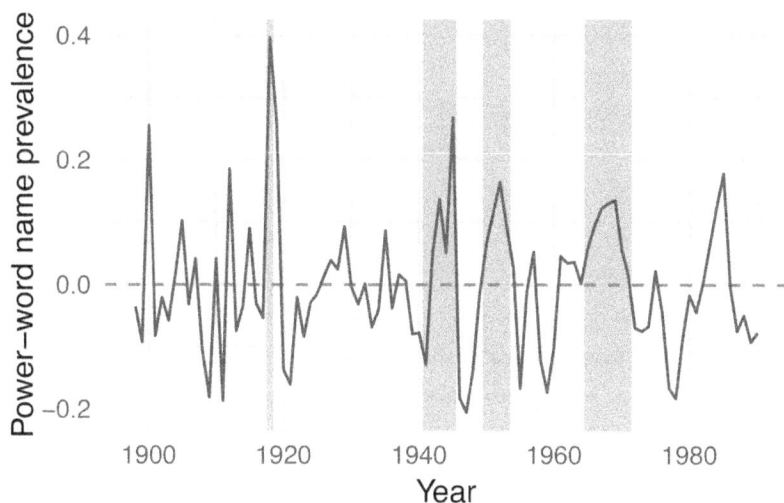

FIGURE 4.7 Detrended use of words associated with power as first names, 1898–1990. Shaded areas indicated years with at least a thousand American combat deaths.

common words conveying potency were as names each year, subtracting out the long-run average prevalence of those names.[24] Shaded areas of the figure indicate the years counting as wartime. The highest two peaks of usage of power-related words as names occurred during the world wars, and this does seem to typify a general trend: Formal statistical tests indicate that war years have, on average, a larger share of power-related names than one would expect from the long-term trends.

The Korea and Vietnam conflicts did not see such large upswings in the use of power-emphasizing words as names, but even in those cases the relevant names were more prevalent during the years of most intense fighting than might otherwise have been expected. This is especially noteworthy given that, unlike the world wars, neither conflict resulted in an unambiguous victory for the American side, and both wars faced widespread public disapproval.[25] The turn toward words that conjure power does not seem to require the country to be swept up in a universal jingoistic euphoria. It could be, of course, that it is mostly supporters of a controversial ongoing war who are likeliest to choose names with more muscular everyday meanings, but even wars triggering public ambivalence appear to inspire some turn toward power-evoking names.

SEEING THE WORLD

Although the wars that the United States has fought have been the most significant wellspring for names relating to world affairs, other international figures and events sometimes also show up in detectable ways. Earlier chapters foreshadowed this: Figure 3.4 shows *Hoover* first gaining widespread use amid Herbert Hoover's humanitarian relief efforts in Europe in the late 1910s and early 1920s, and chapter 2's discussion of states as productive sources of names also applies to countries, such as *Australia*, *Armenia*, or *India*. Another perennial favorite source of names, historically, was royalty. During an era when monarchies often combined real power with their wealth and glamor, trying to capture some of their blue-blooded aura for one's children was a natural tendency, especially when some prince or princess was capturing headlines. Royals' goodwill tours of the United States repeatedly met with popular adulation and a wave of namesakes, just as later heads of state would travel the world in attempts at public diplomacy.[26] The Infanta Eulalia, younger sister of the king of Spain, for example, visited the country to reach the World's Columbian Exposition in 1893, spurring a sharp increase in girls named *Eulalia*.

The dazzling pageantry of royal weddings and coronations could similarly catch public attention. A particularly vivid example was the 1906 marriage of the king of Spain to Queen Victoria's granddaughter Victoria Eugenie, generally known as *Ena*, one of her many middle names. A wedding-day attempt to assassinate the groom with a bomb missed its target but killed some thirty others and wounded scores more, adding layers of sympathy to the sheen of aristocracy. *Ena* promptly shot up in popularity (figure 4.8).[27] By contrast, the name of her new husband, *Alfonso*, experienced little parallel boom, though it did see a more modest increase in

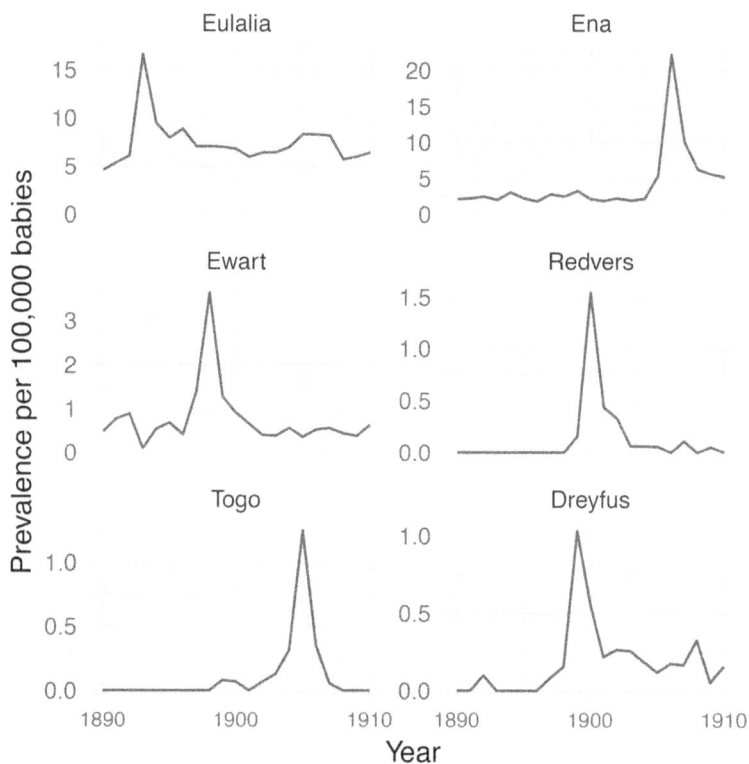

FIGURE 4.8 Prevalence of selected international affairs names, 1890–1910.

1907, the year after the wedding. This may suggest that princesses had a special cultural magnetism even before the Disney-industrial complex, but princes' names could also surge in popularity given the right circumstances. When the Danish prince Carl, on being offered the crown of newly independent Norway, not only insisted that the Norwegians have a popular referendum favoring the establishment of a monarchy but also took a venerable Norwegian name on acceding to the throne, the resultant outpouring of affection extended to the United States, producing a wave of babies sharing his new regnal name, *Haakon*.[28]

Royals were not, though, the only international figures that Americans latched onto as sources for baby names. Although waves of names honoring the king and princess set tended to be particularly large, several other figures attracted American name-givers. As with the domestic politicians examined in chapter 3, overseas politicians could be a source of names. For instance, enough parents were paying attention in 1898 when Britain's former prime minister, the Liberal William Gladstone, died that his distinctive middle name, *Ewart*, was bestowed on dozens of American boys. (*Gladstone* saw a parallel surge, about half the size of *Ewart*'s.) Sometimes these names, like *Trieste* as an Italian-inflected name during World War I, appeared in particular subcultures or regions: *Laurier* saw some use in Quebec-adjoining corners of Maine and New Hampshire when Wilfrid Laurier was Canada's prime minister, and *Eamon* and to a lesser extent *DeValera* ticked up noticeably in popularity among Irish Americans as Éamon de Valera helped lead the successful political campaign for Irish independence.[29] (The popularity of *Eamon* might also have drawn on another independence leader, Éamonn Ceannt, who signed the proclamation of the Irish Republic and was executed by the British.)

Similarly, just as names celebrated military leaders of wars that America itself fought, they marked the heroes of other countries' conflicts (figure 4.8). The British fighting in the Second Boer War was notoriously inglorious, sinking into a grueling attrition that presaged World War I's Western Front while seeing mass use of concentration camps, but the role of Robert Baden-Powell (later famous for his role in founding both the Boy Scouts and the Girl Scouts) in fending off of the Siege of Mafeking in 1899 drew some parents to the name *Baden*, and General Redvers Buller's overall leadership prompted a similar increase in the use of *Redvers*. Only a handful of American parents went the other direction, naming their children *Kruger* after the leader of the Boers; this lower popularity could reflect either less support for the merits of the Boer cause than for the British or a feeling that Boer names did not sound as natural in American English.

Then again, parents could venture quite far from traditional British heritage names to honor a military hero: After Japanese Admiral Tōgō Heihachirō smashed the Russian fleet at the Battle of Tsushima in late

May 1905, essentially ending major fighting in the Russo–Japanese War, the popularity of *Togo* as a name leapt (figure 4.8). One might reasonably suspect that a name like *Togo* would, like *Trieste*, be particularly popular among the ethnic group most connected to the international events involved. Several of the children named *Togo* indeed have typically Japanese family names and live in places—Hawaii and California—with relatively large Japanese American populations. American examples of the name from *Togo* before the Russo-Japanese War even more consistently come from such populations. But most of the children named *Togo* in the United States in 1905 did not: The turn toward the name transcended region and ethnicity. Random examples include Togo Thomas (born May 27 in Virginia), Togo Fisher (June 10, Kansas), and Togo Morris (July 9, Texas). Even as widespread, explicit prejudice greeted ethnic Japanese in the United States—mere weeks before the Battle of Tsushima, the Japanese and Korean Exclusion League was founded in San Francisco, and the so-called Gentlemen's Agreement to restrict Japanese immigration became part of American government policy later in the decade—some people were willing to hail a Japanese leader for his success, even at the risk of associating their child with an unpopular ethnicity.

Attention to happenings outside the English-speaking world can also be seen in a name like *Dreyfus*. It was never a common name, even at its peak being an order of magnitude rarer than *Eulalia* through this period (figure 4.8). But it was deeply associated with the Dreyfus Affair, when a French captain, Alfred Dreyfus, was convicted in 1894 of treasonously spying for Germany and spent years imprisoned in brutal conditions in French Guiana before a media and social uproar later in the 1890s led to another trial and pardon in 1899 (and, later yet, Dreyfus's exoneration). That trial corresponded to a substantial increase in the use of the name *Dreyfus*, which for years thereafter remained more popular than it had been before the matter came to public attention. Dreyfus was Jewish, and so, like Admiral Tōgō, came from an ethnic group that often faced animus in the United States—yet name-givers, even those with no obvious personal connection to Judaism, proved quite willing to invoke him.[30]

THE NAME OF THE FOES

The potential for discrimination against ethnic groups such as the Japanese or Jews hints that names do not just show enthusiasm for individual name-sakes or for timely topical concepts like power and dominance; they also reflect international politics in what they avoid. In particular, many names have associations with specific languages, cultures, and countries. When relations between the United States and a given country deteriorate or rup-ture, names linked to that country might easily find themselves in disrepute; even parents who like a name on its own terms may feel obliged to avoid the tainted national associations. That is, although names of a given ethnic background may become more or less common for many reasons, name-givers' antipathy for a culture—or their expectation that friends and neigh-bors might feel such antipathy—will likely dissuade them from using names that they connect with that culture. This sort of popular rejection of an entire national heritage famously happened with Germans during the World War I, for example, as with the example of sauerkraut as liberty cabbage. This anti-German mood fed into the reduced use of German-origin names for children: Figure 4.5's *Wilhelm* is only a particularly freighted example.[31] But was the World War I case a one-off, or do names more generally reflect public sentiment toward a country? And when, and for how long, do ethnic names respond to these sorts of foreign policy events?

Generalizing across all an ethnicity's names requires being able to iden-tify the set of names that might connect to a culture or country, analogously to identifying words relating to power for figure 4.7. The most straightfor-ward approach relies on the ethnic origin of names: A name that originated in a particular country and culture can measure responses to that back-ground. Names' national origins have, to be sure, drawbacks as barometers of sentiment toward a country, even beyond the usual "people choose or avoid names for many possible reasons" caveat. Trying to assess discrimi-nation based on rejection of the national names falters when the adversary's language background is indistinguishable from the United States': Look-ing for general declines in names of British origin during the War of 1812 or ethnically Confederate names during the Civil War is unlikely to be very fruitful. For other cases, the opposite problem holds, with names from a particular ethnic background too rare to meaningfully trace. This might apply, for example, to Vietnamese names as the United States spiraled into fighting with North Vietnam.

In any case, the relationship between language and nationality is often ambiguous: A German-language name might reflect Swiss origins, for example. More generally, just because a name had a particular origin does not mean the American public still links the two. For instance, *Anastasia* was originally Greek, but some of its most visible appearances in twentieth-century American culture relate to the daughter of the last Russian czar so that it may associate more with Russian than with Greek in the American public's mind. Many other names have been assimilated into seeming thoroughly American without any particular ethnic connection, regardless of their historical or etymological origin. These sorts of pitfalls need consideration, but the language backgrounds of names still offer insight about public attitudes toward their associated countries. To have a consistent coding rule, the ethnic origins of names are taken as those given at Behind-thename.com, acknowledging nationality as perceived by name-givers may not have aligned with this source's categorization.

German-origin names had been maintaining a relatively stable share of the population in the years before World War I. They started dropping appreciably in 1917, however, when the United States entered the war. Strikingly, however, the decline continued not only into 1918 but also for several years after the war; the proportion of names did not stabilize—at a lower plateau than its prewar rate—until the mid-1920s (figure 4.9). This contrasts with other measures of cultural cachet, such as the rate of appearance of different composers on symphonic concert programs, where the turn against Germans (and Austrians) was sharp but short lived.[32] Even if orchestral managers felt comfortable welcoming German influences, name-givers remained more cautious. Some of this wariness may have reflected the longer-term declines in the use of ethnically distinctive names and in ethnic Germans' share of the total population, restoring German names to the downward trend they had generally shown for the twenty years before

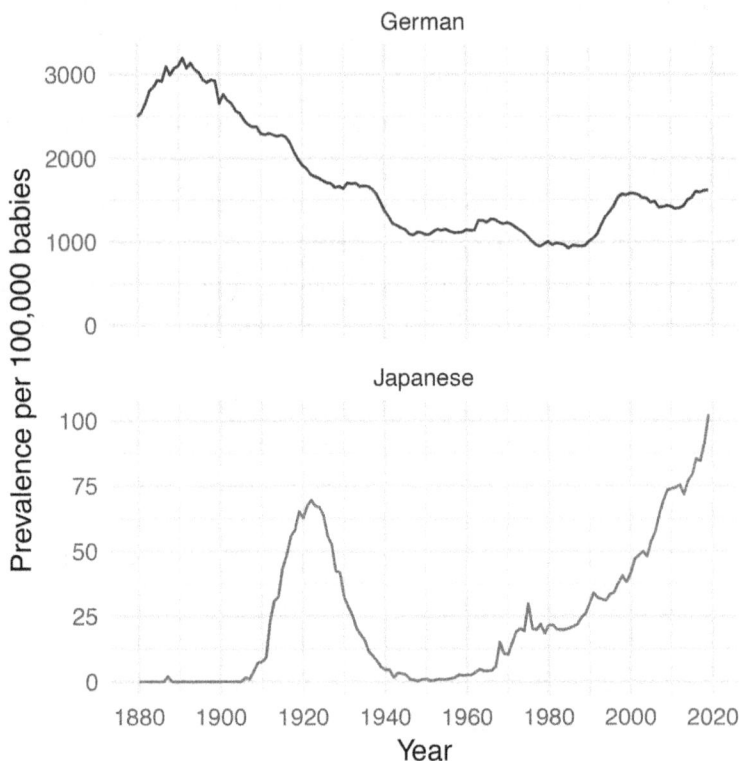

FIGURE 4.9 Frequency of German- and Japanese-origin names, 1880–2019.

1910: The lurch downward might merely have been catch-up for a few years when the taste for German names held up better than might otherwise have been expected.

Still, the reversion to trend occurring just when German–American relations fell apart seems indicative. In the same way that Americans turned more to nationalist names when the country faced international peril, those of German heritage might actually have felt more inclination to express their Germanness through names than they otherwise would during the early years of the war, when Germany and Austria were fighting but the United States was not yet directly involved (see, again, how the name *Wilhelm* surged in the mid-1910s in figure 4.5). Such an impulse would plausibly dissipate for those with joint German and American identities once the war was not simply a question of European hostilities but also involved the new homeland. Even for those who still sympathized with Germany, expressing support for anything German with something as visible as a name would risk a hostile reaction.

That outcome can be compared to what happened with German names in World War II. Then, as in World War I, the rate of German names had previously been holding steady, seeing very little change between the mid-1920s and the mid-1930s even amid the social upheaval of the Great Depression and the rise of the Nazi regime in Germany. Yet that constancy quickly vanished as bilateral relations soured. This decline, however, did not wait until the start of active hostilities. German names began receding in 1937 before Germany's 1939 invasion of Poland kicked off the European theater of the war and several years before the United States entered the conflict. This decline could again be catching up with the previous trend, the previous years of stable use of German names being the real anomaly. It might also be measurement error if people found it relatively easy to rename very young children who had initially been given names that seemed like a good idea at the time but subsequently proved embarrassingly Teutonic. It could also reflect a growing discomfort with publicly expressing German identity as popular sentiment increasingly favored intervening against Germany and as prominent German–American organizations fell into disrepute as they very publicly and stridently embraced National Socialism.[33] By the time Germany declared war on the United States, German names had little further to fall, especially because most of the putatively German names that remained most popular in the early 1940s had plausibly lost their German roots and assimilated into English: names such as *Carl* (especially when spelled with a *C* rather than the traditional German *K*), *Wilma*, *Paula*, and *Leo*. One of the key exceptions of a popular German name, *Marlene*, was strongly associated with the German actress Marlene Dietrich, who famously repudiated the Nazi regime and self-exiled to the United States, and so represented resistance to rather than embrace of the Nazi government. Names that were likelier to read as uncomplicatedly Germanic—*Fritz, Greta, Ludwig, Werner*—became, by contrast, much less popular than they had been just a few years earlier. And, of course, *Adolf* saw a stark fall in popularity.

This can be contrasted with the history of Japanese names (see figure 4.9). Unlike German names, these had at the time rarely broken out from people with Japanese ancestry. As the *Togo* discussion noted, widespread anti-Japanese sentiment typified the United States. Consequently, names such as *Hiroshi, Masao,* or *Yoshiko* almost always went to babies with a typically Japanese family name and, often, with parents listed as Japan-born in census records. As the population of Japanese Americans grew, such names became more common. In the early 1920s, however, the fashion turned starkly against distinctively ethnic first names (though other names were often combined with a middle name that was more traditionally Japanese). By the outbreak of war, then, visibly Japanese names were already relatively rare. Still, their frequency dropped in 1942 to less than half the 1941 level.[34] That year was when popular anti-Japanese hysteria reached its height, encapsulated in the deportation of many Japanese Americans to internment camps. In 1943, though, Japanese names rebounded to only slightly below their 1941 level, and they remained relatively common in 1944 and 1945 before swiftly dropping again thereafter, not reattaining prewar prevalence until the 1960s. This pattern could be because those stuck in the largely monocultural internment camps felt less pressure than they had in 1942 to suppress their Japanese culture. However, the patchy birth records available from Hawaii, where relatively few of the ethnically Japanese population were deported to camps, hint that the decline in Japanese names might have been similarly brief there. Japanese names' slow recovery is not surprising given their rarity before the war and some Americans' lingering animus toward all things Japanese while the Pearl Harbor attack was a recent memory. But Japanese names such as *Akira, Kenji,* and *Kenzo* did eventually rise again, influenced by the increasing reach of Japanese popular culture in North America.[35]

Germany and Japan generally loomed largest as antagonists during World War II: Public-opinion surveys at the time tended to contrast the two as the primary military adversaries.[36] Yet they were not the only countries the United States fought against. One might expect names associated with less-demonized enemies to face fewer headwinds from war. It does in fact turn out that names associated by this measure with Italy, the third member of the Axis Powers, showed a different pattern altogether: They actually became more common as relations between Italy and the United States curdled into warfare. This increase, though, largely reflects the popularity of a single name, *Sandra*, during the war years: It is much the most common Italian-origin name by this measure during the 1930s and 1940s. Although the name does derive from forms such as *Alessandra* that were more specific to families with Italian backgrounds, *Sandra* had spread across ethnic groups in its rise to popularity in the 1930s (take, for example, the future Supreme Court justice Sandra Day O'Connor, born in 1930). Such diffusion suggests that the name may have lost its Italian overtones in the public imagination; figure 4.10 therefore includes a dotted line showing the frequency of Italian names other than *Sandra* as well as the solid-line distribution including the name.

Even without the anomalous *Sandra*, Italian-origin names did not become less common during the war. Although they had become less common through the 1930s, that decline halted around 1940 and soon went into reverse. Italy, that is, did not seem to suffer anything like the hit to its American reputation that, even before the revelation of the worst Nazi atrocities, German culture did. Nor did Italian names seem to suffer any prolonged stigma from their association with a wartime opponent: They continued to prosper in the decades after the war, with or without *Sandra*, and by the 1960s were more common for American babies than ever before. Indeed, the first name *Benito* of the Italian fascist dictator Mussolini had by 1946 already recovered from the mild depression in popularity it endured during the war, and it retained its popularity thereafter—a marked contrast to its German analogue *Adolf* or even World War I's *Wilhelm*.[37]

A yet different sort of pattern might be expected from Russian names. The Soviet Union was an ally in World War II, but one whose communist ideology prompted suspicion among some Americans. After the joint effort to defeat the Nazis, Soviet–American relations rapidly turned into the Cold War, during which relations were generally tense but with an ebbing and

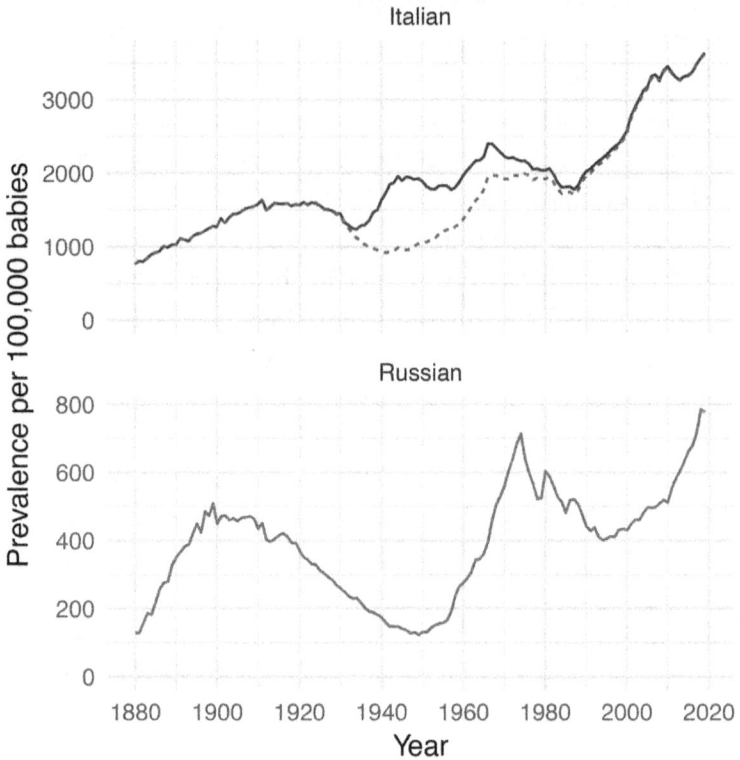

FIGURE 4.10 Frequency of Italian- and Russian-origin names, 1880–2019; dotted line indicates total excluding *Sandra*.

flowing of active antagonism. The standard account has anti-Soviet panic having already set in by the later 1940s, deepening into the McCarthyite mania by 1950. After several years of confrontation culminating in 1962's Cuban Missile Crisis, both sides worked to thaw relations, with the détente policy of the 1970s both causing and resulting from reduced hostility.[38] Thereafter, however, relations deteriorated again with the 1979 Soviet invasion of Afghanistan and the buildup of explicitly anti-Soviet military capacity in the 1980s during Ronald Reagan's presidency. Only toward the end of that decade, as the Gorbachev regime loosened domestic restrictions, did the flare-up of rivalry fade, and the collapse of the Soviet Union soon thereafter reduced the role of Russia as Americans' foreign policy bogeyman.

Do baby names affirm this pattern of relations? Russian names have previously been taken as a way of emphasizing foreignness: One theory holds that Russian Czar Peter the Great is known in English as *Peter* rather than *Pyotr*, whereas his brother is *Ivan* rather than the analogously Anglicized *John*, precisely because *Ivan* reads as foreign whereas *Peter* does not and historians have wanted to emphasize Peter's pro-Western impulses.[39] In the late nineteenth and early twentieth century, the prevalence of Russian names mostly tracks the share of American parents who were Russian born: increasing as migration from Russia increased, then plateauing before an abrupt drop in the early 1910s, and beginning a steady, relentless slide downward from around 1920 (figure 4.11). The alliance years of World War II did see a rough pause of that decline, but after the war Russian names continued to become less popular before bottoming out in the 1947–1951 period. Even as Cold War paranoia remained widespread through the rest of the 1950s, Russian names became more common, slowly at first, but with gathering speed. The abrupt halt of this increasing popularity, too, comes a few years before the standard narratives about the so-called second Cold War, in the early- to mid-1970s. Russian names only resumed their upward trajectory a few years after the Cold War. Notably, these episodes when Russian names became less popular roughly correspond to when public-opinion surveys suggest less positive views of the Soviet Union.[40]

The trajectory of naming may indicate that policymakers tended to trail public opinion in openness to Russia. Russian names, that is, tended to gain popularity somewhat in advance of more cooperative policy toward the Soviet Union, and tended to lose popularity somewhat before policy became more combative. But the trends may once again be distorted by historically Russian names that had shed any ethnic connotations. Several of the most popular Russian names were variant spellings of names common across ethnic backgrounds (e.g., *Tanya* or *Sonya*), or seemed to enter America without specific reference to Russian (e.g., *Tamara*). To focus on names that more clearly read as being from the wrong side of the Cold War tracks, figure 4.11 presents the prevalence of a dozen selected names more likely to evoke the

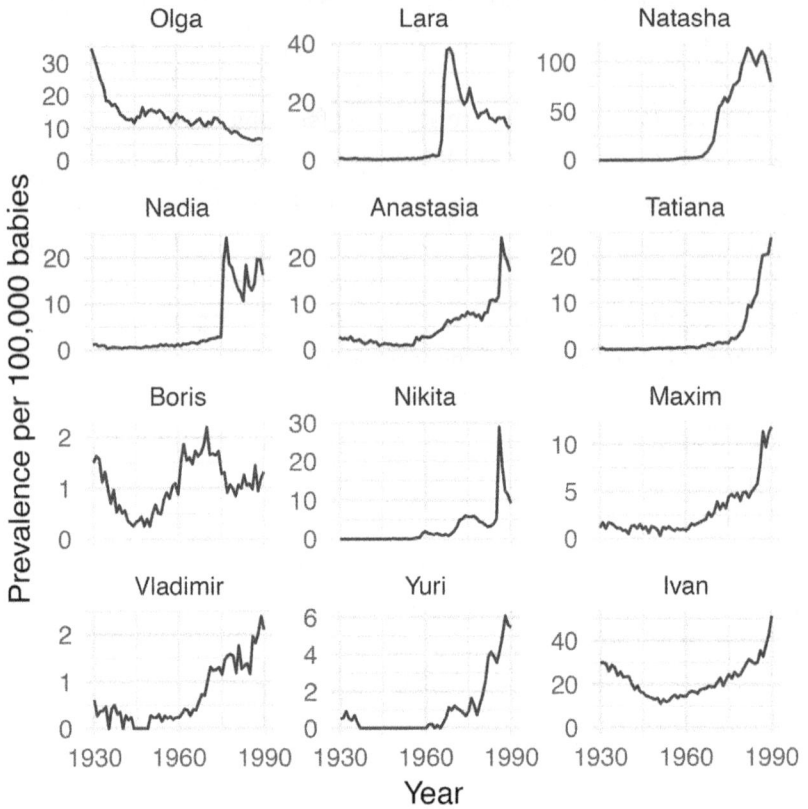

FIGURE 4.11 Frequency of Russian-associated names, 1930–1990.

Eastern Bloc. These are mostly Russian in their entrée into American culture, though the cases of *Nadia* and *Nikita* are instead associated with people from non-Russian Eastern Bloc ethnicities; Americans' sometimes inexact geography may mean that the names felt Russian in any event.

The figure suggests that names from disfavored ethnic associations could break out into mass popularity just like any other if some cultural figure carried the name: for those swooning over Julie Christie as the heroine *Lara* in the 1965 film *Doctor Zhivago*, the story's Russian setting perhaps read more as exotic background color than a political statement (the name barely budged in 1957, when the novel came out). Similarly, Yuri

Gagarin's becoming the first person in space in 1961 (and, even more, his accidental death in 1968), Nadia Comăneci's dominating performance at the 1976 Olympics, or Elton John's 1985 song *Nikita*, impressed Americans enough to show up in children's names. But even without a popular culture hook to propel a sudden rocketing of popularity, many Russian-tinged names—*Ivan, Tatiana, Anastasia, Maxim*—started climbing in popularity after around 1960, if not as markedly as they did after the mid-1980s. It is even possible that the increased acceptance of Eastern Bloc names made it easier for the names that did have more abrupt surges to do so, and indeed for some of the popular culture usages to occur: A song about a *Nikita* might have been a harder sell in 1955 than in 1985.

Many Russian-seeming names then generally did seem to follow predictable patterns, becoming more common as international relations emerged from the iciest depths of the Cold War and tending to come into sudden fashion only in response to specific public figures or fictional characters. Even amid McCarthyism, however, these names did not go away. Some nonconformists actively seemed to embrace the Soviet tenor of certain names. Although *Nikita* might be most notable for its post–Elton John spike, it also subtly tracked the career of Nikita Khrushchev. It was barely in evidence in the United States until Khrushchev succeeded Joseph Stalin as the Soviet Union's leader in 1953. Thereafter, it became more common, and particularly blossomed in 1959 when Khrushchev undertook a much-publicized tour of the United States, with everything from a tour of an Iowa farm to a near-diplomatic incident when Khrushchev raged at being denied admittance to Disneyland.[41] Just as the whistle-stop tours of nineteenth-century royals had often left a trail of namesakes, so did later tours by world leaders, and in *Nikita*'s case the effect was enduring.[42] Even though it was not a particularly popular name during Khrushchev's tenure—its annual appearances were in the scores, not the hundreds—it carved out a niche. That niche may have been subversive, in the manner of naming children *Debs*, rather than just appreciation of the aesthetic qualities of a name in the news: A noticeable number of the mid-century *Nikitas* who are traceable in public records are from Black families active in civil rights movements.

This strand of African American naming presaged (primarily) Black American celebration of other anticolonial figures, such as *Kwame* (following Ghanaian independence leader Kwame Nkrumah) and *Kenyatta* (echoing Kenya's Jomo Kenyatta). These names did start appearing with some regularity when their respective namesakes took power in their home countries, but they did not particularly flower until the social upheavals of the late 1960s relating to civil rights and colonial liberation (see figure 4.12). At that point, a range of radical political leaders saw a surge of namesakes—not just from contemporary Africa, but also from Latin America (as in *Che* Guevara, the Argentine doctor famous for his role in the communist takeover of Cuba) and the more distant past (such as *Toussaint* Louverture, the leader of the Haitian Revolution). Nor were leaders the only source of

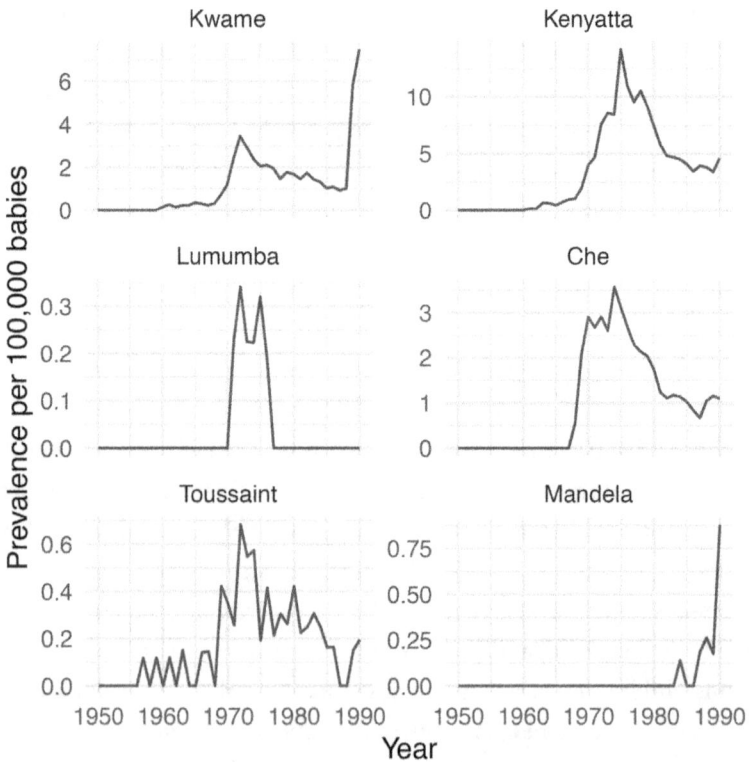

FIGURE 4.12 Frequency of names of anti-imperialist figures, 1930–1990.

anti-imperialist names; parents also chose names such as *Kinshasa*, the newly Africanized name of the capital of the country of Zaire (later the Democratic Republic of the Congo), whose own resonances were boosted by being the site of a famous 1974 heavyweight boxing championship that doubled as a Back-to-Africa cultural celebration.[43] Although the vogue for naming children after the most radical leaders dissipated over the course of the 1970s, other leaders of decolonization, such as Nelson Mandela, could later periodically break through into the American naming scene. Notably, these international figures of Black liberation saw a distinctly earlier, though also smaller, vogue than names from American civil rights leaders such as *Martin* or *Malcolm*, which saw their main burst of popularity in the 1980s and 1990s (likely bolstered by the names' appearances in popular culture, such as Spike Lee's 1992 movie *Malcolm X* or the 1992–1997 television series *Martin*).

Even when foreign policy appears in naming patterns, then, it may sometimes be about domestic politics: The struggles for civil rights and social equality centered less on the unifying, patriotic identities that war and other struggles had previously emphasized. But then, politics was always less likely to stop at the water's edge—as the formulation went about even fierce rivals presenting a shared front in foreign policy—when polarization and partisan identities became permanently inflamed, as happened over the last decades of the twentieth century. These resurgent domestic political conflicts would emerge in names as the Cold War wound down and long after, as the next chapter explores.

5

CULTURE WARS (CA. 1980–2020)

The Meagan *revolution . . . A triumph of individuality . . . Palins . . . Cultural signifiers of right and left . . . Gender ambiguity leans Republican . . . Kennedys and Clintons*

Meg was a common enough name in the nineteenth century—think *Little Women*—and indeed dated back centuries as a nickname for *Margaret*. But the further development of *Meg* into *Megan* was almost unknown in the United States; it had stayed largely in Wales, where -an is a common suffix of endearments and nicknames (turning *Elizabeth* into *Bethan*, for instance). Only around 1960 did *Megan* start gaining traction in the United States. Use of the name did not reflect any specific trigger that launched it to a quick prominence. Instead, it picked up steam at a gathering pace, becoming an ever more common name for girls through the 1970s before rocketing in the 1980s to becoming one of the ten most popular, a position it held intermittently from the middle of that decade to the mid-1990s before gradually cooling off as a naming trend. Figure 5.1's upper panel graphs this prevalence.

With swift growth as it rose and a relatively short time at the top of the naming charts, *Megan* typifies a common pattern of girls' and women's names that become widespread, how they—notwithstanding the long dominance of *Mary*—often flourish only briefly before slipping back into relative rarity. *Megan* also exemplified the related pattern of experimentation when girls' names tend to spawn especially riotous profusions of variants upon becoming popular. The most common alternative spelling was *Meghan*, but more than fifty other renditions reached the five occurrences per year threshold to qualify for reporting by the Social Security Administration.[1] Even once name-givers decided that something sounding like *Megan* was the right choice for their child, then, they had many options as to how to spell the name. Several possible considerations could shape the choice, consciously or otherwise. Parents could strive for uniqueness, or conversely try to fit in with the crowd. Or they might want to formulate some name that would simultaneously honor the child's great-aunts *Mae* and *Ann* (or Mae West and Ann-Margret, for that matter) by including those three-letter groups in the name, or aim for what they assumed was a more Irish or authentic form by incorporating the letters *gh*.

Or, of course, they could be influenced by politics. During the 1980s heyday of *Megan*, the U.S. president was Ronald Reagan. *Megan* literally echoed *Reagan* with their usually rhyming pronunciations (though variant ways of saying each name, such as with an *ee* sound in either name's first syllable, exist). The similarity was even stronger with the commonest spelling variant other than *Megan* and *Meghan*: *Meagan*, the president's surname with just one letter changed. Because the explicit homage of *Reagan* had as of the 1980s barely emerged as a common girl's name—and because, as chapter 3 suggests, mainstream social norms had by the later twentieth century come to see the incumbent president's surname as a name as somewhat cringeworthy choice—*Meagan* offered a somewhat subtler way to pay tribute to an admired politician. Indeed, it may not be a coincidence that the *Meagan* spelling started to appear disproportionately in California in the late 1960s when Reagan was governor there, though admittedly California in the 1960s blazed many cultural trails.

If *Meagan* really did draw on support for Reagan, one might expect it to be more common in places dominated by conservative Republicans, given that the name-givers giving the name in such places were likely to welcome the Reaganite association themselves and to think their neighbors would also do so. One might additionally expect the same outcome as a result of negative partisanship. In that case, it was not that Reagan supporters sought out the echo of *Reagan* in *Meagan*, but that Reagan opponents recoiled from something that reminded them of the president or that they thought risked offending their neighbors by doing so, so that relatively Reagan-hostile regions would avoid the *Meagan* spelling relative to people in more Reagan-curious places.

To look for this pattern, we might compare the local percentage of babies given the *Meagan* spelling, out of those named any of the variants of *Megan*, to a measure of how congenial the local politics were to Reaganism. For the latter, I use a commonly used index of state-years' conservatism, one that estimates the percentage of the local population who would have thought of themselves as politically conservative.[2] The bottom panel of figure 5.1 shows the result of such of a comparison for the 1980s—the year of Reagan's initial election and his tenure in the presidency, and hence the presumed period of his greatest prominence. Each point represents one state-year (such as "New York in 1983" or "South Carolina in 1988"), darker shading indicating places with relatively more babies with *Megan*-sounding names. The solid line indicates the linear trend suggested by the data, weighting places more heavily if they had more *Megan*-like names.[3]

Places likely to support Reagan more were indeed more likely to use the *Meagan* spelling. Substantially so—in relatively conservative state-years, the share of parents who spelled the name *Meagan* approached 12 percent on average, more than twice the share in the most liberal state-years. The local-partisanship gap in prevalence of the name *Meagan* was even starker than this, however, because the fraction of *Megan*-like names spelled *Meagan* is a measure that depends not only on the use of the specific *Meagan* spelling but also on willingness to use the *Megan* name in any form. One could also compare conservatism with prevalence of any *Megan*-sounding

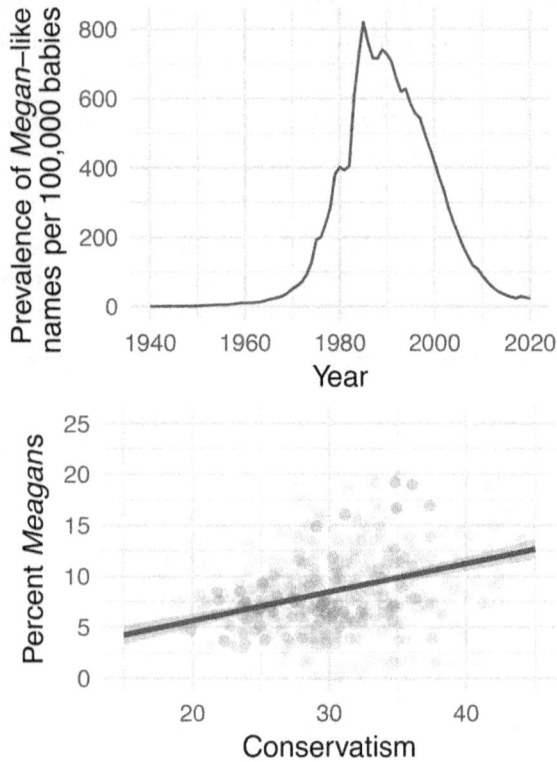

FIGURE 5.1 Prevalence of names sounding like *Megan* (top panel), and share of those names that were spelled *Meagan* for 1980s state-years along with trend line and 95 percent confidence interval (bottom panel).

name, given that the potential rhyme with *Reagan* would be present regardless of the spelling. In that regard, too, residents of Republican-leaning states turn out to be more willing to use names that might carry a whiff of Reaganism.

In this partisan profile, *Meagan* and its homonyms showed an emerging spirit of the age. Partisan attachments grew inexorably stronger for many Americans through the late twentieth and early twenty-first centuries.

People increasingly identified as belonging to one political party and in opposition to the other. Where identities lead, names often follow.

The cultural fragmentation seen in names such as *Megan* having use as Republican, or perhaps pointedly anti-Democratic, symbols also indicated a broader trend of the shared national culture of the post–World War II era fracturing into more independent subcultures. The tendency for people to have fewer social connections in their community, the splintering of major news media sources from a few staid broadcast networks and local newspaper monopolies to the raucous variety of cable news and internet sources, the increased diversity of the United States in ethnicity and other dimensions all mean that the country's people have lived in increasingly separate worlds, with different cultural references and perspectives. Even though America has like any country always had its tensions between a single coherent nationwide society and distinctive political subgroups (the point of chapter 2's discussion of North versus South sectionalism, for example), the balance of forces has by most accounts pulled toward more, and more atomized, division in recent decades, at least relative to the norms of the mid-twentieth century.

Meagan's becoming prevalent in some communities and not others suggests that as communities become more culturally varied, we would expect names to follow suit. Rather than a world in which most of the girls are named *Mary* and *Martha* and most of the boys are named *John* and *James*, names would be more diverse, and less consistent across regions. Many concentration indices measure how varied or unvaried a set of observations distributed across categories is. One common measure squares the proportion of observations in each category then adds the sums, a value that can range from (nearly) 0 for something with many categories all with small proportions of observations, to 1 for something for which all the observations are in a single category. Here, this means looking at what fraction of all of a year's babies had each name, and summing the squares of those fractions.[4] For instance, if half of a population were named *Athos*, one quarter named *Porthos*, and one quarter named *Aramis*, the population's concentration of names would be $(\frac{1}{2})^2 + (\frac{1}{4})^2 + (\frac{1}{4})^2$,

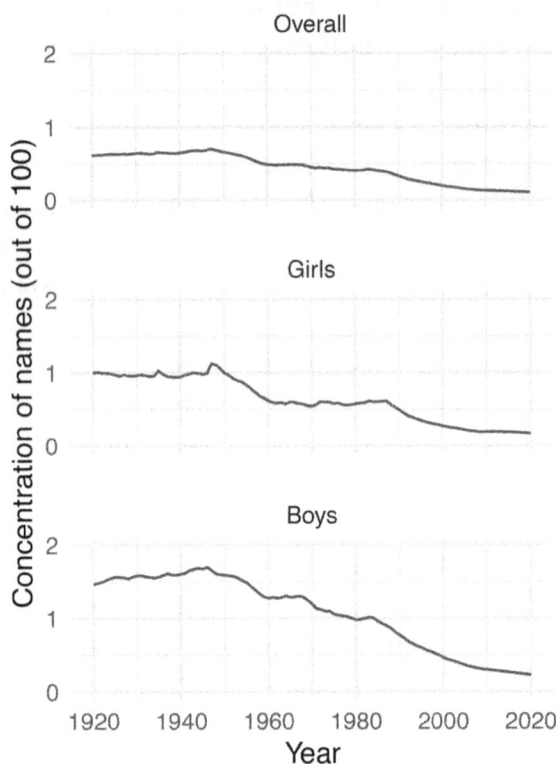

FIGURE 5.2 Concentration of American names in Social Security Administration data, 1920–2020.

which equals ⅜. Higher values of this sum imply greater concentration, or less diversity, of names. I multiply the sum by one hundred to make the scale roughly interpretable as the percentage of the possible concentration observed in each year.

Figure 5.2 presents the index for babies overall, then separately for the year's girls and its boys, for the years from 1920 to 2020. The diversity in babies' names was roughly constant in the years before World War II or perhaps even slightly decreasing as ethnically distinctive names became less common as immigrant populations shrank and assimilated, but thereafter it increased considerably—an increase that further accelerated in the 1980s.

This tendency toward the crumbling of common unified choices in favor of an expanding range of possibilities occurred both among girls' and boys' names, which is especially notable because through the twentieth century the two sexes differed substantially in how diverse their names were. Girls' names often saw more experimentation and originality—take the *Megan* example—but boys' names were more conservative and restrictive: Boys were expected to carry forward the family name, and so most pointedly were much more likely to be given their fathers' names than girls' were to be given their mothers'.[5] Despite the differing processes that produce the levels of variety among girls' and boys' names, though, both broadly followed the same diversifying trend, especially from the 1980s on, and by 2020 the gender gap in name concentration had narrowed to almost nothing.

This society-wide push toward less common names not only reflected a move away from social cohesion into sometimes contending subcultures. It also opened up additional space for name-givers to make choices expressing their political leanings. More choice naturally also made it easier to avoid politically charged names, for those so inclined. As partisan identities devoured ever more social debates, however, the way was clear for politics to show up in names in ever more ways.

NAMES IN THE NEWS

As chapter 3 notes, naming children directly after politicians had fallen out of fashion by the late twentieth century. This was not just a matter of presidential surnames, which were often so distinctive that they klaxoned their political origins. Even more ambiguous or obscure associations with politics could wither enthusiasm for a name. *Donald* had been declining only slightly in popularity in the first half of the 2010s, but once Donald Trump announced his candidacy for the presidency, the falloff accelerated considerably even though the name had many other associations that people might have drawn on other than him. Similarly, *Cruz* had been on an upswing in the early twenty-first century, its popularity having more than tripled in the decade before Ted Cruz was elected to the Senate in 2012. That incipient takeoff immediately halted, the name stalling for two years before retreating somewhat from its previous prevalence.

Nevertheless, although elected politicians had mostly lost their potency as sources of names, name-givers were still willing to call their children after partisan or political figures, and not just through possible transfiguration such as *Meagan*. They simply changed to political figures other than elected officials (see figure 5.3). As a baseline for comparison, consider *Barack*: President Obama swept into office on a wave of euphoria on the election of the country's first African American president, with a coalition of supporters drawing heavily on younger adults who were more likely to be parents. *Barack* might then be expected to show the high-water mark of recent politician names. Indeed, it did experience a sudden if short-lived burst of popularity around the time of Obama's election and inauguration, one that shows up particularly vividly because the name had not previously been at all common in the United States.

Yet at the same time use surged almost ten times as much for another name tied to the 2008 presidential election, *Bristol*.[6] This was the name of a daughter of Sarah Palin, the vice presidential nominee of the losing Republican ticket, a remote enough connection to the election to not historically seem like a propitious launching pad for a name. But Bristol Palin found herself in the news more than the typical family member of a political aspirant when her pregnancy during the campaign—as an unmarried teenager—embroiled her in national conversations about family and morality. What is more, once Bristol Palin brought her name into broad use, it remained there in a far more sustained way than *Barack* did. The seemingly ephemeral political figure proved in the medium term to have much greater staying power as an influence on names than the elected president did, though the recent slow-burn trajectory of presidential names such as *Reagan* and *Kennedy*, and of civil rights figures discussed in chapter 4, suggests that *Barack* may in a few decades become more common.

Names of some other Palin family members also suddenly became more popular, though not to the same degree that *Bristol* did. This was most

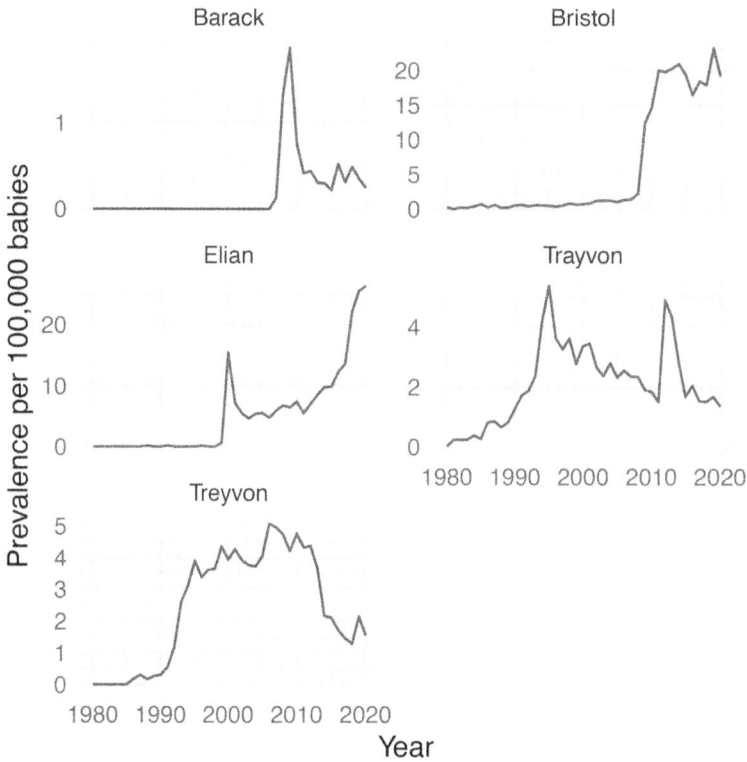

FIGURE 5.3 Prevalence of names related to selected newsmakers, 1980–2020.

visible for Bristol's older brother *Track* (despite Track Palin's being less in evidence during the campaign because he as an Army enlistee was deployed to Iraq months before the election) and especially her younger brother *Trig*, in part because their names had previously been unusual. The names of Bristol's two sisters, *Willow* and *Piper*, were rapidly becoming more common during the years around the election, so it is harder to be sure whether the Palin association in particular encouraged their popularity, though it did not seem to slow their rise any in the way that chapter 3 suggests prominence did for actual politicians' names such as *Carter* or *Clinton*. All the Palin siblings, in short, seemed to attract at least as many namesakes as *Barack* did.

Politics is not just about elections or politicians' families, either. People and ideas that erupted into political news completely outside of campaigns also can shape the American namescape. Take *Elian*. The name has a long and august history, having been the name of multiple ancient saints, and existed as a standard name in Spanish, French, and Dutch. In the United States, though, it was mostly obscure, even though its feminine analogue *Eliana* occasionally gained a bit of popularity.

Then, suddenly, it burst out of obscurity. In late 1999, six-year-old Elián González (whose own name was a fusion of his mother's *Elisabeth* and his father's *Juan*) was found off the Florida coast as one of the few survivors of an attempt to flee from Cuba to the United States; his mother was among those who had perished in the journey. Although a great-uncle who lived in Miami took González in, the boy's father, still in Cuba, demanded custody—backed by Cuba's communist government, and much to the dismay of the mostly anticommunist Cuban American community. An acrimonious controversy climaxed when the federal government sent in heavily armed agents to retrieve González and return him to Cuba, a confrontation captured in dramatic, emotionally charged news photographs. Debate about the government's choices was front-page news for weeks, feeding into Republican suspicions that the incumbent Democratic administration of Bill Clinton was soft on communism. The publicity thrust the name *Elian* into use in 2000 almost as frequent as *Bristol* during Bristol Palin's heyday (see figure 5.3). Although that first surge of *Elian*s was a temporary blip, *Elian* remained far more common after the incident than it had been, and in later years its popularity surpassed even its 2000 figures.

As the examples of *Donald* and *Cruz* make clear, however, a name's appearance in a politically freighted story does not always augur increased use. Such potential for decline extends beyond the narrow set of candidate or officeholder names. This can be seen with the example of *Trayvon*, a widely used name in African American communities starting in the 1990s.

In 2012, however, Trayvon Martin was, while coming back unarmed from an innocent trip to a convenience store, shot and killed by a member of a neighborhood watch. Like *Barack* or *Elian*, the name had a flash of increased use in response to this newsiness. The case of *Trayvon* is complicated, though, because for most of the previous decade it had been losing popularity to the more widespread homonym *Treyvon*—the popularity of which receded sharply on Trayvon Martin's death. Overall, then, names pronounced like *Trayvon* were less popular after the shooting than they had been before, concededly in the context of already fading popularity, though a larger proportion of names with that pronunciation used the *Trayvon* spelling after Trayvon Martin's killing.[7] Although exposure to a name may significantly increase its chance of use, if the associations with a name are negative or painful, its newfound familiarity may not result in popularity.[8] In the case of *Trayvon*, the shooting became entangled with a long history of unarmed Black people suffering violent deaths, as well as with political arguments over the self-defense laws that shielded the shooter from any criminal convictions over the incident. Although this led to *Trayvon* becoming more familiar to many more people, name-givers swiftly began to steer away from it more than they previously had. Even so, the specific spelling *Trayvon* saw a bigger spike in usage than *Barack* had had during President Obama's emergence as a national figure, in another sign of names moving away from electoral politics.

PARTY IS THE MADNESS OF MANY

One might suspect that the political overtones of these news-related names might, like *Meagan* before them, attract some but repel others. For any given name-giver, circumstances could change the appeal of sending political messages. Barack Obama was particularly an icon in Democratic and ethnic minority communities; Bristol Palin was not only the daughter of a star of the conservative Tea Party movement, but also especially lauded among abortion opponents for her choice to give birth rather than terminate her

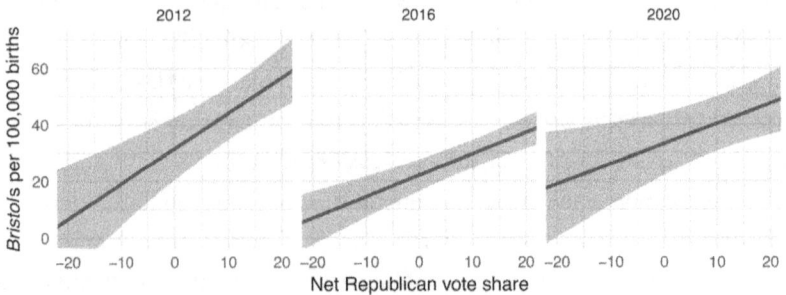

FIGURE 5.4 State-level prevalence of *Bristol*, by state Republican presidential vote compared to the national average. Shaded areas indicate 95 percent confidence intervals.

pregnancy. One might therefore expect people to be more willing to name their children *Barack* in Democratic-leaning areas and *Bristol* in Republican-leaning areas, especially as partisan polarization sharpened. Indeed, the names did not appear equally often in Democratic and Republican parts of the country.

Bristol, for example, has consistently appeared more frequently in states that vote more Republican than in those that vote Democratic. Figure 5.4 shows this, graphing the relationship between the prevalence of the name as a function of how Republican the state-year was, measured by how many percentage points more of the two-party vote the year's Republican presidential candidate got in the state than in the country as a whole. If a state gave the Republican 60 percent of the major-party presidential vote in a year when that candidate got 54 percent of the major-party popular vote, then the state would have a net Republican vote share of 6 percent (60 minus 54). The graph only includes cases where the *Bristol* count is provided by the Social Security Administration and hence where there were at least five examples of a name in a given state-year among girls (or among boys). Several states, such as Hawaii, New Jersey, New Mexico, and all of the states of New England, never have as many as five *Bristols* in a year. (Also, because Bristol Palin rose to fame only relatively late in 2008, few states crossed the five-*Bristol* threshold that year, so too little information is available to clearly see any partisan valence of the name at that point.) With that caveat, though, the name has disproportionately appeared in more Republican parts of the country. It is telling, too, that the states excluded for lack of data are disproportionately from Democratic-friendly parts of the country, and that even in 2008 *Bristol* showed up more often in Republican-skewing Texas than in Democratic-heavy California, despite California's having had considerably more babies born. The figure may perhaps suggest that the intensity of the partisan link is moderating somewhat as Bristol Palin's initial moment of prominence fades from memory and the name's direct associations with a Republican figure become less relevant. Still, even a decade after her emergence, Republican states see higher proportions of *Bristol*s than Democratic states do.

Any tendency for *Bristol* to have become less intensely Republican might be thought to be swimming against the cultural tide. By most accounts, the country's political polarization is only increasing, with ever more cultural and political difference between Democratic and Republican communities.[9] Indeed, evidence of growing differences between states based on their partisan affiliations can be seen in other names, often in ways aligning with cultural fault lines.

Politicians in Republican areas, for instance, often ostentatiously express love of firearms and gun culture, whereas in Democratic areas advocacy for restrictive gun laws is more common. Some reasonably widespread names, especially for boys, invoke firearms: *Gunner* does so perhaps most baldly, but *Beretta*, *Colt*, and *Remington* are prominent gun manufacturers.[10] As usual, the names could have been chosen for names entirely unrelated to those emphasized here; *Gunner*, for example, is a classic Scandinavian name—a variant spelling of *Gunnar* or *Gunder*, the root of the surname of Marge Gunderson of *Fargo* fame.[11] But even many people who simply chose a name because they think their newborn seems coltish, or appreciate *Remington* because of their irrepressible love of 1980s detective comedies, are likely aware of the gun-related resonances, which are widely noted in baby-name books. One might then expect these

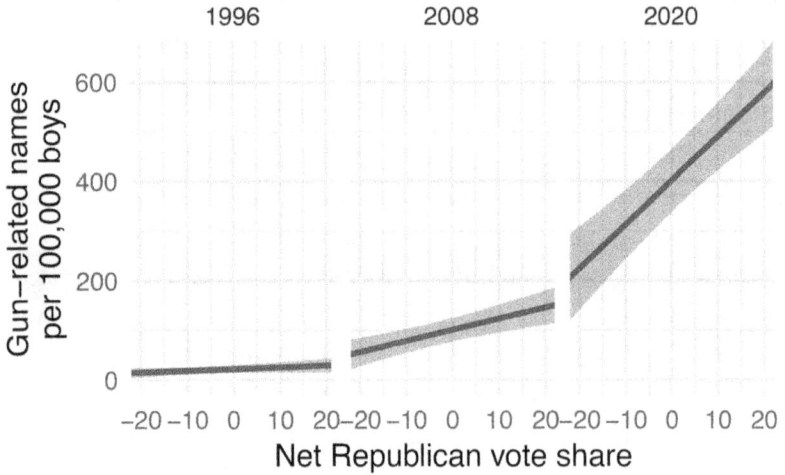

FIGURE 5.5 State-level prevalence of gun-invoking names, by state's Republican presidential vote compared to the national average.

gun-adjacent names to be more popular in Republican areas, given the partisan hue of firearms.

And so they are. These gun-related names have been steadily growing in popularity in recent decades other than a pause in the very last years of the twentieth century, and especially accelerating in the middle of the 2010s. But figure 5.5 shows that throughout this growth they have consistently been more popular in Republican-leaning states, measuring states' Republican leanings, as in figure 5.4.[12] The trend of names' cultural cast increasingly mirroring partisan divides extends beyond gun politics. Another common political-cultural axis of recent decades pits cosmopolitan worldliness against a more national identity rooted in patriotism and Americana: Democrats' rhetoric and culture often emphasize an openness to foreign influences where Republicans prefer to focus on American exceptionalism.[13] One way that names can feed into this spectrum of globalism or nationalism is by invoking cities. Many popular children's names are shared with cities, some of which are in the United States (*Austin, Denver*) and some not (*Paris, Sydney*). The greater sense in Democratic cultures that international associations have a sophisticated prestige presumably increases their likelihood of drawing on foreign rather than domestic names. As cultural polarization has risen, then, one might expect parents who name their children after a city to gravitate more to domestic cities if they live in more Republican-leaning areas and to foreign locales if in more Democratic-leaning areas.

Given the number of named cities in the world, some rule is needed for choosing names that likely link to cities rather than being chosen obliviously to any place name. *Douglas*, after all, is the name of a town in Nebraska as well as the capital of the Isle of Man, but both locations are somewhat obscure—apologies, Douglasites—and unlikely sources for most uses of the name. Any way of defining the set of relevant cities absent unavailable detail about what name-givers were thinking is somewhat arbitrary, though, and potentially prey to ad hocism. To be consistent, the analysis here defines names based on U.S. cities to be those matching the principal cities of metropolitan areas with at least one million people per 2020 Census estimates. For international cities, the analysis uses English-language versions of the names of urban agglomerations estimated in the UN's 2018 World Urbanization Prospects to have at least one million people in 2020.

This set of city namesakes can be criticized both for being under- and overinclusive. Population-based rules for including cities do leave out some reasonably common names that plausibly associate with smaller cities, such as *Stockton* or *Florence* (Florence Nightingale, for one, was explicitly named after the latter city). The rule also excludes secondary cities from metropolitan areas, such as *Camden* or *Oakland*—let alone parts of cities, such as *Brooklyn* and *Chelsea*—though these have all seen use as names. Alongside the omission of potentially important city namesakes is the reverse problem that parents could have hit on these city-matching name choices without ever thinking about this particular association. It seems particularly optimistic to imagine that most Americans are aware of the southern Indian city of *Salem*; similarly, *Alexandria* comes up by this coding rule as an Egyptian city even though many Americans may be just as familiar with its Virginian (or Louisianan or Minnesotan) namesake if they associate it with any place at all. In addition, several major city names, such as

Salvador or *Charlotte*, are themselves named for people or things that are independent sources of names. The idea is, though, that the domestic or international associations would be one of the multiple factors shaping the name choices of parents with particular political viewpoints. By that logic, overseas city names would on average be relatively less likely than domestic ones to attract parents in Republican-leaning cultures even as those parents also weighed other considerations in their name choice—and this difference would be expected to have increased in recent decades as cultural attitudes became more partisan and polarized.

Figure 5.6's top panel shows the distribution of U.S. and non-U.S. city names as of 1980, the circle sizes proportional to how many babies in the data were given the name that year. The vertical line gives the average value of the names, the shaded area indicating the 95 percent confidence interval of that average. At that point, foreign cities were actually somewhat more common in Republican-leaning states than in Democratic-leaning ones, though the difference was not large enough to provide statistical confidence.

The situation evolved over the following decades, however. Figure 5.6's bottom panel shows the analogous results from 2020. The set of cities popular as namesakes changed somewhat in the interim. For example, *Cleveland* largely disappeared after having been relatively popular, especially in African American communities, and *Boston* latterly appears as a child's name though it had been absent from the 1980 numbers.[14] Although the city names in general became more common in Democratic-leaning areas over time, perhaps a consequence of the increasing urban-rural partisan split, that Democratic lurch was especially large for names invoking cities outside the United States. This is, to be sure, partly a reflection of states with large Latin American immigrant communities having become more Democratic, the states having most of the children named *Rosario, Salvador,* and *Santiago* having shifted drastically. Because these names are plausibly among the likeliest of this set to have been given without any thought of the associated city, that perhaps biases the results toward overseas cities showing up as Democratic. On the other hand, many of the other less squarely city-oriented names (*Alexandria, Austin, Charlotte, Orlando, Paris, Salem*) work

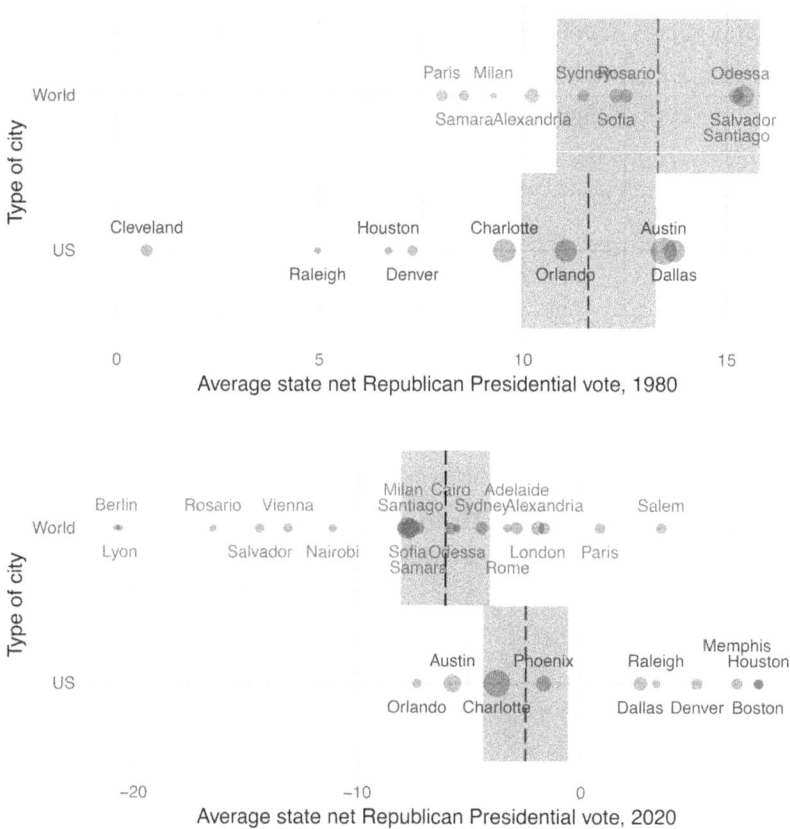

FIGURE 5.6 Average state Republican margin of victory in presidential vote for city-based names, in 1980 (top panel) and 2020 (bottom panel). Dashed vertical line indicates year's group average, with 95 percent confidence interval shaded; circle size indicates frequency of names across reported states in the given year.

against the hypothesis here, having a partisan distribution less in line with the hypothesis than most more straightforward city names. Although these complications advise caution about estimating the precise size of the effect, the results still suggest that as party affiliations have become more tied up with cultural signifiers and international orientation became a Democratic signifier, the geography of names has shifted as well.

These tendencies for names suggestive of particular sides in the culture war—guns are now for Republicans, internationalism for Democrats—to blossom in places with a particular partisan leaning are notable. Still, issues and icons can change in their perceived political hue over time. Allusions that were at one point politically neutral can, in response to events, suddenly strike a chord with one political party or another. Or, the gradual rearrangement of political coalitions or the fading of historical memories (as perhaps seen with *Bristol* in its tendency to move beyond Republican areas over time) might pull a reference that previously trumpeted support for one party to lose or even reverse its previous partisan polarity.

Alexander Hamilton, for example, was traditionally seen as a right-leaning figure, the secretary of the treasury who advocated for big-city banking and financial interests in opposition to Jeffersonian backing of the little guy. When Lin-Manuel Miranda adapted Hamilton's story as the basis of his 2015 multicultural musical blockbuster *Hamilton*, though, its protagonist gained cultural and historical standing with relatively left-leaning groups. One might expect tributes to Hamilton to accordingly become more popular in Democratic-leaning areas, either because parents with Democratic inclinations would take a new fancy to the name, because Republicans were put off by the politics of the musical's protagonist, or because people of whatever political persuasion newly think the name would be palatable to their neighbors. Other historical figures have moved in the opposite direction. Winston Churchill as a foreign leader (albeit one with an American-born mother) might traditionally, like the international cities, be thought to have particular attraction for those with more cosmopolitan leanings. He has, though, increasingly been adopted as a hero figure by pundits on the political right and drafted into partisan culture wars, as with a bust of Churchill that recent presidents have removed from the Oval Office if Democratic and restored if Republican. This suggests that *Winston* might be relatively more common in Republican areas than it used to be.

Figure 5.7 shows trends in these names from 2010 to 2020, using the net Republican score as calculated for the 2020 election and with the size of the point indicating the prevalence of the name. *Hamilton* has indeed been

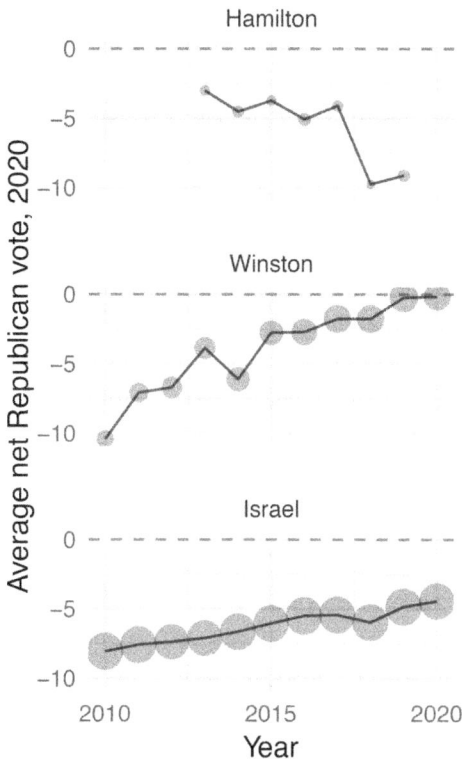

FIGURE 5.7 Average state Republican presidential margin of victory in 2020 for selected names. Circle size indicates number of state-identified observations of the name in the given year.

drifting toward being more common in more Democratic states. *Winston* is more widely used and has gone from being primarily seen in Democratic states at the start of the 2010s to being nearly as common in Republican-supporting states as in Democratic ones by the end of the decade.

Winston and especially *Hamilton* were relatively unusual names during this era, which makes it easier for their partisan complexions to change quickly. But even more widely used names can see changes in the partisan geography of their incidence. Take *Israel*, a name that was long most common among Jewish populations, who tended to concentrate in

Democratic-leaning states. However, support for the country of Israel, long a shared foreign-policy position of both parties, became more partisan as the Israeli government under Benjamin Netanyahu actively engaged in pro-Republican activism in the United States. *Israel* has slowly been seeing more use among social groups beyond its traditional Jewish communities, notably including some conservative Christian groups who see the Zionist project of Israel in line with millenarian goals (or perhaps increasingly find the *God fights* etymology of the name meaningful). As a result, the name grew in prevalence in most of the Deep South over the 2010s even as it became less popular in more left-leaning places such as New York and California. Although *Israel* is still more common in Democratic than in Republican states, its prevalence has become less and less clear of a signal of locally Democratic politics.

Notably, this effect is specific to *Israel*. Other historically Jewish names have mostly not diffused in the same way. Even *Yisrael*, an alternative spelling of the same root name, has not been inching into Republican areas in the same way. Although not conclusive, this suggests that the explicit tie to the country of Israel has been a particular source of *Israel*'s shifting appeal. Nor does the rightward drift of *Israel* seen in figure 5.7 simply derive from a rightward shift among country names in general; a name such as *India* has over the same period had a roughly similar-sized shift in its partisan geography but in the opposite direction, toward more Democratic states.

Names have come to encapsulate a whole range of policy issues and partisan worldviews, as these examples attest: They can conjure culture war issues from guns and religion to cosmopolitanism and partisan heroes.

GENDERED NAMES

Few would be surprised that Republicans might be more attracted than Democrats to names involving guns, or that they have been increasingly the partisan faction expressively identifying with Israel. Such results comport with conventional wisdom about partisan positions. Although it is reassuring that many patterns in names accord with straightforward expectations—if they were constantly bafflingly counterintuitive, it would raise doubts about whether names actually meaningfully reflected political views, and hence about whether writing a book about politics in child names simply wastes everyone's time—they may be able to answer more open questions rather than just confirm existing beliefs.

For example, one perennial topic of interest about baby names concerns unisex names, those widely assigned to girls and boys alike.[15] When discussions on the matter turn to how androgynous names interact with name-givers' political preferences, they often quickly home in on whether the choice of unisex names concentrates among leftist cultures and communities. Some forces do push in that direction, but expectations perhaps should not be so clear-cut: Some processes push in the opposite direction as well, associating androgynous names with more conservative views.

As sociologists have explored extensively, gender has traditionally been one of the clearest associations with names, in the United States as in many other societies.[16] People's names sometimes hint at their race, age, or childhood social class, but for most of American history the relationship between most names and their holder's sex was much more than a hint: If you were to hear about someone named *Eve*, you could confidently expect the holder of the name would be female, whereas an *Adam* was extremely likely to be male. Names would only occasionally provide as much certainty about other demographic categories: You might have relatively confident guesses about the ethnic background of a *Lakisha* or a *Xiuhua* (or a *Yisrael*), but a *Christopher* or a *Lori* or most other names appear widely in children of many ethnicities. Exceptions always existed to the rule that names revealed sex—some people had names that defied common gender roles, and a minority of names that would circulate for babies of any sex—but most names were overwhelmingly identified with and given near exclusively either to girls or to boys.

One of the more reliable laws of American naming, though, is that when widely used names change sex through gradual evolution (rather than reaction to a famous person or fictional character appearing with the name), it is mostly names that were originally given predominantly to boys that first become gender ambiguous and then eventually shift to their non-traditional gender. Names for girls, that is, relatively rarely shift to becoming names for boys. *Aubrey* or *Avery* or *Kendall* or *Morgan* or *Scottie* were in the 1970s almost entirely names for boys; in the 2020s they are predominantly given to girls. Far fewer examples moved in the other direction.[17] This greater propensity for male-to-female evolutions reflects the generally greater social acceptability in the United States for girls to have typically male names than for boys to have typically female; boys with what are perceived to be girls' names violate norms and expectations more than do girls with what are perceived to be boys' names.[18] Thus more pioneers tend to be willing to give their daughters what had historically been boys' names than to give sons what had been thought of as girls' names. Once enough other people follow those early adopters and give the traditionally male name to their daughters, the name becomes ambiguously gendered, people increasingly hesitate to give it to sons, and it is likely to become a female-typed name.

Dissertations can be written about what this says about perceptions of masculinity. What matters most here is that political positions also have long had gender associations in American culture: Conservative culture, with its rough-and-tumble individualism, is traditionally seen as more masculine than liberal culture. Even if contemporary Republican culture celebrates traditional gender roles, it also celebrates women who can take on historically masculine characters.[19] Sarah Palin's initial prominence often positioned her as an aggressive pit bull, for example.[20] Likewise, Republican Senator Joni Ernst rose to fame through advertisements highlighting her love of riding motorcycles and castrating pigs, speaking not just to her rural Iowa bona fides but also to her toughness.

The asymmetry that lets girls have masculine-typed names but tries to keep boys from anything smacking of femininity then leaves room for multiple possible relationships between partisanship and name gender. Parents in areas with more Democratic-dominated cultures may not go out of their way to choose hypermasculine names for their children—names like *Rowdy* or *Tuff* are more common in Republican-dominated areas—but because it requires some cultural daring to give boys androgynous names, most of their sons' names will probably tend to clearly read as masculine. At the same time, although those parents may have little cultural objection to giving their daughters masculine-typed names, they may or may not have the active cultural impetus to do so that more Republican areas' cultures, with their celebration of traditionally masculine values, provide. In this case, the greatest concentration of ambiguously gendered names will arise in girls in Republican areas, so that it might be Republican and not Democratic cultures that end up pushing the trend toward unisex naming.

So much for the theory. What does the evidence say? To measure how gender ambiguous a name is in a year, I calculate what percentage of babies given each name are female as reported by the Social Security Administration. The level of gender ambiguity reflects how close this percentage is to 50: If the name has exactly as many female recipients as male, it gets the maximum score of 100, but if everyone recorded as getting the name in the year is female or is male, the score is zero.[21] Figure 5.8 then plots the average value of this gender-ambiguity scale for all names given in each state for presidential election years since 1976 against the state's two-party Republican vote share in the respective year, so that downward-sloping lines indicate that Democratic states tended to have more gender-ambiguous names, and upward-sloping lines indicate that Republican states did.

Through the 1980s, the line was relatively flat; gender-ambiguous names had no particular association with a state's partisanship. Thereafter, however, partisan leanings began to associate with gender ambiguity, just as they did with names evoking guns or cities from different parts of the world. In particular, more Republican states began to consistently have more gender-ambiguous names, although the relationship tempered somewhat in the 2010s as gender-ambiguity scores rose everywhere. By 2020, the highest gender-ambiguity scores tended to be in Southern states, followed by the rural states of the upper Midwest and Plains, and then New England, the Middle Atlantic states, and California.

If this result stemmed from the logic that masculine names for girls are especially common in Republican-leaning cultures, one would expect that

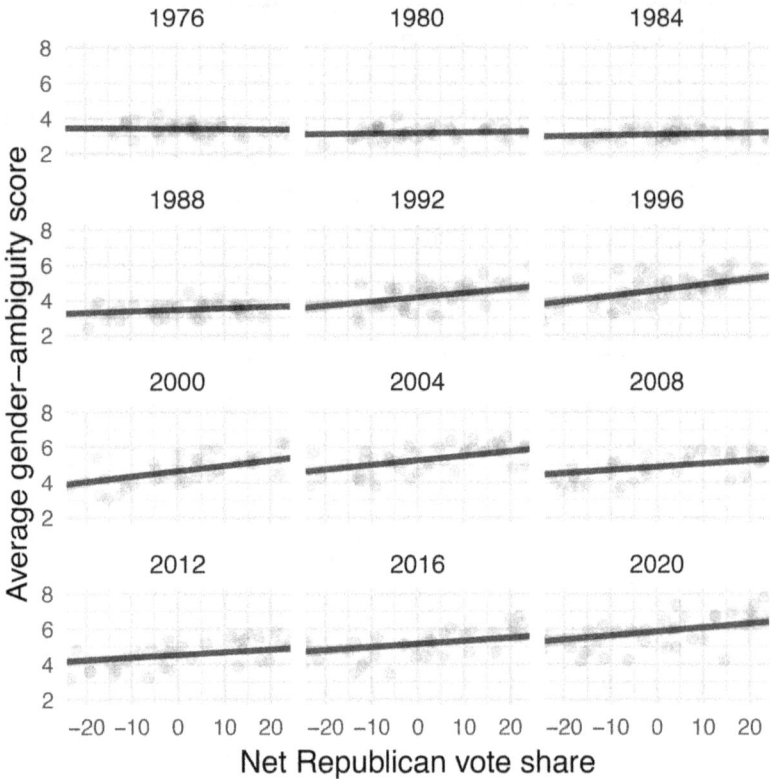

FIGURE 5.8 Average state gender-ambiguity index (0 = name given entirely to babies of one sex in the given year, 100 = name given to equal numbers of babies of each sex in the given year), by relative Republican presidential vote relative to the national trend. Darker points indicate state-years with more births.

mostly girls were receiving the gender-ambiguous names in Republican states, and that boys with gender-ambiguous names would mostly be from Democratic states. Figure 5.9 checks for this pattern, plotting the Republican presidential candidate's share of the two-party vote against the difference between the average gender-ambiguity index of the girls' names and that of the boys' names for a state-year's newborns.

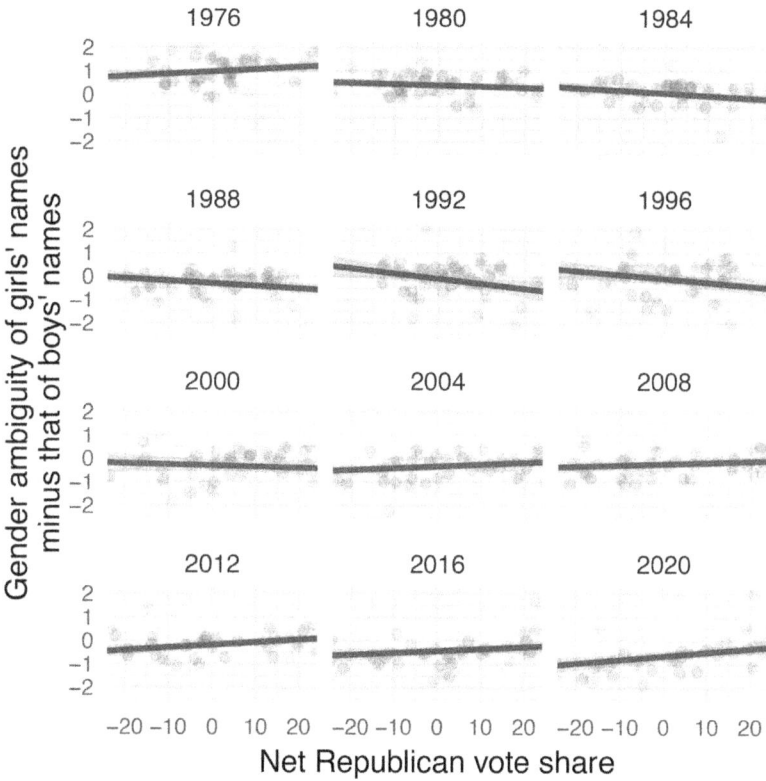

FIGURE 5.9 Relative gender-ambiguity of girls' rather than boys' names, by relative Republican Presidential vote. Darker points indicate state-years with more births.

The results are mixed. From 2004 on, the pattern is as predicted: more Republican states tending to have relatively more gender-ambiguous names for their girls, and Democratic-leaning states to have more gender-ambiguous names for their boys. Before that, though, the tendency is if anything in the opposite direction, though not to the degree that would meet standard benchmarks for statistical confidence (except for a one-off in 1992). The countervailing trend of the earlier eras appears in the data to follow from trends in Mormon parts of the country: Utah, and to a lesser extent Idaho, had a highly Republican population and held on longer to names such as *Jordan*, *Taylor*, and *Tyler* as boys' names even as they transitioned to being increasingly girls' names elsewhere. This obviously contradicts the thought that Republican-leaning areas would be more likely to avoid giving boys names that were associated with femininity. Still, it ends up producing an alternative route to Republican states using more gender-ambiguous names: Perhaps Republican states' more conservative, traditionalist cultures are more likely to stick with more old-fashioned gender associations with names even as more progressive subcultures change their gender associations.

WHITE HOUSE WOMEN

Gender's influence in politics surfaces beyond generic reactions to masculinity and femininity; it can also influence reactions to particular women and men on the political stage. As women have achieved greater political power and visibility, women's names connected to politics have had more chances to become namesakes—for boys as well as for girls, when, for example, the preponderantly male name *Thatcher* is used to honor the British prime minister and free-market icon Margaret Thatcher. Yet the nature of naming patterns means that children might be less likely to be named after prominent political women than otherwise similar political men.

Most crucially, as noted when introducing the *Meagan* example, fashions in girls' names tend to pass faster than those for boys' names.[22] After a few years of widespread use, a girl's name tends to go stale in the public mind. This pattern arises in part because whereas middle-aged men's names are often considered classic, middle-aged women's names are seen as musty. Previously stylish women's names can and do come back into fashion, but it often takes generations for them to do so: *Eva* and *Olivia* and *Emma*, though they never entirely disappeared, faded into near hibernation for most of the twentieth century, only to roar back out of their slumber for the granddaughters and great-granddaughters of their last wave of holders. Despite exceptions, such longer dormancy is a more common pattern than staying at the height of fashion for decades running—as, say, *Michael* did for boys—or having major vogues thirty to fifty years apart. Knowing that a man is named *Michael* (or *Steven* or *Peter*) consequently gives relatively little information about what generation he belongs to, whereas knowing a woman is named *Nancy* (or *Jennifer* or *Brittany*) provides a more confident, though concededly still uncertain, guess.

Women in the prime of their political careers thus tend to have names redolent of their birth year, one that might not feel right for a newborn girl. It was not by chance that, as chapter 3 notes, when political celebrity extended to presidents' families, the feminine examples are of presidential daughters rather than wives. First Ladies generally did not see parallel success as namesakes. *Ruth*, *Esther*, and *Marion* all saw booms in use as they became the names of Grover Cleveland's daughters, even though the sensation of a president marrying in office had not produced the same immediate surge for *Frances*, the name of his bride—and she was a mere twenty-one years old at the time of the wedding, not so old that her name would clearly be unfashionably middle-aged. Only a few First Ladies managed to pull their names from the dormancy or downslope in popularity their names were typically experiencing when their husbands became president. Rosalynn Carter and Melania Trump had names that had not previously been very widespread; their names' having no clear vintage may have spared them the whiff of mothballs and explain why *Rosalynn* and *Melania* sprang to their greatest popularity during their respective holders' time in the White House (the glitz of having been a fashion model may have helped in Melania Trump's case). Neither name really became popular in absolute terms, however, the numbers of babies involved being in the low hundreds.

Jacqueline Kennedy, on the other hand, sparked a phenomenon. The name *Jacqueline* had been in sharp retreat during the late 1950s: Whereas the early years of the decade had seen around seven thousand newborn *Jacqueline*s annually, by 1959 they numbered only about 4,300, a quarter fewer than even three years before. Then began an extraordinary turnaround. In 1960, the year of John F. Kennedy's election, they numbered almost 5,700, a figure that jumped to 11,000 the following year even as the post–World War II baby boom petered out. And this does not include the

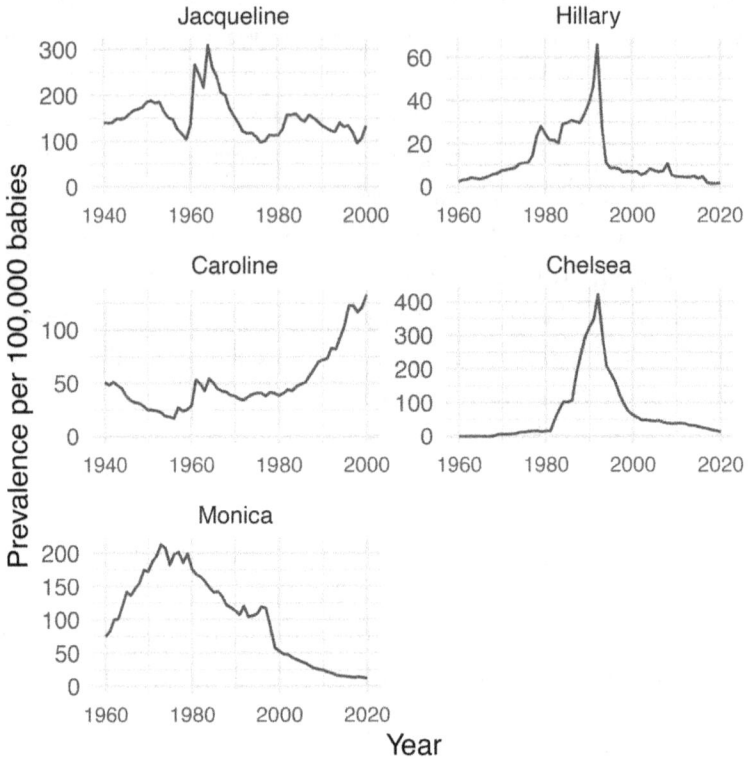

FIGURE 5.10 Prevalence of Kennedy-related names, 1940–2000, and Clinton-related names, 1960–2020.

additional thousands of people named diminutive variants such as *Jackie* or alternative spellings like *Jacquelyn*. A youthful, elegant First Lady connected with many parents' aspirations for their daughters. Although the number of namesakes fell back slightly over the rest of Kennedy's time in office, the name continued to outshine any prevalence it had ever had. And the extraordinary outpouring of sympathy and admiration for Jacqueline Kennedy's fortitude after her husband's assassination launched *Jacqueline* to even further heights in 1964. Only when she retreated from public appearances in the years that followed did her name's remarkable popularity fade.

Only one other First Lady's name took off alongside her husband's election and inauguration at a scale even within an order of magnitude of Jacqueline Kennedy's—*Hillary*, as in Clinton. This similarity between *Jacqueline* and *Hillary* may stem in part from both women's parents having presciently chosen names that were not yet particularly common at the time of naming but would become so over the ensuing decades. This meant both names were relatively close to their peaks at the time their holders appeared on the political scene, only a few years rather than decades out of their highest fashion. Such recent currency contrasts with that of something like *Michelle* at the time that President Obama became a national figure. No matter how widely admired Michelle Obama may have been as First Lady, her name had to overcome starker vintage associations. Having fallen over 90 percent in popularity from its 1960s, Beatles-induced heyday, it saw essentially no detectable increase in use as Michelle Obama began to make the news in the 2000s or throughout her service as First Lady.

Although *Hillary* and *Jacqueline* shared unusual upwellings when their holders became First Lady, differences between their respective trajectories illustrate some of the changes in political culture between the 1960s and the 1990s. *Jacqueline* remained a favorite throughout the Kennedy administration, but *Hillary* utterly crashed after its initial surge around President Clinton's first election. By 1994, the year after Clinton's inauguration, *Hillary* had already dropped in prevalence by more than 80 percent from its 1992 level to its lowest rate since the 1970s. Its use proceeded to fall another quarter the following year. This collapse reflects several factors. Perhaps most pointedly relevant is that, by the 1990s, the First Lady was treated by segments of the media as a much more partisan, political figure than her earlier counterparts had been. As women were increasingly perceived as political actors with potential power and independent views, and as the mainstream media landscape became sharper-elbowed, First Ladies became fair game for increased negative coverage.[23] And Hillary Clinton was not just any First Lady in this regard. She took on an overtly political role, publicly advising her husband on the hotly contentious issue of healthcare reform. This not only embroiled her directly in partisan debates and allowed critiques of her management style even by those who shared her

underlying views, it also betrayed a sort of political ambition that some segments of the public might disdain in women. Partisan overtones and public power could swiftly poison the appeal of a woman's name. Indeed, even
less overt power for the First Lady could inspire backlash. Nancy Reagan's
perceived astrology-inflected influence on her husband attracted some negative comment, though she had largely wielded her authority behind the
scenes. Action as public as Clinton's would face greater pushback yet.

It would be too strong to attribute the swift decline in *Hillary*'s popularity entirely to Hillary Clinton's having stepped into live debates about
health policy and therefore forfeiting the apolitical mantle that had ensured
First Ladies' public esteem. The declining respect for most public institutions, and for presidents in particular, also would likely decrease *Hillary*'s
durability relative to *Jacqueline*. Although President Kennedy could count
on relatively high levels of bipartisan support, especially in the early part
of his term, by the last decades of the twentieth century only grave foreign-
policy crises could raise public approval of the president to what had previously been standard levels. Scandalmongering among a press increasingly
willing to embarrass public figures by airing dirty laundry might along
these lines degrade the personal appeal of figures in the presidential circle.

One way of seeing this might move away from the potentially controversial behavior of presidential wives and instead consider the names of the
daughters of the Kennedy and Clinton households, *Caroline* in the case of
the Kennedys and *Chelsea* for the Clintons. The parallel between the daughters' context is naturally inexact: Caroline Kennedy was barely three years
old when she moved into the White House and so had a small-child
winsomeness that Chelsea Clinton, a month shy of thirteen years old, was
not likely to recapture. Still, during their respective fathers' administrations,
neither daughter undertook anything like public, political advocacy that
would make her an intrinsically partisan figure—yet their names' popularity generally tracked that of their mothers' names.

Caroline, like *Jacqueline*, recovered from the decline that had set in before
it was the name of a First Daughter, more than doubling in prevalence
between the preelection year of 1959 and the inauguration year of 1961. *Caroline* had had a fillip in 1957, just before President Kennedy took office,

when chosen as the name of a new princess of Monaco who also happened to be the first child of the movie star Grace Kelly. Indeed, that may have helped inspire the Kennedys to give their daughter the same name later in the year, but the princess-fueled uptick in *Caroline* naming had already begun to fade by the following year. Its use remained elevated throughout the Kennedy administration and then had another burst of use after the assassination before beginning a moderate decline in popularity. *Chelsea*, on the other hand, had been rocketing in popularity throughout the 1980s, being more than twenty times as popular at the end of the decade as it had been at the start. Its growth was faltering by the early 1990s but abruptly surged again in 1992 when Chelsea Clinton's father became a national figure and won the presidential election. The name's popularity, however, then plummeted. The fall was not quite as spectacular as *Hillary*'s was at the same time, but by 1994 *Chelsea* was less than half as prevalent among newborns that it had been two years before and declined further from there. Even when mindful of the relatively quick changes in fashions for girls' names, this was a strikingly abrupt reversal. Chelsea Clinton might not have been an explicitly political actor, the ardor for an association with her name seemed to cool in a way quite unlike that of *Caroline* three decades earlier or what a name like *Megan* experienced during its post-peak decline.

If names such as *Hillary* and *Chelsea* were closely tied to the approval of the Clintons, one might not just expect variation over time, but across place—*Hillary* could signal partisanship in the same way that, say, a name evoking guns could. Notably, though, the spasm of enthusiasm for *Hillary* and *Chelsea* occurred nationwide, across both Republican- and Democratic-leaning states; although the frequency of use of the names increased more in some states than in others, this variation had very little connection to states' having voted Democratic in the 1992 election, in stark contrast to the later pattern of, say, *Bristol* when it was the name of a family member of a subsequent presidential ticket.

This could as ever reflect an issue of using aggregated, state-level data, if the individuals choosing to give their children a name associated with the Clintons were preponderantly Democrats, but when aggregated up to state-level outcomes the effect is concealed. This is especially likely if

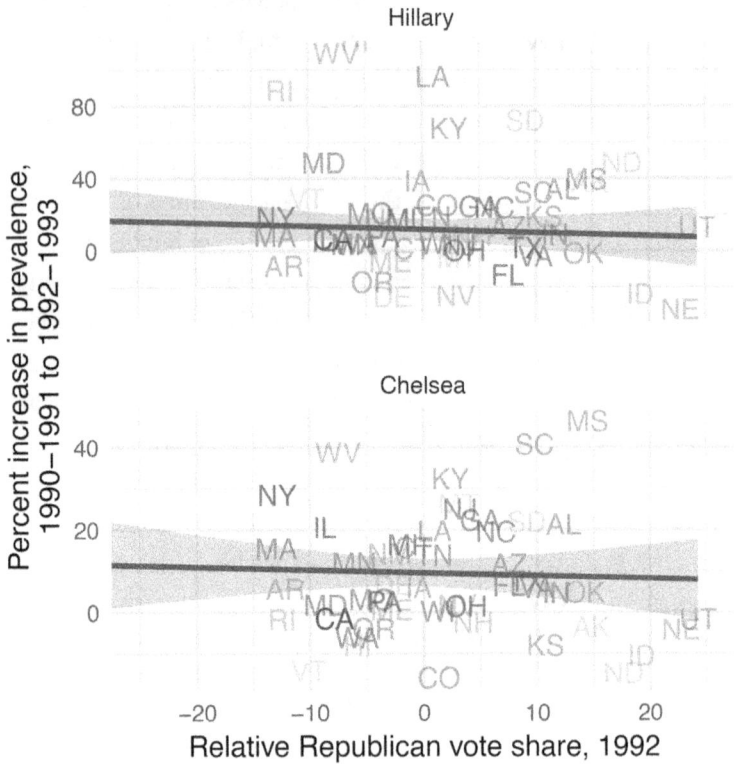

FIGURE 5.11 Increase in relevant names after the Clinton family became nationally prominent, 1990–1993, by state Republican presidential vote. Shaded area indicates 95 percent confidence interval; darker state abbreviations indicate more babies.

Democrats in more Republican areas are particularly likely to use partisan-inflected names, perhaps to assert their partisan identity against the surrounding opposition.[24] It is perhaps notable along these lines that the Republican-leaning states of the Deep South often saw relatively large increases in the use of *Hillary* and *Chelsea* during the campaign years, large African American communities voting heavily Democratic in this era despite (or perhaps because of) White populations' having pulled away from the party.

Detailed data on how specific parents voted and named their children is unavailable nationwide, but some of the problems distinguishing individual-level effects from aggregate outcomes—what social scientists call the problem of *ecological inference*—can be softened by drilling down to more localized data. Smaller geographic units, after all, tend to be less diverse than larger ones, so though the ecological inference problem remains, individual-level characteristics can correlate better with aggregate-level ones. (If a town were 100 percent African American, observations about outcomes there would reflect outcomes for African American individuals, although possibly individuals who do not resemble those who live in more racially diverse towns.) But there is also no relationship between having relative vote for Bill Clinton in 1992 and county-level rates of babies with Clinton-family names in the somewhat smaller units of counties in Texas and California, two states for which birth-certificate data is available: For example, the number of babies named *Chelsea* changed by roughly the same proportion over the 1990 to 1993 period regardless of the local 1992 vote.

Polarization and partisan identification, then, do not always translate into divergent use of political names in Republican- and Democratic-leaning areas—at least, they did not as of the early 1990s. Besides coming from an era before polarization intensified, names such as *Hillary* that have relatively longer histories as conventional first names might read less as political signals than do terms and concepts more recently seeing wide use as names, as in the *Bristol* example. Regardless, the fate of *Hillary* continued to reflect Hillary Clinton's political career after she stopped being First Lady. The name saw noticeable increases in use during the years of her 2008 and 2016 presidential campaigns. Each time she stepped into that public role, though, the name received a smaller increase than the last; into the twenty-first century, the rules observed in chapter 3 of parents seeming less dazzled each time a politician ran for office continued to hold even as the general appeal of presidential candidate names weakened. Indeed, in some ways that old pattern intensified: After each of her defeats, *Hillary* fell substantially in popularity from its level before her campaign,[25] whereas names of figures such as William Jennings Bryan tended to at worst revert to their preelection prevalence.

As a postscript about the names in President Clinton's orbit, one other woman he pulled into the public spotlight who had an outsized influence on naming patterns is worth noting: Monica Lewinsky. News of the affair between Clinton and Lewinsky publicly broke in 1998, in the middle of what had been some good years for *Monica*. Although a quintessentially 1970s name that had been gradually becoming less common, it had been buoyed by being the name of a character in the television series *Friends*, one of the monster pop-culture hits of the 1990s. That had managed to keep the name's popularity relatively stable—until the Lewinsky scandal broke. At that point, the name plunged.[26] It might seem obvious that being at the center of a politically charged sex scandal would torpedo a name's popularity, given that associating one's child with salacious and very highly publicized news has obvious drawbacks. Yet Stanley Lieberman, a titan among scholars of naming trends, expressed uncertainty about whether the scandal would enhance or diminish the popularity of *Monica*.[27] Being much in the public eye often boosts a name's use, and *Monica* did get very widespread exposure as the imbroglio resulted in Clinton's impeachment. But that could not overcome the scandalous associations, perhaps particularly so, some sociologists suggest,[28] for a girl's name, given social emphasis on female purity.[29] Nevertheless, even after *Monica* suffered its post-Lewinsky slump, it did not drop into total disuse. Instead, it ended up almost exactly back on the trajectory it had been on throughout the 1980s, before *Friends* had somewhat revived the name.

An example like this shows the limits as well as the power of political news in driving names, even in an era pervaded by partisanship. Although *Monica*'s popularity did, as figure 5.10 shows, suffer a substantial decline in the wake of the Lewinsky scandal, in some ways it is remarkable how small that decline was, and how many parents contentedly used the name. Even a headline-grabbing event such as a presidential impeachment wrapped up in a sex scandal could not fully deter use of a name at the center of it all,[30] whether because some people remained blithely ignorant of political news or because they philosophically realized that the scandal would pass but their fondness for the name would endure. Still, the tumult did dramatically alter the popularity of a widely used name. Even if this is politics speaking by creating an absence—many of those missing *Monica*s would never know of the fate they escaped, and even their parents might not consciously realize that the Lewinsky affair drove their choice—the combination of high office and gender politics proved potent enough to shape many people's choices about even something as deeply felt as their child's name. At the end of the twentieth century, political currents proved central to many parts of social life, just as they had in past eras when people more baldly named their children after presidents.

6

NAMES, TODAY AND TOMORROW
(CA. 2020–)

Contrarians . . . Social splintering and its consequences . . . Illustrious and ancient names . . . The future of names

On September 12, 2001, shock from the previous day's terrorist attacks overwhelmed much of the United States. At that point, thousands were still missing, and as many as ten thousand people were feared dead. Even without a clear death toll, however, the prime suspect behind the carnage had already been identified: Osama bin Laden, scion of a Saudi construction dynasty and leader of al-Qaeda, had become newly familiar to millions across the country, a focus for fury, contempt, and incomprehension. This sentiment may not have been quite universal, though, because that day one family in Minnesota chose to name their newborn boy *Osama*.

That may have been a coincidence, a long-planned choice made to appear provocative by tragic events. But even if so, it was a noticeable choice, because *Osama* was a somewhat unusual name even before the attack, showing up only as an occasional but not especially common name in Arabic and Muslim communities. Approximately fifty *Osama*s were born in the

United States in a typical year in the late 1990s along with another twenty *Usama*s, an alternative transliteration of the Arabic. Even though its appearance the day after the terrorist attack was particularly arresting, it was not isolated. The name's popularity dropped in 2001 and remained severely depressed for a decade thereafter, but continued to show up in the Social Security Administration's list of baby names in use even during that period and recovered further in the 2010s, after bin Laden's death.[1] It was not just one anomalous family that remained—or perhaps newly became—willing to name a child *Osama*.

As the earlier chapters seek to demonstrate, political movements and events often change a name's popularity; names can get swept up in all manner of social changes, finding themselves suddenly linked to shifting and perhaps uncomfortable associations. This could be seen in cases such as the discussion in chapter 2 of *Savannah* suffering from White flight, or that in chapter 4 of the retreat from German names such as *Wilhelm* during the world wars, or that in chapter 5 of the precipitous drop in the name *Monica* on the eruption of the Lewinsky scandal, among many other examples.[2] A new attention to the fate of the Native peoples of the Americas dimmed the stars of *Columbus* and its feminine analogue *Columbia* over the course of the twentieth century as Christopher Columbus came to be regarded less as a bold explorer and more as a vicious, even genocidal, bumbler. And *Gay*, which used to be quite unremarkable as a name, rapidly declined starting in 1960s as it became increasingly associated with homosexuality; the name basically disappeared by the time of the AIDS crisis in the 1980s. Several offshoots that had previously maintained long, honorable histories as names did the same: *Gaye, Gayla, Gaylene, Gaylord, Gaynell,* and so on.[3] These declines in popularity did not obviously inspire any *Osama*-style countervailing tendency to embrace the newly stigmatized names, even though gay identities and attachments obviously continued to exist.

We have seen examples of contrarian naming before, however. They potentially appeared as far back as the *Royal*s of Revolutionary era and perhaps most pointedly with the *Wilkes Booth*s in the immediate aftermath of President Lincoln's assassination. Thirst for political opponents' tears is certainly nothing new in United States politics, vicious partisan conflict having indeed been nearly a default state for much of the country's history. But as social mores come to favor uniqueness over tradition in naming, scope for political iconoclasm—choosing a name that is openly defiant of prevailing views—increases. Many political actions spur an opposing reaction, and so names appear on both sides of many issues, even those where the sides are unequally popular.

By definition, though, a more popular political cause will have more adherents, and hence more people potentially attracted to names that advertise the cause. As earlier chapters explore, these causes can operate along many dimensions of politics. They can display regional, place-based identities like those in chapter 2, or attachment to particular political leaders and heroes as in chapter 3. They can reflect the nationalism and internationalism of chapter 4, or the partisanship seen in chapter 5. They can express commitment to abstract ideals, as with *Liberty, Justice, Unity,* or *Peace,* but more often these forces are not so explicit. Shading the spelling of *Megan* into *Meagan* to honor the admired figure of Ronald Reagan, or shying away from a Russian-seeming name when international tensions rise, may be entirely unconscious decisions. Still, these stray political impulses, added up across all the newborn babies of a moment in history, can capture even subtle shifts in public sentiment.

The recent tendency toward uniqueness and personal branding in child naming does raise certain difficulties for using names to explore politics, to be sure. The explosive increase in variety of names can obscure connections. For instance, variant name spellings wreak havoc: It may not be obvious that someone looking for names pronounced like *Zachary* should look at or for *Xhaiquirí,*[4] so the recent individualism generally adds noise and chaos to the repertory of names.[5] And the new social freedom offers name-givers so many choices that groundswells of any particular name tend to be smaller and harder to identify.

Yet the profusion of new names also provides opportunities for examining culture and politics. As name-givers feel less constrained by traditional choices, they can allow a broader range of influences and identities, including explicitly political ones, to shape their name selections. Even if some forms of political naming, such as directly using the name of the incumbent president, continue to remain unfashionable, many other elements of politics can slip in. Moreover, long-term cultural forces such as the rise of online social networks in place of local media have to date emphasized the nationalization of politics—though this trend could reverse: One could imagine that alternative algorithms might maximize engagement by encouraging localization rather than uniformity—and a relatively unified nationwide politics makes it more likely that political naming trends in the United States spread widely enough to be noticeable for those who care to look.

ROMAN HANDLES

Although the greater variety of names may make it more difficult to see small blips or interesting individual names—the *Emancipation Proclamations* of the world—it has advantages for comparing regions or ethnicities, or for examining bigger-picture changes. These are legion, for as time and culture change, so do political references. The direction of changes is also often relatively predictable as well as instructive about how society viewed politics, even if any one individual naming choice is not. The analogies that people drew between their current politics and ancient societies can serve as an example.

Classical references abounded throughout educated culture in the post–Enlightenment era.[6] To take one example, Frederick Douglass even in enslavement sought out a wildly popular sampler of rhetoric that included multiple orations attributed to Roman generals, as well as selections from Cato, Cicero, and Socrates.[7] This preoccupation with ancient wisdom showed up in naming, too. The book's introduction mentioned self-consciously ancient selections such as *Pompey* and *Juno* among names slaveowners imposed, and likewise names such as *Flavia*, *Philomela*, or *Ovid* were reasonably common even among the free-born.[8] Greek- and Roman-inflected names were further encouraged by how deeply the Bible saturated many corners of early U.S. society, given that many then-familiar names from the New Testament or early Christian history (*Apphia*, *Archelaus*, *Artemas*, and so on) originated in Greek or Latin.

Easy culture-wide familiarity with ancient history readily helped names express political points as well. For over a century from the late 1700s, many children were named *Cincinnatus*. The name directly honored Lucius Quinctius (or Quintus) Cincinnatus, the legendary ancient Roman who grudgingly assumed dictatorial power to confront a national emergency but swiftly relinquished his political authority to return to his farm after the crisis ended. At the same time, it was a conscious tribute to George Washington, who was seen as having shown a similarly selfless devotion to the republic.[9] The allusion was well-known in nineteenth-century culture, in part because the Order of the Cincinnati was the largest and most prominent of the veterans' organizations of the American Revolutionary War. Although controversial for its quasi-aristocratic hereditary nature,[10] it served as the namesake for everything from a dusting of place names across the country (most notably Cincinnati, Ohio) to General Ulysses Grant's horse during the Civil War.

The position of the classics in national culture eventually declined, though, and the ancient Roman republic and Athenian democracy faded as central frames of reference for thinking about government.[11] Alongside them, names like *Cincinnatus* went, too, even picking up an air of musty pretentiousness. That is not to say that classical names totally disappeared. In fact, they have experienced a strong revival since the year 2000, albeit mostly with choices that were previously rare, invoking figures both historical (*Aurelius*, *Cyrus*, *Leonidas*) and mythical (*Atreus*, *Odysseus*, *Perseus*, *Theseus*).[12] Notably, some of the largest increases in usage of classical names have involved the names of Roman emperors who have borne millennia of generally bad press, *Nero* and *Tiberius*.[13] The notion that someday more parents would want to associate their children with Nero than with Cincinnatus would have baffled observers in the 1700s, but the folk memory of these political figures as political figures has attenuated, and what makes a historical figure admirable may also have shifted.

You perhaps did not need to look at baby names to learn that people of the twenty-first century United States base relatively few major life choices on Suetonius. That unsurprisingness is the point, though: A palpable change in culture such as the reduced use of allusions based on classical references is the sort of major shift that names can help examine or test. This is just another way of saying that names mirror culture; in fact, they are part of culture, which is what gives them the power to reveal social and political identities. Traditional political virtue's no longer correlating with the popularity of ancient figures among name-givers provides another way of seeing just when the public imagination let go of those figures as political exemplars.

In this way, names provide and confirm insights about the politics of everyday life, how real people engage with ideology, parties, and institutions—and, most broadly, identities. Analysts have been increasingly drawn to these sorts of tools, looking at concert programs to examine xenophobia,[14] or examining language used in published books to see how a society's partisan leanings change in response to violence,[15] or asking almost any question imaginable of internet search choices.[16] As more and more of social life moves into virtual panopticons allowing the observation of all significant choices, the possibilities for such behavioral insight into politics increases. Names are a more innocuous example of people expressing their culture because they are more expressly public. They have the additional advantage of being more likely to continue as a core part of life for future centuries as they have for past centuries, and consequently to be relatively comparable over those extended time spans. The social role of a name in the 1700s mostly resembled that in the 2000s, despite all the ways the world changed in the interim.

But names also appeal because they are essentially universal to the contemporary human experience. Everyone can relate to having a name, making them familiar and approachable, which many other indices of political engagement may not be—and accessible because many public-facing applications are available to let anyone readily explore historical trends in naming.[17] When you have a question about past or present views of politics and can think of a name that might speak to the question, tracing the course of the name can offer a quick first answer.

NAME CHANGES

Certain trends, though, may sometimes complicate the use of names to analyze public reactions to events. Names are still tightly bound to identity. As society and the law become more open to people's changing their official names to match their preferred identity—especially in the dimension of gender, because names continue to connect closely to gender despite the increased use of unisex options—it becomes more likely for names to change long after birth, so that the legal name on a revised birth certificate, though better reflecting the wishes of the person involved, may not offer a contemporaneous record of birth-time political views. (This sort of revision also changes the role of the name-giver from the parent or guardian to the user of the name, which adds further inconsistency to comparisons with most names.)

The precedent of allowing changes to birth-certificate information may further open legal and social possibility in the future for more people to alter their official names for any reason—or no reason at all. Even from the narrow perspective of deriving social views from names, such name changes are not all bad in that they provide an additional name selection for the person involved, expanding the number of cases from which information can be extracted. Still, they require additional care in the dating of the names involved and can obscure what is being observed.

In some ways, this change just restores an old caution remarked upon when discussing the days of high infant mortality, when parents more frequently waited for some time after birth to assign a permanent name. Adoption, which also increased the probability of name changes well after birth (but did not inevitably result in such changes), was also formerly more common than now.[18] Those sorts of belated namings, however, still usually occurred in childhood, often quite early childhood, so any misdating would be relatively small. People consciously choosing names that signal their identities as a full-grown adult could by contrast separate the timing of the name-giving from the birth date by multiple decades.

The difficulty is reduced or absent in some sources of information about names, including those relied on here. No practicable method exists as yet to retroactively change the name in a U.S. census record, and the Social Security Administration figures are, at least at present, based on names (and reported sexes) at the time of the original application.[19] In other records, though, name changes can prove a trap for the unwary.

Even so, such changes are another testament to the intensity of feeling and meaning that personal names continue to represent in the United States, and to the social pulse they can therefore offer for the past, present, and future. This book attempts to show some of the range of topics and questions that names might allow you to approach. When people choose a name that proclaims sectional pride, partisan alignment, or support for the president (or the president's assassin)—and when they do not—they tell us something about what they find most meaningful. Although not every name is a *Federal Constitution* or a *Debs*, each one casts a small point of light on what people were thinking and feeling about politics and much else besides.

APPENDIX

METHODOLOGY

The underlying argument of this book is that names can provide insights into what people thought and felt about politics at various points of time and space. Names are not the only source of political information, by any means, but, as discussed in the introduction, they can usefully complement other measures. At its core, then, this is a book about measurement, thinking about some of the variety of potential ways to measure popular attitudes about politics through child names.

That task of measurement requires pinpointing the meaning of names as well as establishing how widely used those names were. Many approaches would be possible here. A qualitative approach might identify parents (or other name-givers) of individual people with some politically resonant name and interview them or, for those who have died or are otherwise inaccessible, search the archives for personal records containing clues about why they chose that name. That tack could potentially offer greater certainty that the child was named after a political namesake, but it is hard to scale with present technologies—and, being time consuming, it is less risky to commit to after first establishing that names do in fact reflect political currents of interest. Interview-based approaches also pose a common problem of retrospective explanation, given that memories about one's exact motivation change over time; further, they suffer from the absence of an obvious control group of people who might have considered a markedly political child name but ultimately did not choose it. The strategy used here, then, turns instead to more quantitative methods, generally counting names of children in large samples with only occasional, brief discussion of specific individuals or the circumstances of their naming.

This strategy relies on large collections of names from across the United States. The country's decentralized, federal institutions preclude any official nationwide record of births, and hence we lack any authoritative compilation of birth names. Vital records are instead collected at the state or even, especially historically, at the local level, to sometimes varying standards of detail and completeness (again, especially historically). In the absence of any exhaustive catalog of given names, the vast majority of the information used throughout this book comes from two major sources, each with its pitfalls.

The first of these sources is the decennial census. Every ten years from 1790 on, the government has tried to count people nationwide, though, as chapter 1 mentions, censuses only started recording the identity, including the name, of people other than heads of household with the 1850 Census. Even then, coverage of residents was not complete. Indigenous populations in their own territories, or "Indians not taxed" as the Constitution put it, were generally not included in nineteenth-century censuses, and many people in pre–Civil War records are listed merely as *Slave*—or, in the official census slave schedules accompanying the 1850 and 1860 censuses, only tallied by sex and age group—rather than by a personal name. Still, the decennial catalog provides much the most complete information about the nineteenth century; some local sources can be more systematic and inclusive for places where they exist, but they are absent for much of the country for great swathes of time.

The national census has additional advantages beyond sheer number of people included. It also consistently comes with information about the race of the people involved, as well as where they were born—which is handy when trying to make sure that we are considering people born in the United States,[1] as opposed to immigrants, whose names are interesting in their own right but less clearly relevant to the questions that animate this book about how people in the United States reacted to events.[2] The census also often indicates, by showing names in the form of first initial plus middle name or by only recording what is officially the middle name, that the middle name was actually the key name for the person involved, and making that name available for study. A birth certificate that recorded someone's name as Addison Mitchell McConnell would not reflect that the name actually used in practice to refer to the child was not *Addison* but *Mitch*. The pro forma first name does have its own interest, but may shed less light on the identity that the people involved felt most emotionally attached to. In general, then, the analyses here treat the middle names as first names in these circumstances. For example, people listed in the census as F. Scott Fitzgerald and J. Edgar Hoover would respectively be treated as *Scott* and *Edgar* in the tallies throughout the book.[3]

The census does have several problems as a data source, though. Just as it comes online earlier than other data sources, it goes offline earlier, too: Individual-level census records are only made publicly available seventy-two years after the census in question. At the time of writing, that means that 1950 is the last census that can be used. Almost all of the rich history of the Cold War era thus cannot be approached with this source as yet, and the post–Cold War period will be locked away for decades to come. Although I use the census figures as the primary source for trends in names before 1950, then, more recent events require other sources.

Even for the century for which census returns are available, some holes beyond excluded categories or the people inevitably missed in an effort to count a whole country's population are notable. First, because censuses only occur every ten years, they are not contemporaneous with births. Instead, the census analyses throughout the book look at people born since the year of the last available census, usually meaning people age nine or younger. That has multiple important consequences. One stems from the quirk that censuses were not always consistent in their timing: Some people could be overlooked by procedural changes in what time of year the census occurred. For example, the United States' fourteenth national census took place in January 1920, but the fifteenth was in April 1930. Anything notable that happened in February or March of 1920 may therefore be overlooked in the counts here. Including ten-year-olds would avoid this problem but has the trade-off of more often producing double counting: Someone born in mid- or late 1919 would be included as a zero-year-old in the 1920 census and a ten-year-old in the 1930 census. This double counting would affect a larger number of people than excluding the children born in the interstices from the occasional censuses that were more than ten years apart (of which the 1920 to 1930 census was the largest). In other cases, the censuses were less than ten years apart, because they moved to an earlier date, which would exacerbate the problem if ten-year-olds were included.[4]

Because the figures reported throughout the book are in terms of proportions, these discrepancies in census date should be a relatively minor issue; in counting *Ethan*s in 1920, for example, the January-, February-, and March-born *Ethan*s presumably go uncounted, but then everyone born that season similarly does, so the *Ethan* proportion of the total will typically be relatively little affected. However, the extent to which different social groups with distinctive naming practices tend to give birth in different times of year—a more severe issue after wider availability of birth control, but still present in 1920—may slightly affect observations for relevant years.[5] Names that themselves have seasonal variation even within social groups will also be affected. This is very common with Catholic saints' names, especially in Spanish-speaking communities; *Valentine* and *Valentina*, for example, are in the United States most common as names for those born immediately around Valentine's Day in mid-February, and *Guadalupe* has an enormous skew toward December births (the feast day of the Mexican Virgin of Guadalupe falling on the twelfth of that month). Other names also have a seasonal valence. Around 45 percent of people in Social Security records named *June* were born in the month of June, when only 8 percent would be expected if names were given without regard to the month of birth.[6] The prevalence of any name with a seasonal pattern is likely to be either over- or underestimated in 1920 depending on the whether the seasonal peak occurred in those missing three months. Fortunately, most names discussed in this text have relatively little seasonal variation, except that the names of electoral candidates discussed in chapter 3 do tend to particularly surge around the date of the election (and of the inauguration, for election winners).

Perhaps more relevant to broader themes is that any political happenings that occurred in the first quarter of 1920 that led to an immediate but short-lived change in naming patterns, as so many passing news events do, would be missed. Two domestic events of those months are, at least in retrospect, potentially noteworthy.[7] One was that Prohibition, the ban on most alcohol sales, went into effect that January but had no obvious effect on relevant names such as *Temperance*. Also, the congressional debate on ratification of the Treaty of Versailles occurred during the key months, the ultimate vote rejecting the treaty held in March. *Versailles* and variant spellings were not common names and do not appear in noncensus sources to have had any transitory attraction during the early months of 1920.[8]

As important as the gaps from inconsistent census timing, using snapshots from every ten years makes for records where an element of hindsight is involved. If families reconsidered their child's originally chosen name and so began calling the child something else at any time before the census, only the new, later name will appear with no indication it was from a later time than the birth date. The child's census name will therefore be associated with the wrong date, anachronistically attached to the birth even though it really derived from a later period. This may be especially likely with politically derived names; the well-established pattern of high hopes for candidates turning into disappointment and opposition after those candidates become incumbent leaders, for instance, makes it very possible that parents could name a child after an office-seeking politician but then regret it when that candidate lost the election or proved deficient in office. Even without a wholesale change of name, many census entries, especially for children, appear to be nicknames rather than the original, formal name; few people insisted on official names in census records until well into the twentieth century. Someone who shows up in the census as *Jeff* may be a *Jefferson*, but is not counted as such in the analyses here (one would not want to count *Jeffreys* or, worse, *Jeffrys* under false pretenses). This potential for name changes means that some names that existed may have been erased from the record available here, and the potential for renaming introduces some uncertainty about when the naming took place, even above the point discussed in the introduction that it was historically common for naming to happen well after the date of birth.

But more pervasive uncertainties obscure when naming happened. A minor but persistent issue is that a few census entries, usually less than 1 percent but varying across time and place, give no indication at all of when the listed person was born. Those cases are omitted from the discussions here because they cannot be confidently attached to any specific time of birth. Even when census enumerations provide information about when people were born, though, most often that is not an actual birth date, but instead age in years. (The 1900 census was an exception, listing years and months of birth. Also, in most censuses, those younger than one year usually have their age reported in months.) This introduces further ambiguity: Someone listed as being five years old in the 1930 Census could have been born in late 1924 or in early 1925. To have a consistent system, this book acts as though censuses happened on December 31 of the census year, so that anyone who is zero years old is assumed to be born in the official census year, one-year-olds are credited to the year before the official census year, and so on. There is additional ambiguity in that, even beyond the inevitable reporting and data-entry errors in analyzing millions of census respondents, people tend to round their responses to an approximate but tidy value when asked questions with numeric answers. This propensity for rounded age reporting is particularly likely among certain groups, such as the illiterate with their reduced access to precise records of age and those in less bureaucratized societies.[9]

These groups make up an increasing proportion of the United States population as one considers phenomena closer to the country's founding. That is, the earlier the census, the more these rounding issues are likely to matter. They are thus of most concern in the 1850 census, the first one

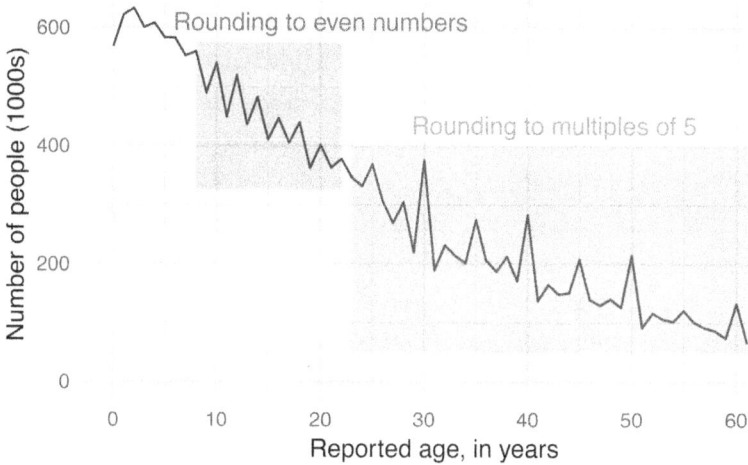

FIGURE A.1 Reported ages in 1850 United States census, showing tendency for imprecise responses.

providing a detailed enumeration of all individuals and hence the earliest used in the analyses here. Figure A.1 shows that census's distribution of responses by reported age.

The distribution does not follow the smooth decline with increasing age that one might expect from a growing population and high mortality rates. Instead, the figure shows many spikes and troughs in the distribution. Some such irregularities may reflect actual irregularities in the age distribution, say if a war or recession triggered a brief baby bust, or if an epidemic with particular lethality for infants swept through society in a year. However, the patterns repeat too frequently, too regularly, and too severely to plausibly reflect real events: Responses instead show signs of rounding. Among children, ages are disproportionately reported as multiples of two: fewer three-year-olds than two- or four-year-olds, fewer five-year-olds than four- or six-year-olds, and so on. This tendency gets even more pronounced for those between ten and twenty years old. Then, after the age of twenty, despite some tendency to still favor even numbers, the main pattern of rounding stretches to multiples of five and, especially, ten. This rounding is even more stark than that seen among children; the figures imply that the ratio of thirty- to thirty-one-year-olds (or forty- to forty-one-year-olds, or fifty- to fifty-year-olds, and so on) is roughly two to one. This pattern creates another reason, beyond the increased probability of names drifting over time, to focus when possible on children born since the previous census. Although the preteenage age bracket also shows some rounding, it appears to be less widespread there and to deflect ages by a relatively small amount.

Focusing on children does sharpen one problem with analyzing names, however. Although names may be less likely to be totally abandoned given fewer years since birth and initial naming, children are, even in the census enumerations, particularly likely to go by diminutive nicknames—not just a problem with *Jeff*, but one for millions of census entries naming *Billy* or *Betty* or *Suzy* or the like, which can be actual given names but often are not. These and other childhood nicknames obscure the birth name and so lead people not to be counted as having the names they were formally given. And if the nickname happens to look like some other name of interest, the other name may be credited with more namesakes than it really had. That issue most obviously binds here in chapter 2, with the names of Civil War generals, one of whom was Jubal Early. Adding a *Y* to the end of a name is a frequent way of forming childhood nicknames and, suspiciously, *Early* shows up frequently in census listings of children just as *Earl* begins to take off in popularity. Quite likely, several of the census *Earlys* really were named *Earl*—indeed, other records list them as such.[10] Any other names being considered that happen to coincide with a nickname might face similar problems of having their prevalence overcounted by the census measure, and the more unusual the name, the more that a few stray nicknames will perturb the analysis. (*Debs* may seem like an unlikely nickname, but then it also seems like an unlikely given name.)

Besides opening up the potential for imprecise dating of births or name changes, the every ten years mode of the data makes for a sample that is incomplete. For much of the era covered by this book, infant and child mortality was appallingly high in the United States.[11] Many children born in 1843, say, would not be alive in the 1850 census and therefore are invisible in this data, which contributed to most age cohorts in figure A.1 tending to be smaller than the one succeeding them, notwithstanding the rounding. Similarly, though likely more rarely, a child whose family relocated overseas before the child's first census, either as permanent or as temporary migrants (for example, as missionaries), would also not be observable in the enumeration. To the extent these sorts of exits from the census population were more common among particular social groups, the estimates of name prevalence will be biased against names from those groups. Unsurprisingly, socioeconomically disadvantaged groups tended to have higher child mortality rates,[12] so such groups are likely to be underrepresented overall, but with a sawtooth cycle: The underrepresentation would be lowest just before the census occurred, but then grow steadily for years earlier in the decade. This inconsistent underrepresentation over time could muddy patterns.

Compounding the difficulty of intermittent coverage, a 1921 fire at the Commerce Department building destroyed virtually all 1890 census records.[13] Instead of looking at anyone nine years or younger in 1890, then, I look at people nineteen years or younger in 1900 to cover the 1880s with census figures. This longer gap will only exacerbate all the problems of the usual ten-year cycle and bring in more of figure A.1's rounding. Similarly, I occasionally venture to report national census figures from before 1841, most extensively in chapter 3, when looking at the use of presidents' surnames. That analysis uses the 1850 census shown in figure A.1 for all years from the start of the sample to 1850; for those born in the 1790s, the sample consists of people who well exceeded the standard life expectancy at birth even of the most prosperous groups within society,[14] and the data is concomitantly likely to be somewhat unrepresentative.

A final difficulty with the census data is that it all derives from handwritten records, which are often difficult to read clearly. No standard tabulation of the names in census returns exists, and one has to divine whether a given entry says *Lois* or *Louis* or *Louise* or *Louisa* or *Lewis*, all of which can look very similar depending on the penmanship. Many judgment calls are involved, and numbers are accordingly approximate whenever the census is the source. I have cross-checked my tallies for a sample of names against large genealogical digitizations of historical census records, and though the numbers usually align closely, they almost never match perfectly. That is, when by my count a name becomes more popular, other databases also report it becoming more popular to a very similar but not precisely identical degree.

The other, noncensus source of name-frequency information derives from the Social Security Administration (SSA). Every year, the SSA releases a list of the most popular given names for newborns and has retroactively released its figures on name prevalence back to the year 1880.[15] Social Security does not release every name; for both privacy and administrability reasons, they only release information about names for which, in the given year, at least five people were born of the relevant name of a particular sex. For example, if seven *Fozzies* were born in a given year, of whom four were female and three were male, none of them would appear in the data; if instead there had been five female and two male *Fozzies*, the females would be visible while the males would not be. (The SSA also releases such counts by state, subject to the same restriction at the state level: If eight females named *Fozzies* were born nationwide, five in California and three elsewhere, only the five Californians would show up in state-level figures even as the national numbers would report the total of eight.) The tally includes versions of a name involving hyphens, spaces, and diacritical marks within a name; *Foz-Zie* and *Fozzié* would both be counted in the *Fozzie* tally. Other variations would mostly not be included, however, and the minimum requirement of five observations goes for each spelling of a name: *Fawzy*, *Fozzi*, and *Phozzee* would not count toward the total of *Fozzies*, and would not appear in the SSA figures at all unless at least five people with the exact variant spelling were born in the given year of a single sex. Although alternative spellings or mistranscriptions are visible in the census returns, if difficult to read with certainty when the handwriting was messy or overly ornate, the omission of rare names from the Social Security figures means variants, or even standardly rendered names that were inadvertently miscopied somewhere in the bureaucratic bowels, can disappear.

The lack of information about rare names is one reason the book's figures concerning names in recent decades tend to be somewhat jumpy when the number of occurrences is few. When names teeter on the brink of the five-per-year threshold, they seem to bounce back and forth between having zero and having several, even if in reality the change might only be four versus five occurrences. A more pervasive problem the exclusion of rare names raises, though, comes from the presentation of figures in terms of rates: occurrences per hundred thousand babies instead of raw counts. Calculating the rate requires an estimate of the total number of babies from which the sample is drawn. When large portions of that sample are unreported, simply adding the total number of observed births will substantially overstate the prevalence of names. The Social Security Administration does supply a count of applications by year of birth, but those figures omit many applications on the basis of incomplete information, which varies over time.[16]

Accounting for the invisible rare names to estimate the total tally involves estimating how many names were likely to have one, two, three, or four observations in a year. The distribution of names tends to follow a mathematical relationship called a power law, such that knowing how often more common names are used is likely to be highly predictive of how often rarer ones are.[17] Figure A.2 illustrates this, showing how many names appear five, six, seven, and so on times in selected birth years from 1900 to 2020. The figure uses logarithmic scales for both axes, unlike most standard graphs (including most of those elsewhere in this book); a fixed distance along an axis represents a constant change in the proportion of the variable being measured, not in raw amount. For instance, along the vertical axis, the distance from the tick at ten and that at one hundred is the same as the tick at one hundred and that at one thousand: Moving that distance represents a tenfold increase in the count of names. When graphed in this log-log form, distributions following a power law approximate a straight line.

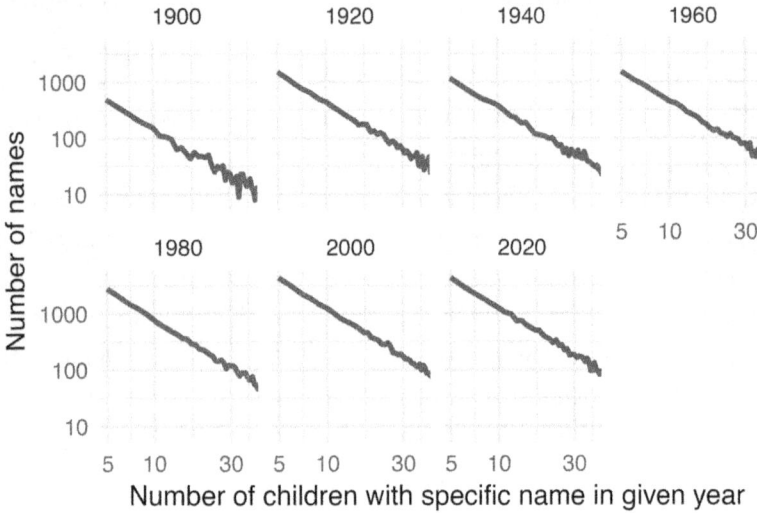

FIGURE A.2 Distribution of name frequencies, selected years, in a log-log plot (i.e., one in which both axes use logarithmic scales).

Such straight power-law lines are evident throughout figure A.2, with allowances for the noisiness of rare events such as names attaining many annual uses, especially in earlier years when the national population was relatively low. Each year has a different line: The larger number of babies in later decades mean that the lines in later years tend to be higher than those from earlier years, and the slope of the line varies alongside the trends in concentration of names noted in chapter 5 (the conformist years around World War II have moderately flatter lines than those from earlier or later periods). Estimating the slope and intercept of each year's straight line over the range of names with five or more observations then provides estimates for counts of names with one, two, three, and four occurrences. As with any extrapolation, the accuracy of this procedure relies on the accuracy of assumptions, particularly the assumption that the power-law distribution that characterizes more common names extends cleanly to rarer names. This assumption is not certain: It might, for instance, be that there are enough one-off typos that the power-law estimate underestimates the number of unique names. The rate of unique names in other data sets does not suggest that major deviations are likely, but they are possible.

The SSA numbers, including those presented in figure A.2, definitionally involve the list of program participants in Social Security (i.e., public pension) programs. These programs did not exist until the Social Security Act of 1935, implementation of which did not begin until 1936, so anyone who had died before 1936 was ineligible for benefits and would be unlikely to appear in this data.[18] Although life expectancies had by the 1930s already climbed substantially from their nineteenth-century levels,[19] Social Security Administration figures will still of necessity exclude everyone born in the first few decades of the country's history, with only gradually increasing coverage—strongly biased at first toward groups that lived longer on average—over the latter part of the 1800s and early 1900s. The agency does not release counts from before 1880 in its standard annual tallies of names precisely because it thinks them too unreliable to be useful.

Even for those alive in or after 1936, however, Social Security does not provide anything like complete coverage of the population. Participation was high from the introduction of the Social Security system, well exceeding projections about uptake,[20] but it was not universal. Although those who worked in some formal employment (rather than as, say, housekeeper or farm laborer compensated in board or in kind—restrictions that, notably for names, skewed the racial incidence of the programs) were obliged to enroll with Social Security,[21] it was not necessary for everyone. People who thought they were ineligible or simply failed to hear about the program may not have signed up. Others may have stayed away on principle, because of opposition to government programs in general or redistribution in particular, because of lack of trust that the program could be relied on, or because administrators discriminated against them.

Even now, registration is not technically mandatory. Many procedures of modern life in the United States are incomparably easier on enrollment with Social Security: Everything from opening a bank account to getting health care comes with requirements, or at least widespread expectations, for a Social Security number. Government programs, the original purpose of the Social Security number, often outright require enrolling with Social Security in ways that will include the name in the database. (If the child's parents want to claim the child as a dependent for tax purposes, for instance, a Social Security number has in recent decades been needed.) Eventually, too, the child is likely to want a formal job that requires payroll taxes and a Social Security account. But none of these are mandatory, and some people who are intensely suspicious of the government and of modern society do avoid them. Even though the vast majority of births in recent decades are included, then, the Social Security records still are not all inclusive.

As the history of the program suggests, Social Security enrollments were at first even more separated in time from a person's naming than a decennial census entry would be. Although people born in the late 1800s could appear in the Social Security registers, when they did so they tended to register with whatever name they used in the 1930s (or later, if they delayed enrolling). Even those who were young when Social Security was enacted were unlikely to register right away; for the first few decades of the program, people tended to sign up for a Social Security number only when they got their first formal job, rarely before their teenage years. Some did sign up earlier, especially after 1970 when banks were obliged to obtain Social Security numbers for all customers. But only in the late 1980s did states launch programs to simplify enrollment in the Social Security system as part of the registration of newborn children, after which point far more children were registered at birth.

These years or decades between birth naming and Social Security registration especially matter because, just as in the census, Social Security long lacked any obligation to use their formal, legal names: People could register under whatever name they saw fit. Laws theoretically banned fraud, but no actual requirement that registrants provide evidence of identity were in place until the 1970s: People could legally use whatever name they liked as long as they were not pretending to be someone else. Instead, whatever was put on the application was taken as true, and no universal mandate to match full or official names was in place. Meanwhile, for parts of the country's

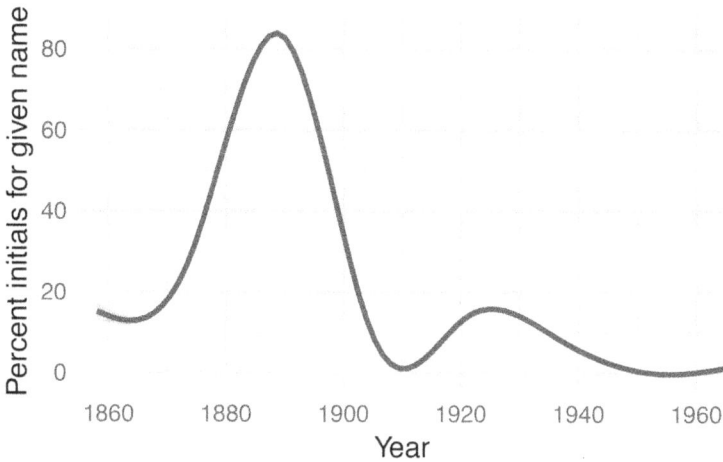

FIGURE A.3 Smoothed (generalized additive model) share of *New York Times* obituaries using initials in place of a given name, 1860–1960.

history, social norms led adult men to use their initials rather than their given names—not just first initial plus middle name as in the F. Scott Fitzgerald example, but all initials before the surname. This is familiar from a wide variety of cultural figures from the first half of the twentieth century who are still referred to in this way: B. B. King, B. F. Skinner, D. W. Griffith, E. E. Cummings, J. D. Salinger, J. P. Morgan, W. C. Fields, W. E. B. Du Bois, and so on. Although some later figures adhered to this convention (such as O. J. Simpson, R. L. Stine, or J. J. Abrams), it was historically much more prevalent.

To see this trend more systematically, consider the set of *New York Times* obituaries presented in figure A.3.[22] In the late nineteenth and early twentieth century, a substantial fraction of the newspaper's obituaries identify the subject by initials.[23] Indeed, for a period initials were the most common way of presenting names. Yet the proportion of obituaries using initials falls to almost nothing after World War II. The long-term fall in initial use is exacerbated by the obituary page's being opened up to a more diverse population of subjects; women, most notably, were far less likely to be identified by initials (except when they took their husband's name at marriage, when they might import their husbands' use of initials using a formulation such as *Mrs. H. L. Mencken*), so the rise of more women into prominent roles contributed to the decline in initials in obituaries. The decline in the rate of obituaries using initials far outpaces the rate at which women gained inclusion, however; even at the end of the sample period, women were far underrepresented, whereas the near-total lack of initial-based entries would require almost all obituary subjects to have been women, if the proportions of men using initials had remained anything like what had prevailed around 1900.

These obituaries, like many of the historical sources, are plainly not representative. People prominent enough to get *New York Times* obituaries are disproportionately well off and from major cultural centers. At the same time, the newspaper noted the death of many non-American figures, so figure A.3 includes entries extraneous to the point here. The use of initials, though, is not simply a tic of cosmopolitan cultural elites influenced by other societies (from India to the Netherlands) or subcultures (such as British writers) that also habitually refer to people by initials. Nor is it just a convention required by the space limitations of obituary headlines or the unusual preferences of some *New York Times* obituary editor. A wide range of other examples from around the country show generally similar patterns. The rosters of the Mormon Tabernacle Choir have relatively comprehensive coverage from 1878 on; the proportion of members identified only by initials quickly rises from a starting level around 10 percent to a peak of more than 30 percent just before 1900 before sliding back to roughly zero from 1940 on, the lower prevalence at the apex relative to the *Times* obituaries partly reflecting that the choir was much more gender balanced than the obituaries were. Similarly, the first (1894) edition of the Iowa State College (now Iowa State University) yearbook lists more than half of the students by their initials, a proportion that rises over the next decade before dropping steeply over the following few years.[24] These proportions again understate the proportion of men in the sample population who used the initial-based styling because Iowa State was coeducational: No student in the college's Ladies' Course used initials, and the women in other, male-dominated majors similarly preferred their names in full to initials. As a last example, the list of mayors, aldermen, and alderwomen of Savannah, Georgia, only rarely saw people entered using their initials until the last quarter of the nineteenth century, at which point the proportion of initial-users rises abruptly, remaining high until around 1910 before beginning a more gradual descent back to near zero. These examples, from different social functions scattered around the country, all converge on the same trend, as seen in figure A.3, with use of initials greatest sometime around the year 1900.

Men in the early twentieth century, that is to say, often publicly identified themselves with initials. When they registered for Social Security as adults, many would naturally continue doing so. At that point, their Social Security record offers little of the information needed for the analyses here. Those who chose the styling of first initial plus middle name are similarly left out. Figures using Social Security names for births from the late nineteenth and early twentieth century then probably understate the relative frequency of most male names and overstate the frequency of female names.[25]

Even for those included in the Social Security database with a full given name, the reports have less information than the census returns in several dimensions: They do not convey most of the administrative and demographic data that the Social Security Administration has about program participants. They do not include any information about race, which would be helpful for assessing how much racial imbalances in the included population skew inferences about the population as a whole. Nor do they consistently include information about place of birth, only about place of registration with Social Security (as encoded in the first three digits of the Social Security number, which was definitive for the first several decades of Social Security's history). Most awkwardly for the analysis here, that could easily include people who were born and named overseas. That is, besides being underinclusive by lacking people who never enrolled or who had too rare a name to make the five-per-year minimum for reporting, the Social Security tallies are, like the *New York Times* obituaries, overinclusive by including immigrants who may not reflect United States birth-naming practices. Even for those born in the United States, infer-ences about place of birth have some inherent uncertainty when using Social Security information from the era when most people registered only years or decades after birth: Having registered with the program while liv-ing in California is entirely consistent with having been born in Maine or Mississippi.

Despite these grounds for caution, the Social Security figures do have some advantages even above the mere (and crucial) fact of being available for recent decades. In contrast to most of the census returns, the Social Security Administration provides year of birth information rather than an age value from which birth year must be uncertainly estimated. Its cover-age of the sex of the holders of particular name is also more complete than the census's, though impressions about that are somewhat distorted by the agency's exclusion from annual tallies of any cases for which the sex vari-able was unavailable. The names have also been precoded by the SSA, so even though the original source of the data was often the same sort of messy or ambiguous handwritten information seen in census returns, an official reading of each entry exists. This makes results more reliably replicable than are attempts to match a particular reading of the census forms.

The Social Security Administration does release parts of its name data in other formats than the annual tallies of popular first names. In particu-lar, the Social Security Death Index (also more threateningly known as the Death Master File), in an effort to limit identity fraud involving use of a dead person's data, releases the names, birth dates, and Social Security numbers of everyone listed in the database whom the agency knows to have died. This has some major advantages over the main Social Security data release. It is not subject to the limitation of requiring five instances of a name (in a given sex) in a year: Even if only one *Fozzie* was born in a year, that person will after dying be included in the Death Index. It provides full names, so that someone who uses the first initial plus middle name styling has a usable name that would not appear in the annual SSA first-name releases. It also, by providing an exact birth date, allows finer-grained con-sideration of timing. An analysis like that in chapter 3 of this book looking at how the use of *Garfield* responded month by month to the events of his run for and tenure in office, for example, would be possible down to the level of the individual day with the Death Index figures. Indeed, the Death Index was the source of the information earlier in this appendix about names such as *June* and *Valentine* appearing particularly among those born in certain times of year.

Unfortunately, the Death Index requires death. It is therefore only confidently usable for years of birth for which everyone involved is likely to be dead—yet still subject to the Social Security limitation of only being usable for cohorts who mostly registered for a program not created until the mid-1930s. The potential for misleading results is especially high for birth cohorts in which many people are still alive in light of the varying life expectancies by sex, race, social class, and other factors that are likely to also influence name choice: If all the men of a birth year are deceased but only 95 percent of the women are, the Death Index will systematically provide too low a prevalence of names given mostly to girls that year and too high a prevalence for many names given mostly to boys.

In addition, the Social Security Administration has considerably restricted access to the Death Index in recent years out of concerns that its availability facilitated fraud.[26] Although the Death Index is still maintained, public releases do not include information about anyone who died after 2014. Because any birth years for which one can safely assume mortality by 2014 are already available in the census figures, which have greater coverage and the ability to isolate those born in the United States, the analyses in this book prefer the census for the relevant eras. However, the Death Index figures get some background use; it was, for example, one source used to check the plausibility of the imputed counts of how many names in the Social Security data saw too few instances to be released in the main SSA source.

The presence of the two data sources, census and SSA, covering different eras can leave an awkward breakpoint at which one switches between the two samples. For the years from 1880 through 1950, both sources are available, though with the Social Security coverage being increasingly tenuous as one considers earlier parts of that period. The rules followed for choosing which data source to draw on was as follows:

1. Within any figure, use a single, consistent data source if possible.
2. If both sources are available for the period under study, use the census.

That is, the strategy for any one figure is to use the more complete census figures if both sources cover the entire period being examined, but (for internal consistency within a figure) to use the Social Security numbers throughout figures that include the recent decades for which the census tallies are as yet unavailable.

The main exception from using one data source for any given figure—the main case where the "if possible" part of rule 1 binds—arises in chapter 3's discussion of the presidency, which attempts to cover the entire sweep of U.S. independence, from the 1700s into the 2000s, to compare the popularity of presidential names across time. In that case, Social Security registrations are completely unavailable for the early decades of the sample and census returns are equally unavailable for the last decades, so that an awkward transition is necessary. Following rule 2 about preferring the census when both are available, census figures are the source of choice until 1950, after which point the Social Security figures become the source. This excludes people born between April 1, 1950 (the official date of the seventeenth census of the United States), and January 1, 1951 (the first birth date for which someone would show up as a 1951 birth in the SSA numbers), so figures for 1950 are less reliable in that portion of chapter 3's discussion.

Fortunately, the results are generally similar if other points are chosen to transition between the two data sources in this instance. Indeed, in most cases, the two sources appear to correspond quite closely in broad strokes over the period for which they overlap, but some circumstances can cause the two sources to provide different numbers. As a concrete example, consider the names *Emmeline* and *Christabel*, the two most prominent of the many politically activist women of the British Pankhurst family (with Emmeline Pankhurst being Christabel's mother). The Pankhursts campaigned for many issues over the years, rising to prominence for their militancy in support of women's suffrage and later barnstorming in support of Britain's efforts in World War I. They were intensely controversial figures, not just for their support of gender equality but also for their use of tactics ranging from hunger strikes to violent destruction, and their fame (or notoriety) extended to the United States, where mother and daughter made repeated lecture tours in the early twentieth century. Indeed, news reports would occasionally refer to them by first name alone and seem to expect that readers would recognize who was being discussed without any further cues. One might then want to explore—how much and how favorable—of an impression they made in the United States: It is plausible that potential name-givers would avoid association with such contentious figures, or that they would be inspired by support for the cause (or causes) to name their children after such leaders.

However, they make for particularly hard namesakes to track in the data. They are longish names, more complicated to transcribe than shorter ones would be, with other names potentially tempting the unwary census enumerator: *Emily* and *Emma* can easily affect the spelling of *Emmeline*—indeed, *Emmaline* was actually more common than *Emmeline* was—and *Belle* can similarly inflect *Christabel*. *Emmeline* and *Christabel* are also easy to misrender because neither name ever became very popular in the United States, despite or because of their literary associations, which adds other complications to measurement.[27] Even if spelled correctly, such unusual names are particularly likely to disappear behind the five instances per year minimum in the Social Security figures, concealing the trajectory of the name's use—and making it look more distinct from the pattern seen in the census figures. In addition, the period of greatest interest for studying views of the Pankhursts occurred well before the Social Security Act passed, when the SSA's coverage of names is spottier than it is for people born later on.

To indicate differences in how these names appear in the two data sources, figure A.4 shows their implied popularity from 1900 to 1940, the census data in solid lines and Social Security figures in dashed lines. The Social Security figures, having smaller samples of names (especially

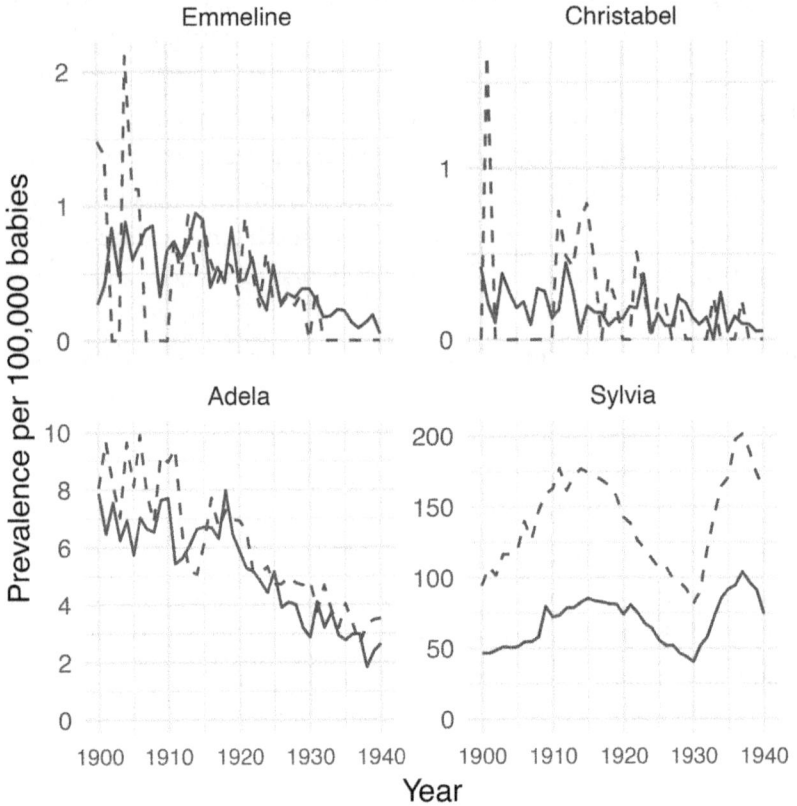

FIGURE A.4 Frequency of use of Pankhurst names, 1900–1940, in census (solid line) and Social Security (dashed line) data.

in the first part of this period) and no reporting of rare names, are decidedly more volatile than the census numbers. Still, the numbers from the two sources roughly track one another. Both for instance show a decline in the use of *Emmeline* between 1920 and 1940.

By contrast, the names of two other prominent Pankhurst women, Christabel's sisters *Adela* and *Sylvia*, were relatively popular. To be clear, this popularity was not solely because they were Pankhurst names: Adela was probably the least known of the family in the United States, despite being a prominent Australian radical, and *Sylvia*'s ascent in name popularity began long before Sylvia Pankhurst was on the scene. These names' greater prevalence smooths the volatility in figure A.4, so they see more identifiably similar trends across the two data sets. *Adela* holds roughly steady for the first years of the century before going into decline from 1920 on. *Sylvia* had more dramatic swings, but in both sources it begins by following the usual arc for a trendy girls' name, rising to a peak in the 1910s before fading, then has an unusual if fleeting bounce back into even greater heights of popularity in the 1930s, perhaps in response to the success in entertainment of women who had been born during *Sylvia*'s first wave. (Sylvia Sidney was a movie actress whose leading-lady stardom almost exactly parallels *Sylvia*'s 1930s success, and Sylvia Froos was a child vaudeville sensation who began recording songs around 1930, for instance.)

Though *Sylvia*'s over-time trend is common to both census and Social Security, the name consistently appears more popular in the Social Security figures. The reason of the disparity is not completely provable, but the obvious source is the frequent use of childhood nicknames in the census records but names used as adults for Social Security information for this era: *Sylvie* occurs vastly more often in the census, following the frequent model of names getting childlike variants ending in -*y* or -*ie*.[28] This more generally suggests that the more commonly a name is reduced to a childhood diminutive, the more it will be undercounted in the census tallies (unless, as with *Early*, it is being counted when it is not wanted).[29] As long as the proportion of children with a particular name who reverted to nicknames held roughly constant over time, the census measure should be internally consistent even if it underreports the official, formal name relative to the Social Security data—but that consistency includes a downward bias.

Even with *Sylvia*-style occasional disagreements between the two sources, however, they are consistent in what would be the central point of the analysis here: None of these names shows a clear effect of Pankhurst prominence. It might be possible if one squints to discern an increase in use of *Emmeline* and *Christabel* in the early 1910s, at a time when they made repeated North American speaking tours, but it is too ambiguous to stand out from the names' general variation, and it is not obvious that the timing of the uptick would be when one would predict it based on the Pankhursts' activities and press coverage. What matters for present purposes, though, is that no distinct sign of a politics-driven change in naming turns up in one of the data sources but not the other.

Although the vast majority of the information examined comes from either the census or the Social Security information, some examples draw on other sources. Chapter 1, in its exposition of the era before either the census or Social Security provides coverage, obviously must do so, but even for some later questions alternative sources are occasionally used to supplement the main analysis. This is mostly so in the discussions of specific people, as when chapter 2 looks into the ancestry of Guiteau Powell to confirm that *Guiteau* was a family name. These sources are, bar the occasional gravestone, contemporaneous records of birth, which circumvent some of the problems of name drift. Chapter 1 primarily looks at records of births and baptisms, which in the 1700s and 1800s were mostly collected by churches. Official, standardized birth certificates did not come into wide use until later—as late as the 1930s in some states, and even after legal requirements were in place, prompt registration of babies was not universal for some time.[30] Both the church and the civil birth records are only sometimes available today, even if they were originally collected: The collection of states, or counties, or parishes that assembled and preserved such records, and then made them public record, is haphazard. As chapter 1 notes, availability tends to be greater in the northern reaches of the country than in the South, which is why that chapter focuses on New England when considering statistical patterns in the 1700s.

Not only is New England a nonrepresentative part of the country—past studies of its early naming culture have emphasized that it was particularly partial to biblical names, likely because of the Puritan history—it is also relatively small. In the pre-1840 period that is the focus of chapter 1, the population was even smaller than it later was, which means fewer births, which tends to mean particularly volatile statistics: A single person with a particular name affects the prevalence much more than one would in most of the book's results. In consequence, the figures in that chapter (and again when looking at *New York Times* obituaries, another case when the sample is far smaller than in any of the census or Social Security explorations) include smoothed averages in addition to or in place of the raw annual rates used elsewhere.[31]

Notwithstanding their smaller sample sizes, these alternative sources occasionally allow for examination of topics impossible with the census and Social Security data. Middle names are a case in point. Neither of the main sources consistently provides middle names, and the annual Social Security lists used for recent decades never do. It is not even possible to infer much from the absence of a middle name or initial in the census, because for most of the period reliant on census data here, middle names existed in the United States but were not particularly common, let alone universal. This is most often demonstrated by pointing to the roster of presidents; only three of the first seventeen presidents had middle names (*Quincy* for the younger president Adams, *Henry* for the elder Harrison, and *Knox* for Polk). Even into the twentieth century, not all presidents had middle names (Theodore Roosevelt lacked one, but presidents have consistently had middle names since William Howard Taft).[32] The rarity of presidential middle names is especially telling because presidents tended to be drawn from the upper social classes, the segment of society that embraced middle names first.[33] In any case, middle names were sufficiently newfangled that in parts of the country it was an open legal question until the second half of the twentieth century whether the middle name had any meaningful role in personal identification at all.[34] A census record that includes no middle name may then mean that no such name existed or that it existed but was not reported—or that the legal middle name was what was given as the first name.

This does not discount the potential value of looking at middle names: I argue elsewhere that they provide special opportunities for examining politics and society because they allow name-givers to choose a name that is somewhat less visible to others and hence less subject to social pressures to be conventional.[35] However, middle names may be less informative for historical than for contemporary analysis, because even when they were present, they often, back in the day, followed their own rules. The presidents are again indicative, with several of their middle names—not just *Knox* but *Birchard, Woodrow, Delano, Fitzgerald, Baines, Milhous, Wilson,* and the senior Bush's *Walker*—being maiden names of the respective holders' mothers. If grandmothers' maiden names are included, add *Quincy* and *Robinette* to the list, as well as the junior Bush's *Walker.* In all, almost half of the presidents who have had middle names had names in this category of mother's or grandmother's maiden name. That was characteristic of middle names, reflecting their original use to indicate family ties among aristocrats. It is a particularly strong convention among the quasi-aristocratic cohort of upper-class men who tended to become president, but it was relatively common in middle names from all social strata relative to first names.

A different set of social rules for selecting middle names could in principle provide information separate from and expanding on first names, but the social rules in question often end up leaving middle names less expressive of most political identities, restricting middle names' use for this book. Given this limitation, and for consistency with the discussions of census and Social Security results where middle names are only patchily available, I mostly set aside middle names even when looking at birth records that consistently record middle names. For example, when looking at the number of babies named *Royal* in the book's opening, the tallies only count those whose first name that was, not cases when it was the middle name. The exception, as noted, is cases in the census data when the first name is reduced to an initial in the record, suggesting that the middle name is the most relevant identifier.

"Counting people with a particular name" might not be a project that immediately suggests the need for tortuous methodological detail, even in arcane academic contexts. Names, after all, have for generations been relatively well recorded in United States public records, so as a characteristic they ought to be simpler to count than many others might; compare trying to tally information about individuals' sexual orientation. And it is true that relatively complete information is available. But, as this appendix suggests, even the relatively straightforward tasks of defining and tallying names can at times require judgment calls, as measuring most aspects of society ultimately does.

NOTES

ACKNOWLEDGMENTS

1. I have no particular animus against *Chisholm v. Georgia* and no explanation why that was the politics-adjacent concept that popped into my head. Maybe the child could go by *Lev* and everyone would think the eponym was Tolstoy?

INTRODUCTION

1. Such a claim for Roosevelt's popularity appears, for example, in Darrell Hartman, *Battle of Ink and Ice: A Sensational Story of News Barons, North Pole Explorers, and the Making of Modern Media* (Penguin, 2023), 140.
2. With apologies to the theologies for which nothing is beyond Theodore Roosevelt's allure.
3. George Beam, *The Problem with Survey Research* (Transaction Publishers, 2012).
4. Eugene J. Webb, Donald T. Campbell, Richard D. Schwartz, and Lee Sechrest. *Unobtrusive Measures* (Sage, 1999).
5. Emilia Aldrin, "Names and Identity," in *The Oxford Handbook of Names and Naming*, ed. Carole Hough (Oxford University Press, 2016), 382–94.
6. Michael Wolffsohn and Thomas Brechenmacher, "Nomen Est Omen: The Selection of First Names as an Indicator for Public Opinion in the Past," *International Journal of Public Opinion Research* 13, no. 2 (2001): 116–39. Stanley Lieberson's *A Matter of Taste: How Names, Fashions, and Culture Change* (Yale University Press, 2000) is another landmark

work using names to analyze social trends and sentiments, though it is relatively uncon-
cerned with political questions.

7. Joke's on you, nineteenth-century parents!

8. Joseph Kasof, "Sex Bias in the Naming of Stimulus Persons," *Psychological Bulletin* 113,
no. 1 (1993): 140–63; Simon M. Laham, Peter Koval, and Adam L. Alter, "The Name-
Pronunciation Effect: Why People Like Mr. Smith More Than Mr. Colquhoun,"
Journal of Experimental Social Psychology 48, no. 3 (2012): 752–56.

9. As one eighteenth-century epigrammatist put it, "I am thankful that my name is obnoxious to no pun." William Shenstone, *The Works in Verse and Prose of William Shenstone,
Esq., Most of Which Were Never Before Printed* (London, 1764), 2:154. Joshua R. Goldstein
and Guy Stecklov, "From Patrick to John F.: Ethnic Names and Occupational Success
in the Last Era of Mass Migration," *American Sociological Review* 81, no. 1 (2016): 85–106;
David E. Kalist and Daniel Y. Lee, "First Names and Crime: Does Unpopularity Spell
Trouble?" *Social Science Quarterly* 90, no. 1 (2009): 39–49; Katheryn Meagher, "Name Dis-
crimination in the Recruitment Process by Recruiters," *International Journal of Social
Science Studies* 3, no. 6 (2015): 20–34.

10. Alexander McQueen, *How to Name Baby without Handicapping It for Life: A Practical Guide for Parents and All Others Interested in "Better Naming"* (McQueen Publish-
ing, 1922). Annotated compendia of given names were not unusual in the 1800s, but
they mostly aimed less at name-givers than at scholars looking into specific contexts (the Bible, Shakespeare, colonial Pennsylvania, and so on). Exceptions from
the United States include Mrs. M. J. Stockwell, *What Shall We Name It? A Dictionary of Baptismal Names for Children, Containing 2,000 Names with Their Meaning and
the Countries from Which They Originated* (New York, 1844), and Julian McCormick,
*The Child's Name: A Collection of Nearly Five Hundred Uncommon and Beautiful
Names for Children; with An Introduction on the Tasteful Use of Christian Names* (New
York, 1899).

11. Richard D. Alford, *Naming and Identity: A Cross-Cultural Study of Personal Naming
Practices* (HRAF Press, 1988).

12. John E. Murray, "Generation(s) of Human Capital: Literacy in American Families,
1830–1875," *Journal of Interdisciplinary History* 27, no. 3 (1997): 413–35.

13. Alford, *Naming and Identity*, 129. From 1917 to 1983, Canon 761 of the Roman Catholic
church's code of canon law prescribed that the pastor when baptizing should add a saint's
name when the name was otherwise insufficiently Christian. That suggests some possibility of nonparental naming, at least for the baptismal name. Since 1983, the relevant
canon is number 855, which less specifically requires that the godparents and pastor "take
care that a name foreign to Christian sensibility is not given."

14. Andrew Arno, "Personal Names as Narrative in Fiji: Politics of the Lauan Onomasti-
con," *Ethnology* 33, no. 1 (1994): 21–34; Mutshinyani Mercy Mahwasane and Thambat-
shira Johannes Tshifaro, "New-Born Baby Naming Practices of the Vhaveṇḍa: A
Sociolinguistic Analysis Perspective," *South African Journal of African Languages* 39,

no. 2 (2019): 175–84; Susan M. Suzman, "Names as Pointers: Zulu Personal Naming Practices," *Language in Society* 23, no. 2 (1994): 253–72.

15. She often went by *Prockie.*

16. There was also at least one *Southern Rights* and an *Equal Rights* (whose father fought for the Confederacy, so *Equal* may be a misnomer for some frames of reference).

17. Winfield Scott also played a role in injecting *Scott* into the United States namescape. Although the name had long been in circulation, its popularity first boomed in the late 1840s and early 1850s, following Scott's exploits in the Mexican-American War. At that time, the name was given to hundreds, perhaps even thousands, more babies than the trend might otherwise have suggested. Even though that burst of popularity waned, the name remained more popular than it had been before the war and seeded many more fathers and grandfathers named *Scott* for future generations to name children after.

18. Even moral philosophers have gotten into the act. See Eldar Sarajlic, "The Ethics and Politics of Child Naming," *Journal of Applied Philosophy* 35, no. SI (2018): 121–39.

19. Superlative examples include Nancy Man's baby-name history blog at https://www.nancy .cc or Laura Wattenberg's broader but often history-focused https://namerology.com.

20. For an overview of toponymy, or the study of place names, see Reuben Rose-Redwood, Derek Alderman, and Maoz Azaryahu, "Geographies of Toponymic Inscription: New Directions in Critical Place-Name Studies," *Progress in Human Geography* 34, no. 4 (2010): 453–70. (The most widespread technical terms for the study of naming people, as this book focuses on, are *anthroponymy* or *anthroponomastics.*) Examples involving the naming of pets include Ernest L. Abel, "Birds Are Not More Human Than Dogs: Evidence from Naming," *Names* 55, no. 4 (2007): 349–53; Mary B. Harris, "Some Factors Influencing Selection and Naming of Pets," *Psychological Reports* 53, no. 3 (1983): 1163–70; and Cynthia Whissell, "Emotion in the Sounds of Pets' Names," *Perceptual and Motor Skills* 102, no. 1 (2006): 121–24; those involving company names include Kee-Hong Bae and Wei Wang, "What's in a 'China' Name? A Test of Investor Attention Hypothesis," *Financial Management* 41, no. 2 (2012): 429–55; T. Clifton Green and Russell Jame, "Company Name Fluency, Investor Recognition, and Firm Value," *Journal of Financial Economics* 109, no. 3 (2013): 813–34; Dawn G. Gregg and Steven Walczak, "Dressing Your Online Auction Business for Success: An Experiment Comparing Two eBay Businesses," *MIS Quarterly* 32, no. 3 (2008): 653–70. This is not an exhaustive list of names that scholars scrutinize. Names for ships and airplanes, names for corporate products, names for astronomical bodies, names for fictional characters: all have been examined for what they say about humans and society.

21. Gregory Clark, *The Son Also Rises: Surnames and the History of Social Mobility* (Princeton University Press, 2014); Paul A. Longley, Justin van Dijk, and Tian Lan, "The Geography of Intergenerational Social Mobility in Britain," *Nature Communications* 12, no. 1 (2021): 6050.

22. Xiaoying Qi, "Neo-Traditional Child Surnaming in Contemporary China: Women's Rights as Veiled Patriarchy," *Sociology* 52, no. 5 (2018): 1001–16; David R. Johnson and

Laurie K. Scheuble, "What Should We Call Our Kids? Choosing Children's Surnames When Parents' Last Names Differ," *Social Science Journal* 39, no. 3 (2002): 419–29.

23. Alberta Fabbricotti, "The Transmission of the Mother's Surname Under the CEDAW," *Diritti Umani e Diritto Internazionale* 2 (2017): 465–76.

24. Meltem Türköz, *Naming and Nation-Building in Turkey: The 1934 Surname Law* (Palgrave Macmillan, 2017).

25. Betsy Rymes, "Naming as Social Practice: The Case of Little Creeper from Diamond Street," *Language in Society* 25, no. 2 (1996): 237–60.

26. For example, Charles Allen Brown, "Symbolic Annihilation of Social Groups as Hidden Curriculum in Japanese ELT Materials," *TESOL Quarterly* 56, no. 2 (2022): 603–28.

27. Raja Jayaraman, "Personal Identity in a Globalized World: Cultural Roots of Hindu Personal Names and Surnames," *Journal of Popular Culture* 38, no. 3 (2005): 476–90.

28. Jorida Cila and Richard N. Lalonde, "What's in a Name? Motivations for Baby-Naming in Multicultural Contexts," in *Contemporary Language Motivation Theory: 60 Years Since Gardner and Lambert (1959)*, ed. Ali H. Al-Hoorie and Peter D. MacIntyre (Multilingual Matters, 2020), 130–52.

29. Terhi Ainiala, "Names in Society," in *The Oxford Handbook of Names and Naming*, ed. Carole Hough (Oxford University Press, 2016), 371–81; Mark Elchardus and Jessy Siongers, "First Names as Collective Identifiers: An Empirical Analysis of the Social Meanings of First Names," *Cultural Sociology* 5, no. 3 (2011): 403–22; J. Eric Oliver, Thomas Wood, and Alexandra Bass, "Liberellas versus Konservatives: Social Status, Ideology, and Birth Names in the United States," *Political Behavior* 38, no. 1 (2016): 55–81. A prominent European analogue is the emergence of the déclassé name *Kevin* across the continent after the release of the American film *Home Alone*. See Gerrit Bloothooft and David Onland, "Socioeconomic Determinants of First Names," *Names* 59, no. 1 (2011): 25–41.

30. Stanley Lieberson and Eleanor O. Bell, "Children's First Names: An Empirical Study of Social Taste," *American Journal of Sociology* 98, no. 3 (1992): 511–54.

31. Oliviu Felecan and Alina Bugheşiu, ed., *Names and Naming: Multicultural Aspects* (Palgrave Macmillian, 2021).

32. Trevor Burnard, "Slave Naming Patterns: Onomastics and the Taxonomy of Race in Eighteenth-Century Jamaica," *Journal of Interdisciplinary History* 31, no. 3 (2001): 325–46; Jerome S. Handler and JoAnn Jacoby. "Slave Names and Naming in Barbados, 1650–1830," *William and Mary Quarterly* 53, no. 4 (1996): 685–728; John C. Inscoe, "Carolina Slave Names: An Index to Acculturation," *Journal of Southern History* 49, no. 4 (1983): 527–54; Iman Makeba Laversuch, "Runaway Slave Names Recaptured: An Investigation of the Personal First Names of Fugitive Slaves Advertised in the *Virginia Gazette* between 1736 and 1776," *Names* 54, no. 4 (2006): 331–62; "Old Slave Names," *Atlantic Monthly* 66, no. 395 (1897): 428.

33. Susan Benson, "Injurious Names: Naming, Disavowal, and Recuperation in Contexts of Slavery and Emancipation," in *The Anthropology of Names and Naming*, ed. Gabriele vom Bruck and Barbara Bodenhorn (Cambridge University Press, 2006), 177–99; Lisa D.

Cook, Trevon D. Logan, and John M. Parman, "Distinctively Black Names in the American Past," *Explorations in Economic History* 53 (2014): 64–82.

34. Joey L. Dillard, ed. *Black Names* (Mouton, 1976); Roland G. Fryer Jr. and Steven D. Levitt, "The Causes and Consequences of Distinctively Black Names," *Quarterly Journal of Economics* 119, no. 3 (2004): 767–805. The distinction is stark enough that race is often confidently inferred from names: S. Michael Gaddis, "How Black Are Lakisha and Jamal? Racial Perceptions from Names Used in Correspondence Audit Studies," *Sociological Science* 4 (2017): 469–89.

35. For example, Elizabeth L. Compton, *An Exploratory Analysis of Personal Naming Practices of Western North American Indians* (MS thesis, West Virginia University, 2004); Linda E. Dick Bissonnette, "Indian Names and Naming Practices in the Sierra Nevada Foothills," *Journal of California and Great Basin Anthropology* 21, no. 1 (1999): 6–16.

36. Abraham D. Lavender, "United States Ethnic Groups in 1790: Given Names as Suggestions of Ethnic Identity," *Journal of American Ethnic History* 9, no. 1 (1989): 36–66; Daniel A. Nakashima, "A Rose by Any Other Name: Names, Multiracial/Multiethnic People, and the Politics of Identity," in *The Sum of Our Parts: Mixed-Heritage Asian Americans*, ed. Teresa Williams-León, Cynthia L. Nakashima, and Michael Omi (Temple University Press, 2001), 111–19.

37. Rajend Mesthrie, "Sociolinguistic Patterns and Names: A Variationist Study of Changes in Personal Names among Indian South Africans," *Language in Society* 50, no. 1 (2021): 7–28. For a sample of discussions among various U.S. immigrant groups and historical moments, see Ran Abramitzky, Leah Boustan, and Katherine Eriksson, "Do Immigrants Assimilate More Slowly Today Than in the Past?" *American Economic Review: Insights* 2, no. 1 (2020): 125–41; Maryann Parada, "Sibling Variation and Family Language Policy: The Role of Birth Order in the Spanish Proficiency and First Names of Second-Generation Latinos," *Journal of Language, Identity & Education* 12, no. 5 (2013): 299–320; Monibo A. Sam, "Maintaining Links with the Homeland through Marriage and Naming: An Exploratory Study among Nigerian Immigrants in the US," *African Diaspora* 10, no. 1–2 (2018): 72–91; Marvin G. Slind, "Child Naming Patterns as an Indication of Assimilation: A Case Study in Eastern Washington's Selbu Community," *Journal of Family History* 46, no. 2 (2021): 191–210; Christina A. Sue and Edward E. Telles, "Assimilation and Gender in Naming," *American Journal of Sociology* 112, no. 5 (2007): 1383–415.

38. Pedro Carneiro, Sokbae Lee, and Hugo Reis, "Please Call Me John: Name Choice and the Assimilation of Immigrants in the United States, 1900–1930," *Labour Economics* 62 (2020): 101778; Vasiliki Fouka, "Backlash: The Unintended Effects of Language Prohibition in US Schools after World War I," *Review of Economic Studies* 87, no. 1 (2020): 204–39; Jürgen Gerhards and Silke Hans, "From Hasan to Herbert: Name-Giving Patterns of Immigrant Parents between Acculturation and Ethnic Maintenance," *American Journal of Sociology* 114, no. 4 (2009): 1102–28; Jürgen Gerhards and Julia Tuppat, "Gendered Pathways to Integration: Why Immigrants' Naming Practices Differ by the Child's Gender," *Kölner Zeitschrift für Soziologie und Sozialpsychologie* 72, no. 4 (2020): 597–625; Sue and Telles, "Assimilation and Gender."

39. Gendered names are traditional in the United States as well. That guide to not handicapping baby for life has seven main commandments, one of which is that a personal name "should indicate the sex of the child beyond a doubt" (McQueen, *How to Name Baby*, 19).

40. For example, see Iceland's *Lög um mannanöfn* [Law on personal names] (1996 nr. 45 17. maí), Denmark's *Navneloven* [Name law], §13(2), or Germany's 1980 *Allgemeine Verwaltungsvorschrift zum Gesetz über die Änderung von Familiennamen und Vornamen* [General administrative regulation on the law on changing surnames and first names] §67. vom 11. August 1980.

41. For example, Xiaopeng Du, Mengchen Dong, Dian Gu, Zhiyong Xin, Jiang Jiang, and Yan Sun, "Difficult Name, Cold Man: Chinese Names, Gender Stereotypicality and Trustworthiness," *International Journal of Psychology* 56, no. 3 (2021): 349–60 [in Chinese]; Jeroen van de Weijer, Guangyuan Ren, Joost van de Weijer, Weiyun Wei, and Yumeng Wang, "Gender Identification in Chinese Names," *Lingua* 234 (2020): 102759 [in Chinese]. In contemporary North America, too, a name's sound varies by sex. See Kimberly Wright Cassidy, Michael H. Kelly, and Lee'at J. Sharoni, "Inferring Gender from Name Phonology," *Journal of Experimental Psychology: General* 128, no. 3 (1999): 362–81; Anne Saxon Slater and Saul Feinman, "Gender and the Phonology of North American First Names," *Sex Roles* 13, no. 7 (1985): 429–40.

42. Lucía Santamaría and Helena Mihaljević, "Comparison and Benchmark of Name-to-Gender Inference Services," *PeerJ Computer Science* 4 (2018): e156; Kamil Wais, "Gender Prediction Methods Based on First Names with genderizeR," *R Journal* 8, no. 1 (2016): 17–37. Even young children infer gender from names. See Patricia J. Bauer and Molly J. Coyne, "When the Name Says It All: Preschoolers' Recognition and Use of the Gendered Nature of Common Proper Names," *Social Development* 6, no. 3 (1997): 271–91.

43. Alice S. Rossi, "Naming Children in Middle-Class Families," *American Sociological Review* 30, no. 4 (1965): 499–513; Lieberson, *A Matter of Taste*.

44. Wilbur Zelinsky, "Cultural Variation in Personal Name Patterns in the Eastern United States," *Annals of the Association of American Geographers* 60, no. 4 (1970): 747. Zelinsky proceeds to list several such names he thinks of as ignorable passing fancies. He does not specify who he thinks the namesakes of each name are, leading back to the problem of names having multiple potential sources and therefore being ambiguous. But his list seems to include several presidents (*Washington, McKinley, Roosevelt*, and likely *Franklin* for Franklin Roosevelt, though it is possible that he instead intends that to refer to Benjamin Franklin), along with a couple of war heroes (*Dewey* and *Douglas*, which I take to refer to Douglas MacArthur) and *Booker* as in Booker T. Washington. All of those cavalierly dismissed names are examples I draw on in this book . . . uh-oh.

45. For instance, Lieberson's *A Matter of Taste*, perhaps the single most influential and widely cited book in recent decades on the sociology of names, does not broach the topic in any sustained way except with an example in his concluding chapter speculating on the fate of *Monica* in the aftermath of its having been engulfed in a presidential sex scandal— the Lewinsky-Clinton affair—shortly before he published his analysis. He was unsure

whether its newfound familiarity would outweigh its potential taint; in the event, it did not, as chapter 5 of this book shows.

46. Barbara Bodenhorn and Gabriele vom Bruck, "'Entangled in Histories:' An Introduction to the Anthropology of Names and Naming," in *The Anthropology of Names and Naming*, ed. Gabriele vom Bruck and Barbara Bodenhorn (Cambridge University Press, 2006), 1–30; Katja M. Guenther, "The Politics of Names: Rethinking the Methodological and Ethical Significance of Naming People, Organizations, and Places," *Qualitative Research* 9, no. 4 (2009): 411–21.

47. Valerie Alia has explored this theme in several works. See, for example, *Names and Nunavut: Culture and Identity in Arctic Canada* (Berghahn Books, 2009).

48. Most *Wilmot Proviso*s were born before the Civil War, which fits with when the Wilmot Proviso was a live issue (be honest: do you even remember what the proviso is these days?). But John and Rachael Ragsdale of Birmingham, Iowa, decided to name their son that in 1878; some records suggest he usually went by *Pro*, although the 1880 Census has him as *Wilmot*. He in turn named his son Wilmot Proviso Junior; Wilmot *fils* lived until 2009, so the name's run in use outlasted the twentieth century. Because I used *States Rights* as the contrasting Southern example, I suppose I should also mention that it also endured into the 2000s through one States Rights Aycock (1933–2007), who shared a name with his great-uncle.

49. In some societies, name choices for explicitly political reasons occasionally become more prevalent. See Robert K. Herbert, "The Politics of Personal Naming in South Africa," *Names* 45, no. 1 (1997): 3–17; "Personal Names as Social Protest: The Status of African Political Names," *Names* 47, no. 2 (1999): 109–24.

50. Štěpán Jurajda and Dejan Kovač, "Names and Behavior in a War," *Journal of Population Economics* 34, no. 1 (2021): 1–33; Katharina Leibring, "Given Names in European Naming Systems," in *The Oxford Handbook of Names and Naming*, ed. Carole Hough (Oxford University Press, 2016), 209–12. Similarly, communist areas such as the former Soviet Union saw widespread naming after Marx and Lenin. See Edwin D. Lawson and Irina Glushkovskaya, "Naming Patterns of Recent Immigrants from the Former Soviet Union to Israel," *Names* 42, no. 3 (1994): 157–80. It is also easy throughout the developing world to find leaders named after communist leaders, such as *Marx* Nekongo, who served in Namibia's Parliament from 1998 to 2015; *Lenín* Moreno, the president of Ecuador from 2017 to 2021; or M. K. *Stalin*, chief minister of the Indian state of Tamil Nadu as of 2024 (for whom, following Tamil naming conventions, *Stalin* is the given name; *Muthuvel Karunanidhi* was the father's name and in the son's name is a patronymic). On the other side of political extremism is the popularity of *Hitler* as a name among Africans. Trevor Noah's *Born a Crime: Stories from a South African Childhood* (Spiegel & Grau, 2016), 194–96. One of my colleagues similarly reports that Hitler Vagner Cândido de Oliveira, a municipal councilor in the city of Juiz de Fora, Brazil, had an absurdly catchy name-based campaign jingle for someone named *Hitler Vagner*. These sorts of names are not exclusively a developing-world phenomenon, either, though figures such as *Marx*

Dormoy, an important French politician of the interwar years for whom a Paris Métro stop is still named, have been rare outside the fringes in recent decades.

51. Political implications did not disappear overnight. Even in the 1940 Census, seventy-five years after the end of the Civil War, Southern Whites were still notably less keen on *Grant* than Whites elsewhere were. For example, the White population ten and under named *Grant* was at that point as large in Nevada as in Mississippi and South Carolina combined, despite the two Southern states together having more than thirty times as many White children.

52. Oliver et al., "Liberellas versus Konservatives."

53. Some formal statistical tests will happen along the way to illustrate that names allow the possibility (and secondarily because academic peer review is a harsh mistress, demanding propitiation via null-hypothesis significance test), but any inferences are a windfall from thinking about the measurement opportunities.

1. BEGINNINGS (CA. 1760–1800)

1. F. K. Donnelly, "A Possible Source for Nathan Hale's Dying Words," *William and Mary Quarterly* 42, no. 3 (1985): 394–96; Henry Phelps Johnston, *Nathan Hale, 1776: Biography and Memorials* (privately printed, 1901), 126.

2. Boris I. Kolonitskii, "'Revolutionary Names:' Russian Personal Names and Political Consciousness in the 1920s and 1930s," *Revolutionary Russia* 6, no. 2 (1993): 210–28. As Kolonitskii notes, the revolution-tinged names can be indirect acknowledgments, as when the French Revolution spawned a wave of names celebrating classical republican heroes such as *Brutus* or *Scaevola*.

3. Jean M. Twenge, Emodish M. Abebe, and W. Keith Campbell, "Fitting In or Standing Out: Trends in American Parents' Choices for Children's Names, 1880–2007," *Social Psychological and Personality Science* 1, no. 1 (2010): 19–25. This book's chapter 5 includes updated data on name concentration (see figure 5.2).

4. Richard R. Beeman, *Our Lives, Our Fortunes and Our Sacred Honor: The Forging of American Independence, 1774–1776* (Basic Books, 2013), 3–4.

5. The title marquis was sometimes used in Scotland, but even there the English names of the rank had largely taken over by the 1700s.

6. La Fayette was not the only prominent marquis. It is theoretically conceivable that names could have been inspired by figures such as the Enlightenment all-rounder Marquis de Condorcet or the, shall we say, libertarian Marquis de Sade. In support of that possibility of namesakes other than La Fayette, one slightly later Vermont baby was explicitly named *Marquis de Montigny*, perhaps as a conflation of the family name (Lévisse de Montigny) and prospective title of the newly adopted heir of the Marquis de Jaucourt. But a substantial fraction of the *Marquis*es have the middle name *Fayette*, or initials D. L. F., or other indicators highly suggestive that La Fayette was primarily the name's honoree.

7. The set of New England names also includes a pair of *Fayette*s and one *Lafayette*, all from after the Marquis's rise to prominence. La Fayette's personal name was Gilbert du Motier, but that name was less publicized, and *Gilbert* may in any case have lacked some of that French *je ne sais quoi*; it did not immediately see the same increase in usage.

8. Emperor Moseley (or Mosely), of Salem, Massachusetts, shared a name with his grandfather, whose given name was his mother's maiden name: G. Andrews Moriarty Jr., "The Emperour Family of Lower Norfolk County (Concluded)," *Virginia Magazine of History and Biography* 23, no. 4 (1915): 439. So this one-off *Emperor* was unlikely to represent any direct celebration of monarchy, but it is of note that the Moseleys did not feel any need to avoid using the name in 1789. Napoléon Bonaparte, on the other hand, spawned a whole heap of *Napoleon*s and *Bonaparte*s before and after he declared himself emperor, but that occurs slightly after the period covered here.

9. These hortatory names, as they are called, never got as gonzo in the New World Puritan tradition as they did in parts of England, particularly the county of Sussex. The most famous exemplars of Sussex's high-hortatory style are from the Barebone family, where a man named *Praise-God*—a figure of some importance in the English Civil War of the 1600s, and with a brother named *Fear-God*—gave his son the in every sense awe-inspiring name *Unless-Jesus-Christ-Had-Died-For-Thee-Thou-Hadst-Been-Damned*. Rather anticlimactically, that son usually went by *Nicholas* (which, to be fair, was his other given name).

10. Gloria L. Main, "Naming Children in Early New England," *Journal of Interdisciplinary History* 27, no. 1 (1996): 1–27; Daniel Scott Smith, "Continuity and Discontinuity in Puritan Naming: Massachusetts, 1771," *William and Mary Quarterly* 51, no. 1 (1994): 67–91.

11. Yvonne Korshak, "The Liberty Cap as a Revolutionary Symbol in America and France," *Smithsonian Studies in American Art* 1, no. 2 (1987): 53–69.

12. Richard D. Alford, *Naming and Identity: A Cross-Cultural Study of Personal Naming Practices* (HRAF Press, 1988); Bertrand Lisbach and Victoria Meyer, *Linguistic Identity Matching* (Springer, 2013), 28–44. In the context of the United States, these sorts of changing or multiple names are for instance important in many Indigenous cultures: Frank Exner [Little Bear], "North American Indians: Personal Names with Semantic Meaning," *Names* 55, no. 1 (2007): 3–15.

13. Iiro Kajanto, "Women's Praenomina Reconsidered," *Arctos: Acta Philologica Fennica* 7 (1972): 13–30; Benet Salway, "What's in a Name? A Survey of Roman Onomastic Practice from c. 700 B.C. to A.D. 700," *Journal of Roman Studies* 84 (1994): 124–45.

14. G. J. R. Glünicke, "The Women of Korea," *Nineteenth Century and After: A Monthly Review* 56, no. 329 (1904): 42.

15. Samuel Gyasi Obeng, "From Morphophonology to Sociolinguistics: The Case of Akan Hypocoristic Day-Names," *Multilingua* 16, no. 1 (1997): 41. Likewise, Annan's middle name, *Atta*, indicated that he was a twin.

16. Valeria Alia, *Names and Nunavut: Culture and Identity in Arctic Canada* (Berghahn Books, 2009), 20–24.

17. Alford, *Naming and Identity*, 40–45. Alford's book is well worth reading: Among the magnificent variety of naming systems he notes is one, said to be used sometimes among Malays, where the child is placed amid seven bananas inscribed with names. The name on whichever banana the child first reaches for becomes the child's name.

18. Ge Gao, "Shall I Name Her 'Wisdom' or 'Elegance?' Naming in China," *Names* 59, no. 3 (2011): 164–74. Gao also notes a trend early in the history of the People's Republic of China for names flatly describing political aims, with meanings such as *aid Korea* or *cultural revolution*.

19. Björn H. Jernudd, "Personal Names and Human Rights," in *Linguistic Human Rights: Overcoming Linguistic Discrimination*, ed. Tove Skuttnabb-Kangas, Robert Phillipson, and Mart Rannut (Mouton, 1995), 121–34; Anne Lefebvre-Teillard, *Le Nom: Droit et Histoire* [The Name: Law and History] (Presses Universitaires de France, 1990); Sarah D. Warren, "Naming Regulations and Indigenous Rights in Argentina," *Sociological Forum* 30, no. 3 (2015): 764–86. Countries also have laws on the choice of surnames (family names). In Norway, if you wish to change your name to one held by two hundred or fewer Norwegians, you must get permission from every last one of those other people with the surname. See Lov om personnavn [Law on personal names], LOV-2002-06-07-19, §3. Denmark has a similar law: Navneloven [Name law], §4.

20. Carlton F. W. Larson, "Naming Baby: The Constitutional Dimensions of Parental Naming Rights," *George Washington Law Review* 80, no. 1 (2011): 159–201; Thomas E. Murray, "The Law and Newborns' Personal Names in the United States," *Names* 47, no. 4 (1999): 339–64.

21. "Henry Irving Suprenant," *New Britain Herald*, May 6, 2020. Lest I leave anyone out, *Zreinu* and *Xzarweoasz* have another sibling, *Kesla*.

22. Even in 1850 and 1860 when censuses do name most people, some were excluded: The census had separate "Slave Schedules" that only very rarely gave names of the enslaved.

23. Robert Gutman, "The Birth Statistics of Massachusetts during the Nineteenth Century," *Population Studies* 10, no. 1 (1956): 69–94; Susan J. Pearson, *The Birth Certificate: An American History* (University of North Carolina Press, 2021).

24. *Warren* is a particularly popular name demonstrating the ambiguity discussed, but it represents many such names. *Sullivan*, for example, similarly starts appearing as a name around 1775, though at a somewhat lower rate than *Warren* does. As Irish migration was at the time relatively more rare, it might seem to have fewer immediate namesakes, but the brothers John and William Sullivan both gained political prominence as supporters of the pro-independence cause, and Sullivan's Island, in South Carolina, was in 1776 the site of a significant battle.

25. *Benedict* also got some use in the interval between Saratoga and Arnold's unmasking as a traitor, most famously with New York Congressman Benedict Arnold. In that case, it was a family name; the congressman was related to the general. Rather distantly related, as third cousins once removed: The congressman's great-great-grandfather Stephen was

the younger brother of Rhode Island Governor Benedict Arnold, who was the general's great-grandfather.

26. To be clear, Elizabeth Freeman chose Freeman as her surname; she retained her previous given name.

27. The political motivation could also have honored specific people. For example, Nathaniel Freeman led some Massachusetts protests against British policy and served as a general during the war of independence.

28. Sheldon S. Cohen, "Reuben Harvey: Irish Friend of American Freedom," *Quaker History* 88, no. 1 (1999): 22–39.

29. *Reuben* also does trend upward in popularity, though much less dramatically and from a higher base, in the 1780s.

30. *Polly* does echo the first syllables of *politics*, and one could construct a story that the revolution and constitutional upheaval brought the idea of politics to the fore in a way that might have encouraged the use of *Polly*. One could probably not construct that story with a straight face, though. (And *polyarchy*, though it was a term in use in the eighteenth century, is even more dubious as a possible political allusion.)

31. For example, Todd Estes, "Shaping the Politics of Public Opinion: Federalists and the Jay Treaty Debate," *Journal of the Early Republic* 20, no. 3 (2000): 393–422.

32. Richard B. Morris, "John Jay and the New England Connection," *Proceedings of the Massachusetts Historical Society* 80 (1968): 30.

33. Morris, "John Jay," 31.

2. REGIONAL IDENTITIES (CA. 1850-1880)

1. That this history escaped 1980s moviegoers may reflect that they were not the most discerning public; they made a major hit of *Crocodile Dundee II*.

2. The figures in this paragraph (and analogous figures throughout this chapter) do not include West Virginia births as occurring in the Confederacy.

3. *Savannah* could theoretically have had an additional significance for Southerners in that one potential origin of the name of the river (and thence the city and the children) involves an Algonquian root meaning *southern*. The nineteenth century had only a few baby-name books encouraging readers to obsessively pore over name etymologies, though, so this was probably not front and center in most parents' minds.

4. Around 21 percent of the Alabama-born *Savannah*s in the 1880 Census report at least one parent born in Georgia; the proportion rises to 28 percent when considering only White *Savannah*s.

5. The *Oxford English Dictionary* dates the first use of the term *sectionalism* to 1858, and indeed its use did mushroom in the lead-up to the Civil War (and during the war itself). But the term was clearly in circulation before then. It came up, along with multiple invocations of *sectional prejudice* and the like, in President Pierce's inaugural address in 1853, to cite a particularly prominent use. "The field of calm and free

discussion in our country is open, and will always be so, but never has been and never can be traversed for good in a spirit of sectionalism and uncharitableness." *Inaugural Addresses of the Presidents of the United States from George Washington 1789 to George Bush 1989* (Government Printing Office, 1989), 122. The absence of any effort to explain what *sectionalism* meant suggests the concept was already in wide enough use that Pierce expected it to be readily understood. Other sermons and pamphlets using the term can be readily found; appearances in books start appearing regularly in the mid-1840s.

6. Lori D. Bougher, "The Correlates of Discord: Identity, Issue Alignment, and Political Hostility in Polarized America," *Political Behavior* 39, no. 3 (2017): 731–62; Matt Grossmann and David A. Hopkins, *Asymmetric Politics: Ideological Republicans and Group Interest Democrats* (Oxford University Press, 2016).

7. A local fad can arise without any institutionally powerful source. The area around Eureka, South Dakota, had a whole cluster of *Milbert*s in the early twentieth century, even though the rest of the country has somehow resisted the name's charms.

8. Among children the 1880 Census lists as born in Georgia, *Sherman*'s incidence is fifty-one per hundred thousand for those whose race is given as Black or Mulatto and four per hundred among those deemed Whites. Even some of those White *Sherman*s may not represent Southerners endorsing General Sherman. Sherman Lenfestey, for example, was born to parents from England and Canada who had lived in Michigan for many years, and most other sources render Sherman Rozier's name as *Sermon*, suggesting a mishearing by the census-taker.

9. For example, clothing styles. See Mijeong Noh, Meng Li, Kaleb Martin, and Joseph Purpura, "College Men's Fashion: Clothing Preference, Identity, and Avoidance," *Fashion and Textiles* 2, no. 1 (2015): 1–12. The tendency for White avoidance of Black-associated items appears even among small children. Kristin Shutts, Mahzarin R. Banaji, and Elizabeth S. Spelke, "Social Categories Guide Young Children's Preferences for Novel Objects," *Developmental Science* 13, no. 4 (2010): 599–610.

10. Hundreds of *Union*s were born in the mid-1800s. Although many were Southern (and not just among the Black population), proportionally more were not.

11. *Okey*, though, has almost no geographic correlation with use of Oklahoma-invoking names; it occurred at the highest rates in West Virginia. This may relate to *Okie* so often being seen as an insulting epithet for Oklahomans.

12. Relatedly, *Providence* shows up occasionally as a name, notably as the name of a daughter of Roger Williams, the founder of Rhode Island. But, despite occurring elsewhere in the country, the name receives no discernible use among Rhode Islanders after 1776. This may say something about the appeal of the city of Providence. In fairness, members of the Italian immigrant community there did name daughters *Providensa* and *Providenza*.

13. *Nevada*'s ranking as a top-ten name is especially impressive given that it was relatively often a middle name, following *Sierra*, during the period figure 2.2 presents.

14. Most state names other than *Washington* were primarily given to girls. This may less reflect profundities about gendered associations with state-level governments in

federalism than that many state names end in the letter *A*, which is mostly a feminine name ending in English.

15. This would be another manifestation of the point made in the introduction about highly unusual names (such as *Emancipation Proclamation*) having a clearer source than do more prevalent ones.

16. The *Oklahoma* was the 1880 Census's Oklahoma Vandervert of Chariton, Iowa, who was born in Indian Territory, the later Oklahoma, between older and younger siblings born in Iowa—apparently the name commemorated a brief family sojourn.

17. Here and throughout unless otherwise noted, the coding of regions follows that of figure 2.3: The Border states are, from west to east, Oklahoma, Missouri, Kentucky, West Virginia, Maryland, and Delaware.

18. Frederick Merk with the collaboration of Lois Bannister Merk, *Slavery and the Annexation of Texas* (Knopf, 1972).

19. Bryan Santin, Daniel Murphy, and Matthew Wilkens, "Is or Are: The 'United States' in Nineteenth-Century Print Culture," *American Quarterly* 68, no. 1 (2016): 101–24.

20. The census generally does not record place of birth with any more specificity than the state, so looking at finer geographic scales requires the inference that most people listed as being born in the state where they live at the time of the census were born in or near that place of census residence. With that inference, these patterns play out within states, too. Indiana would be a classic example, noted for its north-to-south gradient of different cultures where more southerly populations in the state derived more from and more closely resembled those of Confederate states. See Nicholas P. Lovrich, Byron W. Daynes, and Laura Ginger, "Public Policy and the Effects of Historical-Cultural Phenomena: The Case of Indiana," *Publius* 10, no. 2 (1980): 111–25. In the data from the 1850 through 1880 Censuses, the Indiana counties whose population-weighted centroid is south of 40 degrees north latitude (a dividing line putting Boone, Hamilton, and Montgomery Counties among the forty-two in the north but Henry and Wayne Counties among the fifty in the south) have 177 state names per hundred thousand babies—excluding *Georgia*, *Virginia*, and *Washington* in this calculation as less clearly state-related—versus 113 per hundred thousand in the northern counties. That is more than 50 percent higher in the state's northern counties. Treating latitude as a continuous variable, a regression weighing counties by number of each degree of latitude further south one goes associates with roughly twenty-three more babies per hundred thousand getting state names other than *Georgia*, *Virginia*, and *Washington* (the 95 percent confidence interval on that estimate ranges from six to thirty-nine babies per hundred thousand).

21. Changes starting around 1860 for the Confederate and Border categories could, here and throughout the chapter, be partly induced by the sudden appearance of West Virginia. That was not yet a state in 1850 or 1860, so anyone born there would in those years' censuses have a listed birthplace of Virginia. Starting with the 1870 census, though, the identification of state of birth would usually list West Virginia. (A few census entries helpfully specify that people were born in "Virginia now West Virginia" or the like,

which may also leave some room for some people to have accurately said their children were born in Virginia even though the relevant territory subsequently became West Virginia.) Various attempts to correct for this change produce similar results to those shown, which may not be a surprise given West Virginia's relatively small population relative to the Confederacy or Border states as a whole.

22. Joanne B. Freeman, *The Field of Blood: Violence in Congress and the Road to Civil War* (Farrar, Straus and Giroux, 2018).

23. As *Catch-22* fans will anticipate, *Major* is the most common military-rank name in the data, about a third more common than *General* (which in turn occurs a bit more than three times as frequently as the third most common military name, *Colonel*).

24. Memorializing given names' tendency to arise immediately before fading contrasts with the much-noted pattern that most statues and monuments commemorating the Confederate cause did not appear until decades after the war ended: Heather A. O'Connell, "More than Rocks and Stone: Confederate Monuments, Memory Movements, and Race," *Social Forces* 100, no. 4 (2022): 1479–502. Some of the difference in timing stems from the cost of building expensive monuments amid the devastated postwar economy of the South, but the names may also express distinct aspects of war memory or sectional difference.

25. To be sure, children were named after many major battles. *Antietam, Chickamauga*, and *Gettysburg* are findable in the records, for instance. (*Shiloh*, with its biblical connections, had been in occasional use even before the war, though its use did increase thereafter the associated Civil War battle. Both *Spotsylvania*s I know of were also born before the war.) Battle sites did not seem to be especially gendered, being given as names to either girls or to boys.

26. The honoree of the name was clearer when parents chose the first-and-middle combination *Elmer Ellsworth*, in the fashion of *Fort Sumter*, and this was also a widespread choice: Elmer Ellsworth Brown, Elmer Ellsworth Burns, and Elmer Ellsworth Jones were all prominent authors of the early twentieth century.

27. A Virginian [John Esten Cooke], *The Life of Stonewall Jackson: From Official Papers, Contemporary Narratives, and Personal Acquaintance* (New York, 1863), 17, 108.

28. Ulysses Grant was promoted to full, four-star general in 1866, shortly after the war, and other Union generals from the Civil War attained the rank in the 1880s. The list of included Federal generals includes John C. Frémont, Ulysses Grant, Henry Halleck, George McClellan, George Meade, Philip Sheridan, William Tecumseh Sherman, Winfield Scott, George Thomas, and John E. Wool. See Frederick Phisterer, *Statistical Record of the Armies of the United States* (Charles Scribner's Sons, 1886), 247–48. The corresponding list of Confederate generals includes Richard H. Anderson, Simon Bolivar Buckner, Pierre G. T. Beauregard, Braxton Bragg, Samuel Cooper, Jubal Early, Richard S. Ewell, Nathaniel B. Forrest, Wade Hampton, William J. Hardee, A. P. Hill, Theophilus H. Holmes, Jonathan B. Hood, Thomas J. (Stonewall) Jackson, Albert Sidney Johnston, Joseph E. Johnston, Robert E. Lee, Stephen D. Lee, James Longstreet, Jonathan C. Pemberton, Leonidas Polk, E. Kirby Smith, Alexander P.

Stewart, and Richard Taylor. See Robert Crooke Wood, *Confederate Hand-book: A Compilation of Important Data and Other Interesting and Valuable Information Relating to the War between the States, 1861–1865* (New Orleans, 1900), 43. Because the Confederacy had two generals *Johnston* and two generals *Lee*, the twenty-four Confederate generals involve only twenty-two distinct names.

29. This rescaling of each name to one hundred weights each name roughly equally; going by raw numbers of names per hundred thousand babies overwhelmingly tracks the changes in the most common names, especially *Thomas*. The annual average within each region is smoothed using a loess procedure, the same smoother used in chapter 1.

30. General Bragg's first name, *Braxton*, proved more persistent than *Bragg* did, but for consistency the figure focuses on surnames.

31. These names ultimately also derive from John Wilkes, one of the namesakes of Wilkes-Barre (along with his fellow parliamentary supporter of colonial rights Isaac Barré).

32. Thomas Reed Turner, *Beware the People Weeping: Public Opinion and the Assassination of Abraham Lincoln* (Lousiana State University Press, 1991), 90–99.

33. Following the book's standard procedures, reports about *Wilkes* and *Booth* here ignore people whose first name is given as *John*, so the children where the census spells out the full set of given names *John Wilkes Booth*—such as John Wilkes Booth Winston, born in Texas around 1865; John Wilkes Booth Sharp, born in Georgia in 1871; and John Wilkes Booth Wagoner, born in West Virginia around 1873—are excluded. So are a suspicious number of children reported as having given names *John W. B.*, *John W. Booth*, the given-name initials *J. W. B.*, or the like.

34. The post-assassination increase in the gap between the two regions in their rate of *Wilkes* and *Booth* namings is statistically significant at the two-tailed $p < .001$ level.

35. Or so most records suggest. The 1900 Census has him born in April 1866, a year after the assassination. It is also possible that the child was not named at birth, but still.

36. Thomas R. Baker, *The Sacred Cause of Union: Iowa in the Civil War* (University of Iowa Press, 2016); Lindsey R. Peterson, "'Iowa Excelled Them All:' Iowa Local Ladies' Aid Societies on the Civil War Frontier, 1861–1865," *Middle West Review* 3, no. 1 (2016): 49–70.

3. POLITICAL CELEBRITY (CA. 1860–1940)

1. "The Anecdotal Side of Mrs. Cleveland," *Ladies' Home Journal* 15, no. 7 (1898): 1. She also trumped Mark Twain, the series' third subject.

2. Ruth Cleveland had died of diphtheria as a child, so was unable to sue in the way Babe Ruth the baseball player could.

3. Though not totally unknown. The stuntman Kermit Maynard, for example, was born in Indiana in 1897, before the Roosevelts came to national prominence.

4. This is not to imply that pop-culture naming touchstones only arose in the late nineteenth century—the New England birth data used in chapter 1 shows *Emily* first emerging as a popular name in 1794, the year Ann Radcliffe's *The Mysteries of Udolpho*, with

protagonist Emily St. Aubert, became a massive bestseller. *Pamela* and *Clarissa* also experienced eighteenth-century booms as the titular heroines of Samuel Richardson novels. But even mammoth bestsellers such as *Uncle Tom's Cabin* struggled to generate as many namesakes as would even relatively minor films later on.

5. Theda Bara herself indirectly reflects the trend of names deriving from politicians' penumbras. Her birth name was Theodosia Burr Bara, after Vice President Aaron Burr's daughter.

6. The process went both ways. When actors adopt professional names, choices currently trendy with new parents are likely to appeal. For example, the heyday of *Bette* was slightly before Bette Davis's emergence as a celebrity; she (née Ruth Elizabeth) chose the name at the start of her career.

7. For a similar phenomenon in the context of television, see Markus Prior, "News vs. Entertainment: How Increasing Media Choice Widens Gaps in Political Knowledge and Turnout," *American Journal of Political Science* 49, no. 3 (2005): 577–92.

8. Marguerite Cassini, *Never a Dull Moment* (Harper Brothers, 1956), 95–97.

9. For example, Jean H. Baker, *Affairs of Party: The Political Culture of Northern Democrats in the Mid-Nineteenth Century America* (Cornell University Press, 1983); William E. Gienapp, "'Politics Seem to Enter into Everything': Political Culture in the North, 1840–1860," in *Essays on American Antebellum Politics, 1840–1860*, ed. Stephen E. Maizlish and John J. Kushma (Texas A&M University Press, 1982), 14–69.

10. For example, Krzysztof Kułakowski, Piotr Kulczyckia, Krzysztof Misztal, Antoni Dydejczyk, Piotr Gronek, and M. J. Krawczyk, "Naming Boys after U.S. Presidents in 20th Century," *Acta Physica Polonica A* 129, no. 5 (2016): 1038–44; Stanley Lieberson, *A Matter of Taste: How Names, Fashions, and Culture Change* (Yale University Press, 2000), 70–73.

11. Conversely, the people listed in figure 3.2 may not be a complete tally of relevant presidents: *Jefferson* had its biggest peak when Jefferson Davis headed the Confederate states. *Davis* also flourished then.

12. For instance, *Addison* (derived from Adam-son, as *Harrison* comes from Henry-son) and *Benson* were already circulating as names in the United States in the 1700s: notable political examples include New York Lieutenant Governor Addison Gardiner (1797–1883) and Boston Mayor Benson Leavitt (1797–1869).

13. Similar results hold when looking at the logged ratio, rather than the difference, of name prevalence to look at proportional rather than absolute changes in the two-year periods.

14. Other partisan-adjacent names' continued use suggests that declining use of presidential names does not primarily result from polarization, even though recent decades' increasingly negative partisanship might be expected to contribute to name-givers' reluctance to invoke a president in way names that might prejudice others against the child. The timing of the decline would in any case be a surprising fit for polarization-driven story, because presidential names were already rare by the 1950s and 1960s, often seen as a relatively unpolarized era.

15. This possibility relates to what psychologists call mere exposure effects, when having seen a name or word makes it more attractive: Robert B. Zajonc, "Attitudinal Effects of Mere Exposure," *Journal of Personality and Social Psychology* 9, no. 2 (1968): 229–33.
16. For further discussion about Winfield Scott as a namesake, see the introduction.
17. Fillmore was also put forward as the candidate of the moribund Whig Party. The national convention that produced this nomination, however, represented only a small rump of the party, which had already mostly disintegrated. See Michael F. Holt, *The Rise and Fall of the American Whig Party: Jacksonian Politics and the Onset of the Civil War* (Oxford University Press, 2003), 951.
18. If you can call Maryland "middling."
19. Robert Urbatsch, "The American Public's Attention to Politics in Conflict and Crisis, 1880–1963," *Journal of Interdisciplinary History* 46, no. 2 (2015): 225–44.
20. Elizabeth Carlson, "Finding Partisanship Where We Least Expect It: Evidence of Partisan Bias in a New African Democracy," *Political Behavior* 38, no. 1 (2016): 129–54.
21. See also examples as *Cleveland* gaining many fewer new namesakes on Grover Cleveland's second inauguration relative to its tally at his first.
22. In this, naturally, they track the relatively small vote shares for third-party candidates, but do argue against a hypothesis that followers of third-party candidates might be especially passionate and hence disproportionately likely to name children after their favored candidates.
23. Note that this is the actual count, not the usual rate per hundred thousand babies mostly used elsewhere in this book, because the period covered in figure 3.5 is short enough that the number of births remained relatively constant at around 120,000 per month.
24. James A. Garfield, "Pons Asinorum," *New-England Journal of Education* 3, no. 14 (1876): 161.
25. "Garfield on Polygamy," *New York Times*, June 18, 1880.
26. The degree of rise is likely understated here. Recall once more that it was relatively common in the nineteenth century for babies not to be named for weeks to months after their births. Some *Garfield*s who were born in early 1880 thus may reflect his subsequent rise to popularity. Also, the appendix's discussion of inaccuracy of birth years in census records may apply all the more strongly to records of specific months of birth: Vague recollections of specific months of birth likely scramble what were actually later births into earlier months and vice versa, diminishing the differences within the year.
27. Candice Millard, *Destiny of the Republic: A Tale of Madness, Medicine and the Murder of a President* (Anchor, 2011).
28. G. Scott Morgan, Daniel C. Wisneski, and Linda J. Skitka, "The Expulsion from Disneyland: The Social Psychological Impact of 9/11," *American Psychologist* 66, no. 6 (2011): 447–54.
29. Emphasizing how unusual these had been as first names, they were often the presidents' middle names, as in the cases of (Stephen) Grover Cleveland, (Thomas) Woodrow Wilson, and (John) Calvin Coolidge.

30. Monika L. McDermott and Costas Panagopoulos, "Be All that You Can Be: The Electoral Impact of Military Service as an Information Cue," *Political Research Quarterly* 68, no. 2 (2015): 293–305; Albert Somit, "The Military Hero as Presidential Candidate," *Public Opinion Quarterly* 12, no. 2 (1948): 192–200; but see Peter Karsten, "Veteran Electability to the Presidency: A Critique of the Somit Thesis," *Armed Forces & Society* 38, no. 3 (2012): 486–99.

31. Pierce's case may also be worth noting because some names from his inauguration year are unusually likely to reflect personal rather than political sympathy: Pierce witnessed the near-decapitation of his only surviving child, Benjamin, in a train accident between his election and the inauguration.

32. As will Donald Trump, once the naming information becomes available following the start of his second term.

33. As with the military-leadership variable, other choices of coding of these borderline cases does not make a great difference to results.

34. Granted, Franklin Roosevelt looked pretty sickly by his fourth inauguration, and many insiders were relatively confident he did not have long to live. See Robert H. Ferrell, *The Dying President: Franklin D. Roosevelt, 1944–1945* (University of Missouri Press, 1998).

35. Once again, alternative measures produce similar outcomes.

36. The underlying model coefficients for how much presidential names rise over the two years up to inauguration are, for military-veteran status, 18 (standard error [SE] = 9.4; p = .06); for having been elected, 17 (SE = 9.7, p = .09); for being reelected, 2.6 (SE 7.5, p = .73); for being from the South, 9.0 (SE = 7.6, p = .25); for year of inauguration, 7.2 (SE = 3.8, p = 0.06); and for year of inauguration squared, -0.0019 (SE = 0.00099, p = .06); the intercept is -6,812 (SE = 3,607, p = .07). The coefficients for change in name popularity between year of inauguration and four years later are, for size of inauguration peak, -0.82 (SE = 0.11, p = .00); for military-veteran status -19 (SE = 6.4, p = .01); for having been elected, 2.0 (SE = 6.8, p = .77); for being reelected, 16 (SE = 5.0, p = .00); for being from the South, 1.2 (SE = 5.3, p = .82); for having died in office, -3.5 (SE = 7.1, p = .62); for year of inauguration, 1.2 (SE = 2.9, p = .67); and for year of inauguration squared, -0.00034 (SE = 0.00077, p = .66); the intercept is -1,137 (SE = 2,794, p = .69).

37. Less lofty political figures also follow presidents in the variant naming practices discussed earlier: newborns are often given politicians' first names, as with *Adlai* after Grover Cleveland's second vice president, Adlai Stevenson, in 1892, or the name of defeated candidates, such as *Thurman* after Allen Thurman, Cleveland's 1888 running mate and main campaign surrogate in an era when it was considered unseemly for presidential candidates themselves to actively seek votes.

38. Patrick Hanks, Kate Hardcastle, and Flavia Hodges suggest that *Morton* also saw use among Jewish name-givers as an analog for *Moses*. See *A Dictionary of First Names* (Oxford University Press, 2006), 303.

39. Christopher A. Cooper and H. Gibbs Knotts, "Defining Dixie: A State-Level Measure of the Modern Political South," *American Review of Politics* 25 (2004): 25–39.

40. Melanie J. Springer, "Where Is 'The South?' Assessing the Meaning of Geography in Politics," *American Politics Research* 47, no. 5 (2019): 1100–34.

41. The Oklahoma governor was not closely related to the South Carolina (or Tennessee) Haskells. His set of Haskells mostly lived in New England, though the governor was born in Ohio.

4. FOREIGN AFFAIRS (CA. 1898–1990)

1. This fits in with a broader tendency to name children after those, including relatives and acquaintances as well as public figures, slain in war: Nicolas Todd and Baptiste Coulmont, "Naming for Kin during World War I: Baby Names as Markers for War," *Journal of Interdisciplinary History* 52, no. 1 (2021): 55–67.

2. Colin Powell and Joseph Persico, *My American Journey* (Random House, 1995), 13.

3. *Jasper* followed a similar trajectory as a boy's name, though by most accounts the given name *Jasper* is etymologically unrelated to the name for the gem, deriving instead from the Persian word for *treasurer*.

4. Associating one's baby with a place of shocking defeat might be surprising, and it may not have been parents' immediate reaction either. For states with 1941 birth-certificate data available to allow day-by-day tracking of name usage, *Pearl* was less common as a first and as a middle name in December's second week than its first (that is, in the week immediately following the attack than in the week before), though too few examples arise to draw statistically meaningful conclusions. In other semi-unpleasant associations that encouraged a gemstone baby name, *Ruby*'s similar long slide briefly reversed in late 1963 and 1964, after Jack Ruby shot Lee Harvey Oswald.

5. The prevalence of *Victoria*, relatedly, jumped in both 1918 and 1945, the years of triumph at the end of each world war; *Victor* did, too, although it had also risen earlier in World War II before dipping in 1944, so its end-of-war kick stands out somewhat less.

6. Mary Seeman argues that *German* was so distasteful that it damaged the English-language prospects of the name *Gerard* as well by mere resemblance (whereas in French *Gérard* could be popular, lacking any comparable sonic echo of the French word for German, *allemand*). But then, she also claimed names starting with Ger- or Gr- were reminiscent of the roar of a lion. See Mary V. Seeman, "Psycho-Cultural Aspects of Naming Children," *Canadian Psychiatric Journal* 17, no. 2 (1972): 149–51.

7. Gabriel A. Almond, *The American People and Foreign Policy* (Praeger, 1960).

8. John R. Oneal and Anna Lillian Bryan, "The Rally 'Round the Flag Effect in US Foreign Policy Crises, 1950–1985," *Political Behavior* 17, no. 4 (1995): 379–401.

9. Marcus M. Wilkerson, *Public Opinion and the Spanish-American War: A Study in War Propaganda* (Louisiana State University Press, 1932); John Maxwell Hamilton, Renita Coleman, Bettye Grable, and Jaci Cole, "An Enabling Environment: A Reconsideration of the Press and the Spanish–American War," *Journalism Studies* 7, no. 1 (2006): 78–93.

Even before the United States entered the war against Spain, interest in the Cuban war of independence was expressed through names. Ada Ferrer notes the case of *Maceo*, after the rebel leader Antonio Maceo. Ferrer discusses the name in the context of African Americans celebrating a Black fighter against oppression, and she is correct that the relative prevalence was higher among children not identified as White. It is worth noting, though, that White babies also saw a substantial uptick in the use of *Maceo* just as General Maceo won renown, a relatively rare instance in the years around 1900 of Whites in the United States naming children after figures of other racial origins (though see, among other things, this chapter's discussion of *Togo*). See Ada Ferrer, *Cuba: An American History* (Scribner, 2021), 150.

10. Stanley Lieberson, *A Matter of Taste: How Names, Fashions, and Culture Change* (Yale University Press, 2000).

11. And, possibly, after the war. The Spanish naval commander at Santiago, Pasqual Cervera y Topete, won esteem after the hostilities ended, especially once the national media turned on the leaders of the United States military it had at first patriotically celebrated. See Lori Bogle, "The Spanish American War's 'Most Durable Hero': Admiral Pasquale Cervera and Popular Heroic Values in the United States, 1898–1909," *War & Society* 36, no. 2 (2017): 98–119. *Pasquale* did become substantially more common as a name shortly after the war ended, though this mostly seems to reflect a growing Italian American population rather than direct commemoration of the foreign admiral.

12. To return to the question posed in the introduction about whether Roosevelt was really the most popular figure in the country, *Roosevelt* barely registering as a source of namesakes relative to *Dewey* suggests not. It is true that *Roosevelt* is more unwieldy and less similar to previously circulating names, so it might be a heavier lift to make popular. But it did make a considerably greater lift after the war, which suggests that Roosevelt's popularity had not broken out particularly far during the war itself. Although this naming pattern is not clinching proof about Dewey's popularity relative to Roosevelt's, it provides one possible objective indicator for assessing that comparison.

13. C. Lombroso, "An Epidemic of Kissing in America," *Pall Mall* 18, no. 76 (1899): 544–47.

14. Serbian ethnic communities might naturally find Serbian names congenial. But few if any babies in the United States were named *Putnik* after the storied chief of the Serbian general staff, an analogue to *Joffre* or *Foch*. Nor did other famed Serbian figures of the war, such as the infantrywoman Milunka Savić or the Serb-nationalist assassin Gavrilo Princip, inspire many obvious namesakes in the United States.

15. Formally, Clemenceau's title was president of the Council of Ministers, but he was widely referred to as the prime minister in English news accounts to distinguish his office from that of France's separate, largely ceremonial office of president. Additionally, *Clemenceau* was at least relatable to the longtime name *Clement*.

16. For a deeper exploration of World War I sites as names in the Australian context, see Mark Connelly and Jessamy Carlson, "Naming, but Not Shaming: The War Names Phenomenon, 1914–1920," *Critical Military Studies* 7, no. 4 (2021): 384–96. Especially in Australia, but even other parts of the English-speaking world including occasionally the

United States, the Gallipoli campaign spurred use of the name *Dardanella*: Not all of the war's battle-site names came from the Western Front. The fields of France loomed larger than the other theaters of war in United States names, however.

17. Harold D. Lasswell, *Propaganda Technique in the World War* (Knopf, 1927).

18. Italian Americans had form in this. In 1896, when Giuseppe Galliano perished in one of Italy's hapless compulsions to be comprehensively defeated by Ethiopia's army, many children were christened *Galliano*.

19. Calling *Peace* "reasonably common" may depend on the time scale used: Almost all of the *Peace* babies were born in the space of a week in the middle of November, just around the armistice—and indeed *Armistice* was almost as common a name during that month (and continued popping up for the next few years, though not as frequently as in late 1918 and early 1919).

20. Names in some non-English cultures (e.g., Han Chinese) habitually use common words as names as well.

21. Philip J. Stone, Dexter C. Dunphy, and Marshall S. Smith, *The General Inquirer: A Computer Approach to Content Analysis* (MIT Press, 1966). The dictionary is available online.

22. Concededly, words change in connotation over the decades, and even at any one time people disagree on meanings. Although the General Inquirer list of words is relatively middle of the road for this sample, having been developed toward the middle of the study period, the static word list will miss any linguistic drift that made words relate more or less to power. Such random miscoding should bias the analysis against finding a significant association between wars and use of power-invoking words as names.

23. Meredith Reid Sarkees, "Defining and Categorizing Wars," in *Resort to War: A Data Guide to Inter-State, Extra-State, Intra-State, and Non-State Wars, 1816–2007*, ed. Meredith Reid Sarkees and Frank Whelon Wayman (CQ Press, 2010), 39–73.

24. The long-run trend is calculated using a lowess smoother, like those used in chapter 1.

25. John E. Mueller, *War, Presidents, and Public Opinion* (John Wiley, 1973).

26. Benjamin E. Goldsmith, Yusaku Horiuchi, and Kelly Matush, "Does Public Diplomacy Sway Foreign Public Opinion? Identifying the Effect of High-Level Visits," *American Political Science Review* 115, no. 4 (2021): 1342–57.

27. Tragic deaths often got royals attention in the United States, just as with the presidents in chapter 3. *Mercedes*, for example, leapt in popularity as a name choice in 1876 when the Queen of Spain—named *Maria* but known as Mercedes of Orléans—died two days after her eighteenth birthday.

28. The Scandinavian *aa* sounds roughly like a long English *O*: the pronunciation of *Haakon* is such that baristas in the United States mostly render it as *Hogan*.

29. *Porfirio*, by contrast, seems to gain wider use after the toppling of the Mexican dictator Porfirio Díaz. This may have been an expression of nostalgia for the relative stability of his reign compared with the years of conflict that followed his overthrow, or increased use of a name once it was no longer associated with an active despot. In a mirror image of *Laurier*, *Porfirio*'s popularity was regional, in its case concentrated in the southwestern United States among parents with Spanish family names.

30. Today the controversy surrounding Dreyfus's conviction mostly concerns the case's blatant anti-Semitism. Yet the overwhelming majority of the newborns named *Dreyfus* were from the South, not a region known as culturally philo-Semitic in the Jim Crow era. Nor is its Southern cast driven by births in Louisiana, with its heritage ties to French culture. Part of the appeal to Southerners may instead have drawn on attitudes toward Catholicism. The Dreyfusard faction tended to be anticlerical, which chimed with widespread anti-Catholic sentiments in the South. See Charlton Moseley, "Latent Klanism in Georgia, 1890–1915," *Georgia Historical Quarterly* 56, no. 3 (1972): 365–86.

31. Vasiliki Fouka, "How Do Immigrants Respond to Discrimination? The Case of Germans in the US during World War I," *American Political Science Review* 113, no. 2 (2019): 405–22.

32. Barbara L. Tischler, "One Hundred Percent Americanism and Music in Boston during World War I," *American Music* 4, no. 2 (1986): 164–76.

33. Leland V. Bell, "The Failure of Nazism in America: The German American Bund, 1936–1941," *Political Science Quarterly* 85, no. 4 (1970): 585–99; Adam J. Berinsky, Eleanor Neff Powell, Eric Schickler, and Ian Brett Yohai, "Revisiting Public Opinion in the 1930s and 1940s," *PS: Political Science and Politics* 44, no. 3 (2011): 515–20.

34. Martin Saavedra, "Kenji or Kenneth? Pearl Harbor and Japanese-American Assimilation," *Journal of Economic Behavior & Organization* 185 (2021): 602–24.

35. And of popular culture not directly from Japan: The blips on figure 4.9 in 1968 and 1975 with more-prevalent Japanese names reflect years when a singer of part-Japanese descent, Tamiko Jones, respectively released a self-titled album and her highest-selling one, sparking increases in the use of *Tamiko* and variants such as *Tamako*.

36. Hadley Cantril, "Opinion Trends in World War II: Some Guides to Interpretation," *Public Opinion Quarterly* 12, no. 1 (1948): 30–44.

37. Mussolini had himself been named politically, in honor of the liberal Mexican president Benito Juárez (ruled 1858–1872). The popularity of *Benito* as a name in the interwar United States generally parallels Mussolini's rise.

38. In something of a mirror image of using names of figures identified with communism to examine how people felt about the Cold War, we could also look at the names of foreign figures to see how much those figures were identified in the public mind with communism. For example, *Fidel* soared in popularity in 1959, the year of the Cuban Revolution that put Fidel Castro in power. (He also took a much-publicized tour of the United States that year.) *Fidel*'s prevalence was still substantially above its pre-Revolution rate through 1960 and 1961, but by 1962, when in the wake of the Bay of Pigs invasion Castro's communism and Soviet affinities were clear, it had fallen back to its previous levels. The name did, however, experience a larger and more sustained resurgence starting in the late 1970s that traces attitudes to communism in the United States: As détente took hold, *Fidel* became more common before dropping dramatically in the Reagan years then becoming more popular than ever with the end of the Cold War and not falling back to 1960s prevalences until the 2010s.

39. Michael David-Fox, Peter Holquist, and Alexander M. Martin, "What's in a Name?" *Kritika: Explorations in Russian and Eurasian History* 4, no. 4 (2003): 779–81.

40. Choichiro Yatani and Dana Bramel, "Trends and Patterns in Americans' Attitudes toward the Soviet Union," *Journal of Social Issues* 45, no. 2 (1989): 13–32. Yatani and Bramel do express ambivalence about the quality of polling about attitudes toward the Soviet Union, but names' tracking of the public-opinion surveys provides an alternative source of evidence pointing in the same direction.

41. Lawrence J. Nelson and Matthew Schoenbachler, *Nikita Khrushchev's Journey into America* (University Press of Kansas, 2019).

42. This contrasts somewhat with the experience of *Leonid*. That name similarly had one of its bigger years when Khrushchev's successor Leonid Brezhnev visited the United States in 1973 for a summit with Richard Nixon, but Brezhnev never had Khrushchev's shoe-brandishing, we-will-bury-you draw. *Leonid* consistently trailed *Nikita* in popularity, barely registering in the statistics most years, and faded quickly after the 1973 visit.

43. Lewis A. Erenberg, "'Rumble in the Jungle': Muhammad Ali vs. George Foreman in the Age of Global Spectacle," *Journal of Sport History* 39, no. 1 (2012): 81–97.

5. CULTURE WARS (CA. 1980–2020)

1. They were, in declining order of popularity with the number of reported occurrences between 1940 and 2020 in parentheses: *Megan* (439,079), *Meghan* (95,780), *Meagan* (41,564), *Meaghan* (14,041), *Maegan* (9,148), *Meghann* (3,788), *Magen* (3,346), *Meggan* (2,927), *Magan* (2,739), *Meagen* (1,182), *Maeghan* (1,064), *Meegan* (979), *Maegen* (875), *Megann* (797), *Megen* (682), *Maygan* (612), *Meighan* (564), *Mehgan* (543), *Maghan* (496), *Megyn* (459), *Maygen* (398), *Meggin* (345), *Megin* (294), *Meagon* (240), *Maigan* (239), *Meeghan* (235), *Meghin* (193), *Magon* (179), *Megean* (174), *Meaghen* (172), *Megon* (161), *Meigan* (147), *Meaghann* (145), *Meghen* (135), *Meggen* (133), *Meygan* (125), *Maigen* (109), *Maghen* (108), *Magin* (74), *Megahn* (64), *Meghaan* (36), *Maeghen* (32), *Magean* (20), *Meagin* (17), *Meahgan* (16), *Maegann* (12), *Maegon* (10), *Meagann* (10), *Megghan* (10), *Meghyn* (10), *Maghann* (6), *Megaan* (6), *Maggen* (5), *Maigon* (5), *Mayghan* (5), *Meagyn* (5), *Meghean* (5), and *Meghon* (5). Some exponents of these names might not have thought of them as versions of *Megan*, and conversely some names I did not interpret as a *Megan* variant might have been so considered by those choosing the name.

2. Peter K. Enns and Julianna Koch, "Public Opinion in the US States: 1956 to 2010," *State Politics & Policy Quarterly* 13, no. 3 (2013): 349–72.

3. Gory methodological details: States with fewer than five *Meagans* are assumed to have zero, as usual with Social Security data (see appendix), and the state-year prevalence of *Meagan* is adjusted by the national prevalence of *Meagan* nationally in the given year—as seen in figure 5.1's top panel, this varied substantially, especially early in the decade as *Megan* leapt to prominence—to account for secular countrywide trends. These

adjustments make little difference to the result, though they explain the horizontal bands of points at the bottom of the graph: Those are states coded as having zero *Meagan* births in different years. The District of Columbia is included as a state. The slope of the best-fit line given in figure 5.1's bottom panel is 0.28 (that is, for every four percentage points more conservatives in the population, the share of *Meagan* spellings goes up by approximately one percentage point), with a standard error of 0.03.

4. As noted, for most figures in this chapter, the primary source is the Social Security Administration, which discards names with fewer than five observations in a sex-year. This means that the concentration indices will overstate the true concentration: Names are in fact even more varied than the numbers here indicate. That upward bias persists over time, however, so for examining year-on-year trends, the index is still meaningful. Correcting the data by imputing numbers of rarely used names with a power law—see the appendix—produces a very similar trend to that in figure 5.2.

5. Stanley Lieberson and Eleanor O. Bell, "Children's First Names: An Empirical Study of Social Taste," *American Journal of Sociology* 98, no. 3 (1992): 511–54.

6. *Bristol* echoes chapter 4's *Dewey* in likely having its wide acceptance expedited by rhyming with existing names, notably *Crystal*. The advantage for naming would be especially great because *Crystal* was generally a girl's name, as *Bristol* would be in the years after Palin's emergence as a public figure.

7. Potential homonyms widespread enough to be included in the Social Security data include—and you may want to bail out now if you thought the *Megan* endnote was over the top, because we are about to embark on another long list with name counts over the 1940 to 2020 period in parentheses—*Trevon* (13,866), *Travon* (6,484), *Treyvon* (3,730), *Trayvon* (3,214), *Trevaughn* (848), *Traevon* (748), *Traivon* (246), *Trevaun* (236), *Treavon* (230), *Trevonn* (216), *Travaughn* (158), *Travonn* (52), *Treyvaughn* (46), *Treyvan* (38), *Treyvonn* (37), *Trevahn* (24), *Trevohn* (16), *Treivon* (12), *Travaun* (5), and *Trevhon* (5). This list excludes similar names apt to be pronounced with an extra vowel, in three syllables (*Travian, Travien, Traeveon, Traevion, Traiveon, Traveion, Traveon, Traveyon, Travion, Travyon, Trayveon, Trayvion, Treavion, Treveion, Treveon, Treveyon, Trevian, Trevien, Trevion, Trevyon, Treyveon, Treyvian, Treyvion*) and two-syllable names where the most common ways of sounding or stressing the vowels in English diverged from *Trayvon* (*Traeven, Traevin, Traevyn, Travan, Traven, Travin, Travyn, Trayven, Trayvin, Treaven, Tresvon, Trevan, Treven, Trevin, Trevun, Trevyn, Treyven, Treyvin, Trivon, Trovon, Troyvon*). Some users of these names could use a pronunciation matching that of *Trayvon*, but most of the names are rare and do not particularly affect the discussion. Note also that although these lists formally incorporate names going back to 1940 for consistency, none meet the minimum frequency to appear in the Social Security records until 1965.

8. *Clarence* is another name sometimes said to have become less popular because of political news (e.g., Elie Mystal, "One Supreme Court Justice's Legacy, as Expressed by Baby Names," 2018, https://abovethelaw.com/2018/06/one-supreme-court-justices-legacy-as -expressed-by-baby-names/): It was reputed to have become radioactive in some circles after Clarence Thomas was named to the Supreme Court in 1991 and faced highly

publicized accusations of sexually harassing Anita Hill. *Clarence*, though, was in steep decline for most of the twentieth century and did not ebb noticeably more quickly after 1991 than it had beforehand. This does not rule out a political reaction against the name, but it gives room for doubt. (Perhaps notably, recent uses of the name have tended to disproportionately occur in relatively Republican states.)

9. Emily A. West and Shanto Iyengar, "Partisanship as a Social Identity: Implications for Polarization," *Political Behavior* 44, no. 2 (2022): 807–38.

10. This list and figure 5.5 focus on personal weapons, but *Cannon* (and *Kannon*) is also distinctly more common in Republican-leaning states than in Democratic-leaning ones. That broader link with weapons may somewhat reduce the possibility that the use of gun-related names simply shows that the West is a Republican-dominated region and also has a legacy of cowboy culture (other names with frontierish overtones such as *Boone* or *Stetson* indeed appear more frequently in Republican areas).

11. *Gunner*'s Scandinavian link adds a further hint of aggressive violence: The name derives from a word for *warrior*, and the character Gunnar in ancient Germanic lore is most famous for killing his brother-in-law. To the extent implications of ferocity associate with one party's preferred vision of masculinity, this might reinforce partisan tendencies among those who fanatically scour baby-name books for belligerent etymologies.

12. Because fewer gun-related names appeared in the 1980s and 1990s, their relationship with partisanship is less confidently estimated in those early years, especially in simple models not accounting for the Social Security information's restriction of state-years with few examples of a specific name. However, the point estimates indicate that gun-related names were more common in more Republican states even then.

13. Herbert P. Kitschelt and Philipp Rehm, "Secular Partisan Realignment in the United States: The Socioeconomic Reconfiguration of White Partisan Support since the New Deal Era," *Politics & Society* 47, no. 3 (2019): 425–79.

14. Even if chapter 4 showed that *Ruby* could get some mileage out of being the name of an assassin-slayer, Boston Corbett may have been a wee bit too eccentric to have made many name-givers enthusiastic about it. Which, yes, I did look for, but no obvious *Boston*s or *Corbett*s came of it. One Corbett Lincoln Baker was born in Barton, New York, in February 1865, two months before Boston Corbett became famous; it is theoretically possible his parents did not settle on his name until April when Boston Corbett came on the scene, but Corbett was a common local surname around Barton, so that seems a more likely basis for the name.

15. Stanley Lieberson, Susan Dumais, and Shyon Baumann, "The Instability of Androgynous Names: The Symbolic Maintenance of Gender Boundaries," *American Journal of Sociology* 105, no. 5 (2000): 1249–87; Herbert Barry and Aylene S. Harper, "Evolution of Unisex Names," *Names* 30, no. 1 (1982): 15–22. Barry and Harper, in particular, continued to write for decades about names that obscured gender.

16. For examples and overviews of the sociological literature on names and gender, see Jane Pilcher, "Names and 'Doing Gender': How Forenames and Surnames Contribute to

Gender Identities, Difference, and Inequalities," *Sex Roles* 77, no. 11 (2017): 812–22; Claire Etaugh and Colleen Geraghty, "Both Gender and Cohort Affect Perceptions of Forenames, but Are 25-Year-Old Standards Still Valid?" *Sex Roles* 79, no. 11 (2018): 726–37; Gerianne M. Alexander, Kendall John, Tracy Hammond, and Joanna Lahey, "Living Up to a Name: Gender Role Behavior Varies with Forename Gender Typicality," *Frontiers in Psychology* 11 (2021): 4038.

17. Of the names that the Social Security administration reports at least a hundred cases of in both 1970 and 2020, the fourteen names with the largest shifts in sex distribution all became more female typed. In addition to the examples listed in the text, these include *Stevie*—the champion sex-changer, going from only 2 percent of newborns so named in 1970 being female to 96 percent in 2020—*Blair, Harley, Quinn, Ivory, Taylor, Paris, Jade*, and *Kelsey*. The largest female-to-male shift among names with at least a hundred cases was that of *Joan*, the fifteenth-biggest shifter by this measure. Notably, though, the historically popular girl's name *Joan* was pronounced differently from the rising boy's name *Joan*, with the former mostly having only one syllable and the latter, reflecting its Catalan origins, usually having two. The distinctive pronunciations probably lessened how much name-givers worried about giving a male child a female-typed name. The degree to which name shifts went male to female in the fifty years to 2020 is admittedly extreme, but other eras and samples find the same general pattern of more male-to-female name changes. For instance, replicating the calculation for the 1920 to 1970 period instead of 1970 to 2020 finds six female-to-male shifts among the fifteen most-changed names (*Robbie, Frankie, Mickey, Ollie, Jessie, Willie*). But many of those formerly female names were historically nicknames more often than first names, which is a problem of using Social Security data for information before the mid-twentieth century: The 1920 names were not recorded as official records at the time of birth whereas most of the 1970 names were, skewing the comparison. In any case, even in the fifty years from 1920 the names whose sex incidence shifted most dramatically generally followed the male-to-female rule (e.g., *Leslie, Kelly, Shelby, Meredith, Merritt*).

18. Shel Silverstein, "A Boy Named Sue," *A Boy Named Sue and His Other Country Songs*, RCA LSP-4192 (1969).

19. I have written elsewhere about how voters respond to electoral candidates, female or male, with names that read as masculine; see R. Urbatsch, "Feminine-Sounding Names and Electoral Performance," *Electoral Studies* 55 (2018): 54–61.

20. Katie L. Gibson and Amy L. Heyse, "'The Difference between a Hockey Mom and a Pit Bull': Sarah Palin's Faux Maternal Persona and Performance of Hegemonic Masculinity at the 2008 Republican National Convention," *Communication Quarterly* 58, no. 3 (2010): 235–56; Dustin Harp, Jaime Loke, and Ingrid Bachmann, "First Impressions of Sarah Palin: Pit Bulls, Politics, Gender Performance, and a Discursive Media (Re)Contextualization," *Communication, Culture & Critique* 3, no. 3 (2010): 291–309.

21. For the details of the calculation, the percentage female is subtracted from fifty. The absolute value of the resulting difference is itself subtracted from fifty, and the result

multiplied by two. A name for which 90 percent of the recipients in the year are female then gets a gender-ambiguity score of $2 \times (50 - |50 - 90|) = 20$ and, symmetrically, a name for which 10 percent of the year's recipients are female gets a score of $2 \times (50 - |50 - 10|) = 20$. A name for which 75 percent of the recipients are from one sex similarly gets a gender-ambiguity score of $2 \times (50 - |50 - 75|) = 50$. Because the Social Security Administration does not reveal counts when a name gets fewer than five recipients of a sex in a year, this measure can be quite uncertain for rare names: If five female cases are reported in the data but no male cases, the true ambiguity score could be anywhere from zero, if there were in fact no males given the name, to eighty-nine, if four males were. This issue should not much affect the state-level gender-ambiguity scores: A rare name will get very little weight in any state's distribution of names, and it would only be observed as being present in the state if all five of the nationwide females happen to be from that state (because the Social Security Administration also conceals state-level totals less than five in a sex-year). But I treat all the unobserved names as having had zero observations, which will consistently bias the ambiguity scores downward from what would be calculated if all information were available.

22. Stanley Lieberson, *A Matter of Taste: How Names, Fashions, and Culture Change* (Yale University Press, 2000), 87.

23. Lisa M. Burns, *First Ladies and the Fourth Estate: Press Framing of Presidential Wives* (Northern Illinois University Press, 2008); Liz Watts, "Magazine Coverage of First Ladies from Hoover to Clinton: From Election through the First One Hundred Days of Office," *American Journalism* 14, no. 3–4 (1997): 495–519.

24. I somewhat more expansively consider similar dynamics with the name *Reagan* elsewhere. See R. Urbatsch, "Nominal Partisanship: Names as Political Identity Signals," *PS: Political Science & Politics* 47, no. 2 (2014): 463–67.

25. For more on *Hillary* and the 2016 campaign, see Stefano Ghirlanda, "Trends in First Names Foreshadowed Hillary Clinton's Electoral Defeat," *Cliodynamics* 8, no. 1 (2017): 48–58.

26. This was not *Monica*'s first go-round as a hostage to political fortune. In 1978, Equatorial Guinea's founding president—the brutal, capricious dictator Francisco Macías Nguema—reportedly decreed that no child could be given the first name *Monica* after his wife of that name fled the country (Jesus de las Heras, "La esposa del presidente Macías puede estar en España," *El País*, February 1, 1978). This alleged proscription went out even though *Monica* was the name of Nguema's own daughter; perhaps fortunately, he had shipped that daughter off to North Korea for Kim Il-Sung to raise, as one does. Subsequent revelations suggested, however, that the senior Monica's departure might just have been a presidential plot to smuggle embezzled money out of the country rather than a wounding betrayal of the president, with *Monica* never really banned (Jesus de las Heras, "Cinco mujeres en la vida del dictador," *El País*, August 12, 1979). Then again, Nguema had at one point prohibited all non-Indigenous names as part of a policy of Africanization, so *Monica* might have been caught up in that even if it was not specifically

forbidden. In short, Equatorial Guinea has a fascinating history, and more books about the United States should have endnotes that dilate on it.

27. Lieberson, *A Matter of Taste*, 263–66.

28. Tristan Bridges and Philip N. Cohen, "What Can Baby Names Tell Us About #MeToo?" *Inequality by (Interior) Design*, 2018, https://inequalitybyinteriordesign.wordpress.com /2018/01/18/what-can-baby-names-tell-us-about-metoo.

29. Purity culture was relatively ascendant in the 1990s, especially in evangelical circles. See Sara Moslener, *Virgin Nation: Sexual Purity and American Adolescence* (Oxford University Press, 2015).

30. More peripheral names in the scandal, like *Tripp* (surname of Linda Tripp, who recorded and betrayed Lewinsky's confidences) also experienced very little setback to their popularity.

6. NAMES, TODAY AND TOMORROW (CA. 2020–)

1. *Usama* did not recover enough popularity to return to the Social Security listings in the 2010s.

2. Pun about name-dropping not intended.

3. *Lesbia* was never as popular as *Gay*, but regularly was given to a few children per year in the early decades of the twentieth century. It has also become less apparent in the records in recent decades.

4. Archivists and genealogists have developed several phonetic algorithms to try to identify equivalent or homophonic names; the most prominent, Soundex, has seen wide use for over a century. Some though not all Soundex variants would match *Zachary* with *Xhaiquirí*.

5. In statistical terms, the increased variability or dispersion of names reduces confidences about most inferences regarding them. This is somewhat counteracted by the increasing national population over time leading to more newborns in any given year and hence more names to consider, a larger sample size that all else equal increases the possibility for confident inferences.

6. Andrew Watson, "Changes in American Court Advocacy during the Long Nineteenth Century: Classical Influences, Their Decline, Similarities and Comparisons with England and Wales," *Journal on European History of Law* 11, no. 1 (2020): 14–21; Caroline Winterer, *The Culture of Classicism: Ancient Greece and Rome in American Intellectual Life, 1780–1910* (Johns Hopkins University Press, 2002).

7. Caleb Bingham, *The Columbian Orator* (Baltimore, 1811).

8. *Philomela* is, to current sensibilities, a somewhat unsettling choice of name for a child. The most prominent Philomela in the classical canon was a mythical Athenian princess whose brother-in-law raped her then cut out her tongue to prevent her reporting his transgression. She proceeded to weave the saga into a tapestry to expose him. The gods then turned her into a bird.

9. Thomas Nelson Winter, "Cincinnatus and the Disbanding of Washington's Army," *Classical Bulletin* 51, no. 6 (1975): 81–86. As usual, some parents went further and used Cincinnatus's full name, most famously with Lucius Quintus Cincinnatus Lamar, who achieved high rank in all three branches of the U.S. government (as senator representing Mississippi, secretary of the interior, and justice of the Supreme Court) and represented the Confederacy as a diplomat. *Lucius*, though, was a widely popular name both in classical Rome and in the modern English-speaking world, which makes it harder to pinpoint as relating specifically to Cincinnatus.

10. Cassius [Ædanus Burke], *Considerations on the Society of the Cincinnati* (Philadelphia, 1783). Contextualizing that example, Ædanus Burke, who wrote under the *Cassius* pseudonym to strenuously object to the Cincinnati opening up a hereditary class distinction, owned slaves: Even those who seemed to have no objection to genetic determinism of social standing with respect to slavery baulked at the new organization. Burke might merely have been self-servingly hostile to class hierarchies only when he was not in the upper rank, but some who were eligible for membership, including George Washington himself, commented unfavorably on the society's embrace of primogeniture. (Then again, Washington's childlessness might have made it easier for him to deride a social network that passed advantages through the family line: The hereditary system would by this cynical logic have given him more value had he had children.)

11. John A. Magni, "The Decline of the Classics and their Place in Future Curricula," *Pedagogical Seminary* 20, no. 1 (1913): 23–44.

12. Classical words not historically much used as personal names, such as *Sirius*, have also increasingly been applied to children.

13. *Gaius* also became much more popular at roughly the same time, though the link to the primary emperor of that name is more questionable given that he is mostly remembered by the nickname *Caligula* (which has also become more common than it once was, but remains very rare). It may be notable that vilified classical women have not seen a parallel naming revival: *Nero* has been much more widely used than *Agrippina* and *Messalina* have.

14. Jonathan Rosenberg, *Dangerous Melodies: Classical Music in America from the Great War through the Cold War* (Norton, 2019).

15. Tamar Mitts, "Terrorism and the Rise of Right-Wing Content in Israeli Books," *International Organization* 73, no. 1 (2019): 203–24.

16. Seth Stephens-Davidowitz, *Everybody Lies: Big Data, New Data, and What the Internet Can Tell Us About Who We Really Are* (HarperCollins, 2017).

17. The introduction notes two particularly accessible resources. The author Laura Wattenberg currently provides a number of interactive tools about the history and geography of baby names at her website, Namerology.com, and Nancy Man has a long-running blog about name history at Nancy.cc.

18. Anjani Chandra, Joyce Abma, Penelope Maza, and Christine Bachrach, "Adoption, Adoption Seeking, and Relinquishment for Adoption in the United States," *Centers for Disease Control and Prevention Advance Data* 306 (1999): 1–14.

19. The Social Security Administration does process changes of name (and sex, which is relevant not only to the perceived gender of a particular name but also to whether the name appears too rarely in a sex-year to meet the rules for having its information released in Social Security name counts), and it is conceivable that regulations could in the future allow backdated revision of the annual name-prevalence counts.

APPENDIX: METHODOLOGY

1. Note, however, that at various points places that we do not currently think of as being in the United States, such as the Panama Canal Zone, were counted as part of United States.
2. Names sometimes changing on immigration would further complicate the use of migrant data here.
3. The examples in this sentence are hypothetical: In reality, censuses from the childhoods of the most famous people with these names list Francis S. Fitzgerald and John E. Hoover, not the middle names by which they became better known, so they would count as *Francis* and *John*.
4. The official census date was June 1 (or June 2 when June 1 was a Sunday, as happened in 1890) from 1830 to 1900, April 15 in 1910, January 5 in 1920, and April 1 in the decades from 1930 on. But the entire count did not take place on the year's official date. It commonly took several weeks, or even months, to reach everyone. Although the census explicitly sought information as it had been on the official census date, inaccuracies inevitably crept in when people were asked to record details such as ages that had changed between the date of the question and the date being asked about. People who were born or died between the official census date and the actual enumeration are especially likely to be inaccurately recorded or not recorded at all.
5. Kasey S. Buckles and Daniel M. Hungerman, "Season of Birth and Later Outcomes: Old Questions, New Answers," *Review of Economics and Statistics* 95, no. 3 (2013): 711–24.
6. *June* is, in fairness, exceptional among the common month names in this regard. Around 37 percent of the *April*s were born in April, 25 percent of those named *May* were born in May (as were 17 percent of *Mae*s), and 16 percent of those named *August* were born in August: all substantially more than would be expected by chance, but less dramatically than was the case for *June*. (The months of May and August each having thirty-one days also slightly reduces the degree to which the associated names are overrepresented when compared with the thirty-day April and June.) Indeed, the *August* result is barely larger than, for instance, the propensity for people named *Carol* to be born in December (the Christmas carols and all), and smaller than the propensity for *Noel*s or *Holly*s to be. *Natalie*, with its relation to natal/natality/nativity, also gets a substantial December bump.
7. Important events of course happened abroad as well. Those on the left might have wanted to celebrate Hjalmar Branting's formation of the world's first social-democratic government (in Sweden), and those on the right the Kapp Putsch (in Germany) or inauguration of Miklós Horthy (in Hungary), for example. No relevant names actually appear to

respond to these events, however—*Hjalmar* does see an uptick in use in early 1920 relative to its generally declining baseline, but that uptick is not large enough to be statistically distinguishable from random noise.

8. Versailles L. Sidney (née Snell) appears in Social Security records as born in January 1920, but her tombstone gives her birth date as 1919. Even if that one case were in early 1920, the period in question would not have had notably more cases of *Versailles* than surrounding months did.

9. Karen Oppenheim Mason and Lisa G. Cope, "Sources of Age and Date-of-Birth Misreporting in the 1900 U.S. Census," *Demography* 24, no. 4 (1987): 563–73; Henry S. Shryock and Jacob S. Siegel, *The Methods and Materials of Demography* (U.S. Bureau of the Census, 1980), 204–5.

10. For instance, the Early Reber of Adams County, Indiana, in the 1900 census applied for Social Security as Earl Reber and is identified on his gravestone as Earl J. Reber, and the Early Maupin of Boone County, Missouri, listed in the 1870 Census has a gravestone that identifies him as Earle Marvin Maupin.

11. George Alter, "Infant and Child Mortality in the United States and Canada," in *Infant and Child Mortality in the Past* ed. Alain Bideau, Bertrand Desjardins, and Héctor Pérez Brignoli (Oxford University Press, 1997), 91–108.

12. Daniel Scott Smith, "Differential Mortality in the United States before 1900," *Journal of Interdisciplinary History* 13, no. 4 (1983): 735–59.

13. Kellee Blake, "'First in the Path of the Firemen': The Fate of the 1890 Population Census," *Prologue: Quarterly of the National Archives* 28, no. 1 (1996): 64–81.

14. J. David Hacker, "Decennial Life Tables for the White Population of the United States, 1790–1900," *Historical Methods* 43, no. 2 (2010): 45–79.

15. Frank Nuessel, "A Note on Popular Baby Names on the Social Security Website: An Important Onomastic Resource," *Names* 65, no. 1 (2017): 45–50.

16. See "Social Security number holders," https://www.ssa.gov/oact/babynames/number USbirths.html.

17. Aaron Clauset, Cosma Rohilla Shalizi, and M. E. J. Newman, "Power-Law Distributions in Empirical Data," *SIAM Review* 51, no. 4 (2009): 661–703. In a power-law relationship, the count of names given to exactly n babies has a constant ratio to the count of names that are given to exactly $k \times n$ babies for any constant k: If half as many names appear twelve times as appear nine times, then we would expect half as many names to appear sixteen times as twelve times, because $16/12 = 12/9$. Power-law relationships in real-world data tend to break down when looking at very large (and rare) counts of events, but that concern is less applicable here because the imputation in the Social Security figures is at the opposite end of the scale, where names have very small counts.

18. Grace Abbott, "The Social Security Act and Relief," *University of Chicago Law Review* 4, no. 1 (1936): 45–68. The Social Security Administration in its early years relied on hand-recorded self-reports for birth dates, and either that or the subsequent data-entry process produced some entries from earlier in history (especially a large number of people ostensibly born in the year 1800). Some Social Security birth years from the early period

might even be intentionally misstated as people responded to the incentive to claim to be older in order to receive a pension sooner: Robert D. Young, Bertrand Desjardins, Kirsten McLaughlin, Michel Poulain, and Thomas T. Perls, "Typologies of Extreme Longevity Myths," *Current Gerontology and Geriatrics Research* 2010, no. 1 (2010): 423087, 9.

19. David W. Smith and Benjamin S. Bradshaw, "Variation in Life Expectancy during the Twentieth Century in the United States," *Demography* 43, no. 4 (2006): 647–57.

20. Carolyn Puckett, "The Story of the Social Security Number," *Social Security Bulletin* 69, no. 2 (2009): 55–74.

21. Gareth Davies and Martha Derthick, "Race and Social Welfare Policy: The Social Security Act of 1935," *Political Science Quarterly* 112, no. 2 (1997): 217–35.

22. This discussion relies on the official index to *New York Times* obituaries, which suggests the newspaper's coverage may have been intermittent: The annual number of obituaries abruptly plummets by 90 percent for around fifteen years starting in the mid-1880s and another fifteen years from the mid-1920s.

23. As befits an appendix fixated on measurement, this raises a host of questions about how to categorize the obituaries' use of initials. Sometimes the headline provides alternative names for a person, the official name alongside something they were more commonly known by, as for example with Samuel Clemens and Mark Twain. If either name features a written-out moniker beyond just initials—even if what is written out is a nickname or other non–birth name rather than the formal given name—this analysis counts the person as not using initials. Thus I count as not using initials figures such as J. P. Richardson, also identified as The Big Bopper, as well as many nuns and monks whose religious name involves a given name, as in *Brother Anthony*. The *Brother* points to another wrinkle, that many of the names are provided alongside a title of some sort. The *New York Times* helpfully abbreviates most titles (writing Prof., Capt., and Gov. rather than Professor, Captain, and Governor) in ways that make them distinctive—Brother shows up as Bro.—though some titles are written out or treated inconsistently. The counts here treat anything that is more common as a title as a name as a title, though it is possible that something like *Bishop* or *Cardinal* was in fact a given name on occasion. (*Dean* is only assumed to be a title if it is followed by two or more initials.) As ever with names, edge cases arise; with *Mother Mitchell (A. Mitchell)*, I assume that *Mother* is a title and *Mitchell* in both appearances is a surname, but either of those assumptions could be incorrect; the person could have been familiarly called *Mother* in the same way that Grandma Moses was called that, and *Mitchell* is a given name that could have been adopted as a religious name, though because no important Catholic figure's name is usually written as *Mitchell* (it can, etymologically, be a rendering of *Michael*, as in the archangel, but is not commonly used as such in the religious context) that would be an unlikely interpretation of Mother Mitchell. Finally, though I generally do not take abbreviations, such as *Wm.* for *William* or *Geo.* for *George*, as initials, I do count multiletter compounds that include particles: *McA.*, as the traditional initial for a name like *McAdoo* or *McArthur*, is interpreted to be an initial.

24. The yearbook was published by the college's junior class and took the year of graduation of that class. The 1894 yearbook therefore appeared in 1893.
25. Children were less likely to adopt the initials-for-name style, so the fashion for using initials is less relevant to the census data, in which the analysis mostly looks at those age nine or younger. However, the destruction of the 1890 Census and consequent use of those up to age nineteen from the 1900 Census—when the use of initials was near its peak prevalence—may mean that the issue does affect births from the early 1880s.
26. Alessandro Acquisti and Ralph Gross, "Predicting Social Security Numbers from Public Data," *Proceedings of the National Academy of Sciences* 106, no. 27 (2009): 10975–80.
27. Emmeline was the title heroine of a 1788 novel by Charlotte Smith that enjoyed popularity throughout the nineteenth century; Christabel Pankhurst's parents named her for a character from a Samuel Taylor Coleridge poem.
28. Representative examples of specific people who appear as *Sylvie* in the census but *Sylvia* in the Social Security records include those recorded in the census as Sylvie Feeler (born in Indiana in 1904; her married name, used in Social Security records, was *Sylvia C. Wigger*), Sylvie Lad (born in Georgia in 1914; *Sylvia Ladd* in Social Security records), or Sylvie Paulsen (born in Idaho in 1927; her married and Social Security name was *Sylvia Likes*).
29. This project has very much pressed upon me Hazlitt's aphorism (in a quotation, sometimes alleged to be from Thomas Browne) that "A nickname is the heaviest stone that the devil can throw at a man." See William Hazlitt, *Sketches and Essays* (London, 1839), 222.
30. Susan J. Pearson, *The Birth Certificate: An American History* (University of North Carolina Press, 2021).
31. When computationally feasible, that smoother is a loess model, which is totally nonparametric: It algorithmically follows the data without any constraint. With the *New York Times* obituaries, I resort to a generalized additive model, which imposes some functional constraints on the smoothed line, fitting the smoother as a series of splines.
32. President Truman's middle name was famously *S*, in an effort to honor both his grandfathers, but even in that case there was a middle name, if a reductive one.
33. Stephen Wilson, *The Means of Naming: A Social and Cultural History of Personal Naming in Western Europe* (UCL Press, 1998).
34. Percy S. Morris, "The Middle Initial," *Dicta* 37, no. 6 (1960): 361–67.
35. R. Urbatsch, "The Social Desirability of Rallying 'round the Flag," *Political Behavior* 42, no. 4 (2020): 1223–43.

INDEX

Page numbers in **bold** denote figures.

GPSR Authorized Representative: Easy Access System Europe, Mustamäe tee
50, 10621 Tallinn, Estonia, gpsr.requests@easproject.com

www.ingramcontent.com/pod-product-compliance
Lightning Source LLC
Chambersburg PA
CBHW021857020426
42334CB00013B/364